TEACHING AND LEARNING FROM WITHIN

How can teachers grow into more natural and authentic role models for promoting the excitement of learning with their students? How can they draw the best out of their students and support their human potential? This book addresses these significant questions through the lens of a process called *core reflection* – an approach that focuses on people's strengths as the springboard for personal growth and serves every human being involved in education, including students, teachers, school principals, and university faculty. This approach supports the essential role of authenticity in the development of the whole person. It has been used in contexts around the world and has shown great promise in helping to re-chart the course for education and to re-think its purpose in global and democratic societies.

Teaching and Learning from Within first looks at the current educational context and the need for core reflection, introduces the theory and its linkages to previous studies in numerous disciplines, and provides a deeper explanation of the model along with specific examples of how the theory works in a framework of education. Next, it presents various applications in multinational research and practice – with teachers, with students and schools, and with teacher educators. The conclusion highlights ongoing work in core reflection around the world along with future plans, opportunities, and resources for professional development and research.

Bringing together theory, research, and practice on a topic of growing interest in the field of reflective inquiry in teacher education, this book does not assume that education or relationships are about mastering a set of techniques based on a particular theoretical model. In contrast, it links theory and practice by highlighting *the experience and strength of the person,* showing how personal and professional growth can become connected in a deep learning process. For additional information on core reflection visit www.korthagen.nl

Fred A. J Korthagen is Emeritus Professor of Education, Utrecht University, The Netherlands.

Younghee M. Kim is Professor, School of Education, Southern Oregon University, USA.

William L. Greene is Professor, School of Education, Southern Oregon University, USA.

TEACHING AND LEARNING FROM WITHIN

A Core Reflection Approach
to Quality and Inspiration
in Education

Edited by
Fred A. J. Korthagen
Younghee M. Kim
William L. Greene

 Routledge
Taylor & Francis Group
NEW YORK AND LONDON

First published 2013
by Routledge
711 Third Avenue, New York, NY 10017

Simultaneously published in the UK
by Routledge
2 Park Square, Milton Park, Abingdon, Oxon OX14 4RN

Routledge is an imprint of the Taylor & Francis Group, an informa business

© 2013 Taylor & Francis

Library of Congress Cataloging in Publication Data
A catalog record has been requested for this book

ISBN: 978-0-415-52247-2 (hbk)
ISBN: 978-0-415-52248-9 (pbk)
ISBN: 978-0-203-12140-5 (ebk)

Typeset in Bembo and Stone Sans by
Florence Production Ltd, Stoodleigh, Devon, UK

To our loving families, and to all the
children and teachers in the world.

May this book contribute to more shining eyes.

The Editors

CONTENTS

FOREWORD

This book presents a powerful, holistic approach to learning and how it has been successfully used with students and teachers in the United States and the Netherlands. *Core reflection*, based in positive psychology, allows the individual to work from their inner beliefs and strengths. It is truly an inside-out approach to change. Using a collegial approach, the teacher or coach works with the individual (e.g. teacher or student) to identify their core beliefs and strengths. This process helps the person bring their behavior in line with their core values and thus to live what Parker Palmer has called the "undivided life."

One of the strengths of the book is that it is filled with examples of how this process works. The three main sections of the book focus on how it has been used with teachers, students, and teacher educators. As a teacher educator, I found the last section particularly relevant. The authors describe how this approach was brought to the School of Education at Southern Oregon University and how a significant number of faculty participated in its use. Core reflection was developed in the Netherlands by Fred Korthagen and Angelo Vasalos, and they were invited three times to the US to give workshops on the approach – once in Chicago and twice at Southern Oregon University. Professors Younghee Kim and William Greene were central to bringing core reflection to their university, and they write about their own experiences and share their own thoughts during the process. In Chapter 11, Professor Greene describes core reflection this way: "It's about the opportunity to be who you really are or really want to be. Some people might call it *self-actualization*. Some people might call it *authenticity*, some might call it *flow*, but I'm not sure it's any of those things exactly. I think it's about being human, being very natural in responses, and being very present."

I was impressed that the Dean also participated in the process and wrote, "It was only through my self-study work through the lens of core reflection that

I was able to sustain my sense of self and stay true to my core values." Again, the book is filled with various examples of how core reflection has been used and thus provides ample evidence that this approach can make a difference in the lives of teachers and students.

I have been working in the area of holistic education and contemplative education for many years. One of the challenges in this work is finding language that invites rather than separates, and one of the strengths of core reflection is the language. The central term 'core' is not problematic and thus allows people to enter the process in a non-threatening manner.

The attempts at educational reform for the past several decades have focused mainly on testing and accountability measures; yet, there is a sense that nothing has really improved in education and teacher education. With the emphasis on comparing test scores, discourse about education has taken on a grim, Darwinian feel. This discourse has skated on the surface and not addressed the deeper issues that face teachers. Core reflection encourages us to explore these issues and offers real hope for significant change. It is only when our deepest values are viewed within a positive frame that we can hope to have an education that is truly inspiring and life affirming. Core reflection and the work described in this book gives us reason to make that hope a reality.

John (Jack) P. Miller
University of Toronto

PREFACE

This book is about 'core reflection,' an approach to developing the human potential in teaching and learning. Core reflection focuses on people's strengths as the springboard for personal growth and answers the call for a new educational approach that serves every human being involved in education – including students, teachers, school principals, and university faculty. Following publications on core reflection in Europe, including research-based articles in international professional journals, this book is the first of its kind in English and brings together theory and practice on core reflection.

The research base for the core reflection approach includes published works in positive psychology, clinical psychology, coaching, and reflective inquiry in education. The experience base includes evidence collected from core reflection training courses conducted by Fred Korthagen and Angelo Vasalos in several European countries (e.g. the Netherlands, Belgium, United Kingdom, Ireland, Slovenia), Australia, and the United States.

For the practitioner, this is a very concrete and practical handbook with specific guidelines for how to draw the best out of children, colleagues, and self. This book will be useful to those seeking to improve relationships with co-workers, colleagues, and students and to those seeking to improve the quality and integrity of their own work. The solid research and numerous applications using core reflection presented here can serve as a starting point for further studies in cognitive, emotional, motivational, and behavioral aspects of learning and for professional development in education.

For researchers, this book offers a framework and research evidence to further build on in future studies. The research studies presented in various chapters focus not only on outcomes, but also provide in-depth analyses of underlying learning processes, showing how reflection can be deepened by a holistic perspective on learning.

The book is organized into five parts. In *Part I, Overview: Introduction to Core Reflection*, Chapter 1 opens with a look at the current educational context and the need for core reflection. Chapter 2 introduces the theory of core reflection and its linkages to previous studies in numerous disciplines. Chapter 3 provides a deeper explanation of the model along with specific examples of how the theory works in a framework of education. Next, Chapters 4–12 present various applications of core reflection in multinational research and practice. These are grouped as follows: *Part II, Core reflection with teachers*; *Part III, Core reflection with students and schools*; and *Part IV, Core reflection with teacher educators*. Concluding with Chapter 13 in *Part V,* we highlight ongoing work in core reflection around the world along with future plans, opportunities, and resources for professional development and research. Core reflection is a young theory, developed over the last decade. This is represented by the extensive degree of collaborative work by the editors with many of the chapter authors. There is much potential for its future growth, and we will return to elaborate on that potential throughout the book and in the concluding chapter.

Note

If the book creates the wish to go deeper and learn more about this inspiring approach, and really integrate it in one's daily practices, the reader may experience that there are limits to learning to use core reflection in its full depth from a book. It might then be helpful to follow a brief course or a training workshop in core reflection. If you want to know more about core reflection training or workshops, you can visit the website at www.korthagen.nl or contact the editors.

ACKNOWLEDGMENTS

We are grateful to Naomi Silverman at Routledge who recognized the value of this book and accepted our proposal with enthusiasm and who was available to us frequently throughout the process of our editing. To her we express our deep thanks for her trust, support, and insights that made this book a reality.

We wish to give our deep thanks to Angelo Vasalos for his inspiration, collaboration, and contribution in the co-founding and building of the concept core reflection. We also wish to express special thanks to Jack Miller for his thoughtful and inspiring foreword.

We wish to thank all of the chapter authors whose passion, quality work, and commitment contributed so much to this project. Their research and applications have made this first book on core reflection in English possible. We also wish to express our deep respect for each of the student teachers and teachers whose quotes and voices brought these chapters to life.

We also would like to express our deep gratitude to all the teachers, student teachers, teacher educators, and ultimately children of every age. For them, we hope this book may be used to bring out their shining eyes and joyful hearts, to help them believe in themselves, and to inspire them to realize their potential.

PART I
Overview: Introduction to Core Reflection

This first part of the book consists of three chapters that together lay out a foundation for the rest of the book. Building on a critical view of current educational developments, we start with explaining why we see a need for core reflection. Next, Chapter 2 provides an introduction to the theory of core reflection and its linkages to other theories and disciplines. Chapter 3 provides a deeper explanation of the model and examples of how the core reflection approach works in education. It also summarizes the basic principles of core reflection and its scientific background.

1

TRANSFORMING EDUCATION FROM WITHIN

William L. Greene, Younghee M. Kim, and Fred A. J. Korthagen

This chapter examines educational developments worldwide, taking the historical developments in US education as an exemplar for how the human aspect has gradually disappeared from the realm of teaching and learning. We explain how core reflection aims at overcoming tensions, such as those between the personal and the professional, the technical and the dispositional, the external and the internal. Most of all, core reflection tries to nurture the whole student and teacher, and to give full attention to issues like identity, mission, inspiration, and passion.

The most valuable measure of my development as a teacher has been the growth I have experienced by discovering traits and talents within myself and manifesting them through my work with students. A principle motivation behind my aspiration to become a teacher was the desire to bring out the best in my students. Through the process of teaching, I have discovered that they bring out the best in me. As I have allowed my genuine concern and care for individual students to flourish, I have found myself becoming more compassionate. As I have sought to understand their individual needs and abilities, I have found myself becoming more earnest and authentic. And as I have humbled myself and learned how to plan and provide the best atmosphere and experiences for student learning, I have found myself becoming more effective.

(US graduate of a teacher preparation program that emphasized the core reflection approach)

This book explores what it means to bring out the best in ourselves, our students, those with whom we work, and others in our lives. It is about setting the stage for strengths within each individual to flourish and for deep learning to occur. It is about connecting human hearts and spirits with how we see ourselves and others in our daily practice as educators. Envisioning the expansion of our capacities and potential through strengthening that connection, we present 'core reflection' as an approach to teaching, learning, leading, and professional development that supports the critical role of authenticity in the development of the whole person.

Developed in the Netherlands by Fred Korthagen and Angelo Vasalos, core reflection is based on nurturing the relationship between a person's inner qualities, or core, and her experiences in the outer world (Korthagen, 2004; Korthagen & Vasalos, 2005). The core reflection approach, as it is being used in education, provides a tool for overcoming internal obstacles and limitations that can block our ability to see the many possibilities within ourselves and our circumstances. Core reflection provides a means to integrate, rather than separate, the multiple dimensions of our wholeness as humans – our thoughts, our feelings, our desires and ideals – and to bring the full power and potential of that wholeness to bear upon the experiences of teaching and learning.

In education, interest in holistic development has slowly and cautiously re-surfaced among growing numbers of professional educators. Perhaps this is in response to sagging morale in schools and communities where the measure of educational success has been defined too narrowly to be very meaningful. Or, perhaps it is in response to accountability tactics that have deprived teachers of the sense of professional worth they need to thrive and students of the empowerment they need to excel in their learning. Much talk and research about education is focused on the external and measureable conditions for learning that result in the adoption of, for example, outcomes-based curricula, 'best practice' instructional strategies, or behavioral support programs. Less focus is typically paid to the internal and natural qualities that individuals bring to the context of teaching and learning. We recognize the importance of developing skills and competencies as part of a foundation for learning, but our focus here is on the internal realm as a foundation for learning. This is a realm in which individual strengths and ideals are embraced and where personal growth is supported. This is exactly what core reflection offers, and we believe that this approach orients education toward the requisite conditions for substantive and enlightened transformations to occur.

With prominent national standards in many countries around the world emphasizing content, pedagogy, and test scores, rarely do we see any recognition of the importance for a teacher to understand herself, to engage and expand her awareness and sense of being in the world, and to teach from her soul so she can touch and know the souls of her students. Palmer (1998) asks, "How can schools educate students if they fail to support the teacher's inner life? How can schools perform their mission without encouraging the guide to scout out the inner terrain?" (p. 6). These questions expose a major void in the initial preparation of teachers and in the professional development typically offered for practicing teachers. Evoking and nourishing the inner life of teachers can provide the opportunity for them to revisit their commitment to and passion for teaching because it re-connects them with their core qualities (Korthagen, 2004), their sense of purpose (Intrator & Kunzman, 2006), and their authenticity as an individual (Palmer, 1998). In other words, "the more we are able to nourish our own souls the more our teaching or work will be reenergized and revitalized" (Miller, 2000, p. 5). This book is an attempt to bridge the critical gap between the inward and the outward dimensions of teaching and leadership and to advocate for a greater measure of attention to the inner lives of students and teachers. Such a connection appears in the following example.

> It has been an amazing journey to be able to really sit back and reflect not only on lessons planned and taught, but on me and who I am as a person, deep down. It is the true me that I pass along to my students. It is my compassion, empathy, enthusiasm, silliness, authenticity, drive, commitment, open heart, and many more core qualities that allow me to teach from my heart and be the teacher I have become.
>
> (US student teacher)

The excerpt above is taken from a final 'synthesis' paper at the end of a two-year teacher preparation program in which students engaged regularly in a practice called *core reflection* with their professors. Core reflection, as Chapters 2 and 3 explain in detail, represents a shift from a focus on overcoming problems and deficiencies toward a focus on supporting people's inner cores, and thus on promoting personal strengths and personal growth. The student teacher quoted above and her peers in the teaching program were provided with a chance to explore and integrate how images of their true selves could align with their developing identities as teachers. When teachers can imagine and become who they want to be, the ideals they hold will come into practice. This will directly impact their students' outcomes and achievements. Imagine a teacher who begins to share her core qualities with her students through her daily lesson planning, classroom management, and relationships. It is easy to imagine her practice becoming more engaging and powerful to her students. We believe that this level of authenticity goes hand in hand with providing a safe and enjoyable place to learn.

When learning becomes a joyful or meaningful experience for students, it touches the spirit in ways that cannot always be measured, but that can leave a lasting imprint on their deeper sense of being. We ask:

- How can a teacher grow into becoming a more natural and authentic role model for promoting the excitement of learning with her students?

- How can teachers draw the best out of their students and support their human potential?
- How can teacher education faculty support student teachers to become the best teachers they can be?

We believe these questions are critically significant if schooling is to realize new levels of possibility and potential. This book addresses these questions through the lens of core reflection.

One of the interesting aspects of the core reflection process is that it challenges the apparent dichotomies we, as human beings, usually tend to create within our minds and belief systems. Core reflection highlights the effect of limiting concepts, interpretations, and conclusions we may hold about ourselves and our relationships with others; it also highlights the effects that become manifest when we experience various levels of tension, conflict, and suffering in a personal or professional situation. As we re-chart the course for education and re-think its purpose in global and democratic societies, the core reflection approach can help us challenge and see through polarizing perspectives that may place artificial boundaries on how we look at ourselves and the world; it invites us to focus on embracing and integrating the values, visions, and strengths of (apparently) conflicting realities and concerns. We think the time has come to bring these conflicts to new levels of awareness in teaching and teacher preparation and to look at how we can rise above the tensions and limitations that undermine effective education.

Overview of the Educational Trend in the US

The educational implications of core reflection are both international and multicultural. With that in mind, this section provides an overview of educational trends in the US as an example of similar trends in the public school systems of other countries around the world. The recent history of education in America, as in other parts of the world, has seen ebbs and flows in the priorities of mainstream practice. Over the years, influences on American educational values have come from many philosophical perspectives – some contradictory and others complementary. For example, progressivists, inspired by John Dewey, see the purpose of education as more student-centered and experiential. In contrast, the perspective's represented by essentialism and behaviorism, tend to be more teacher-centered and to value the mastery of a particular body of knowledge and skills. While world events and politics have had a prominent hand in shaping the prevalence of these and other philosophical perspectives and trends in American education since World War II, the last three decades have seen a series of sweeping changes resulting from reports and policies with national scope and influence.

In 1983, the US National Commission on Excellence in Education produced a report called, 'A Nation at Risk: The Imperative for Educational Reform.' This report claimed that American schools were failing academically and in their ability to supply the nation with a competitive workforce. The response to this report led to an increased focus on content standards and graduation requirements for public school students. By the year 2000, academic standards measured through high-stakes tests determined high school graduation criteria in almost every state. With ever-increasing federal influence tied to financial support and accompanying policy mandates, states and local districts attempted to comply with more and more stringent testing and accountability requirements.

The next major iteration of national education reform in the US appeared as the 'No Child Left Behind Act' of 2001 (NCLB). This produced rigorous requirements for state-established curriculum standards and testing across all grades with strict economic sanctions for schools and states that did not comply. With the stakes of their students' test scores even higher, teachers were expected to adapt their curriculum and teaching practice in order to demonstrate student gains on federally-approved standardized tests. Test-based academic achievement often overshadowed other important aspects of students' growth and development. Many in education began to feel disempowered and demoralized believing that the focus of education had become too narrowly defined and, at the same time, short-changed its promise to contribute to a more equitable and just society. Diane Ravitch, once a strong proponent of NCLB and presidential advisor who helped shape its goals and provisions, now writes that with the current emphasis on testing and accountability under NCLB, the broader purposes of education are themselves being left behind:

> At the present time, public education is in peril. Efforts to reform public education are, ironically, diminishing its quality and endangering its very survival. We must turn attention to improving schools, infusing them with the substance of genuine learning and reviving the conditions that make learning possible.
>
> (Ravitch, 2010, p. 242)

From someone as academically and politically influential as Ravitch, her statement represents a sense of having lost something important in education. Remarkably, over the course of her career, she has positioned herself at opposing poles of clashing educational reform measures and beliefs about the purpose of education.

For teachers and administrators who feel as Ravitch does, these tensions come to the forefront of their professional lives and in the everyday realities they face in their schools and classrooms. Some have capitulated and compromised their own ideals to survive in the new era of education, fitting right into what is demanded of them externally and without much resistance. Others fought the tension and recognized their own internal struggle between what they were asked to do versus what they believed right when faced with the standardized, outcome-based definition of learning. Some in this latter group managed to find the strength in their own ideals to make tough choices that did not compromise themselves in the process; this allowed them to retain their locus of control over difficult decisions and to remain authentic in their practice. We believe that the historical trends in US education discussed above can be recognized in other countries as well. Many European countries, for example, have seen a 'back to basics' fervor in which uniform curricula and standardized outcomes – with an emphasis on high stakes tests – gradually came to dominate the landscape of education.

Believing that the greatest personal and professional power comes from teaching and learning holistically, it seems important to ask:

- Where does this power come from?
- How do we support it in a way that teachers can find the strength and the confidence to make decisions that are right in their hearts and right for their students?

This book invites the reader to become more aware of the source and reasons for the tensions we face in our everyday work and to appreciate the possibilities when we teach and learn from within.

Yearning for a Perspective of Wholeness

> I will never give up the good fight for the rights of my students to get the best from me as a teacher. However, I sadly and strongly feel our current direction with assessment is the wrong way and that there are other acceptable ways to move forward which don't take away quality teaching and learning. I love the kids, but the picture on a student's face today, knowing he was the only one not to finish the test, brought tears to my eyes. Wow . . . I guess I had something on my chest.
>
> (Excerpt of an email from a US elementary
> school teacher to his school's principal)

The last decade has been a philosophical battleground for many educators worldwide. Passionate about their work and committed to bringing out the best in their students, teachers like the one quoted above are experiencing a growing unease as their ideals and core values about the purpose of education have been questioned, devalued, or rendered invisible. As a result, burn-out appears to be widespread among new and veteran teachers alike; deep down, many of them wanted to be teachers but the burden of their own unease became too great to bear. There are others who experience similar levels of tension and stress as front-line adjudicators of educational policy and pressure, yet they manage to overcome the personal impact of this and to retain their core mission and commitment to doing what they believe is best for their students. The quote above is an example of how teachers struggle with the inner conflict between their personal ideals and the professional expectations imposed on them by the larger educational enterprise.

Should we be concerned when these teachers, who have rich life experience and a deep sense of commitment to their students, begin to doubt the essence of their work as teachers? The quote above is one example of what is happening in the hearts of many teachers who would define their calling to the profession as empowering students to reach their potential, in all aspects of their being. Perhaps we could ask: Are we doing the right things to nourish and inspire teachers in this effort? If so, what more can we do? If not, how will their students be nourished and inspired in their care?

> Julia was a new teacher. She was also a talented singer with a gift and passion for sharing her beautiful voice in lessons with her first grade students. Imagine Julia's response after being scolded in an evaluation by her principal who said: "You should not be singing songs with your students. They should not be sitting on the rug but at their desks with their attention on you." Torn by the conflict she now felt inside, Julia's first response was to doubt her own efficacy and calling as a teacher and to adhere to the feedback from her principal to avoid conflict and to preserve her career path. Her classroom became a noticeably more somber place. Julia's facial expressions, body language, and level of enthusiasm seemed to diminish as her role became somehow fragmented from the person she knew herself to be. Julia confided in a few close friends that she was considering leaving the profession.
>
> (Real-life example from a new teacher study group, 2008)

Many in education seem to struggle with this tension between the personal and professional, especially when the most deeply personal dimensions of themselves do not seem to align with the professional practices they enact. Do the personal and professional dimensions of teaching have to be disconnected? We see this conflict in some of the most effective teachers, many of whom internalize the pressure to prioritize content over understanding who their students are – their natures, imaginations, curiosities, and the passions they, as human beings, bring into the classroom. It is a conflict that finds its origin in the battleground over the 'purpose of education.' It is a conflict born of an awareness that the reason for choosing to teach has more to do with awakening human potential in one's students than it does about trying to standardize academic achievement at the expense of developing other dimensions of the whole person. When educators realize (or remember) this about themselves, it can be a source of relief to discover what is draining their passion for teaching; on the other hand, it means that their beliefs about the purpose of education may be in direct conflict with the beliefs of their school or district.

How do we sustain the development of important human qualities in our students? How can we honor students' yearning to explore life's most meaningful questions if they do not have access to teachers who inspire them in such a quest? How do we cultivate the conditions that, as Ravitch suggests, make genuine and deep learning possible? If the purpose of education is, as Gandhi and others have said, to draw the best out of people, what is lacking and what is needed to achieve this end? Should we accept fragmented views of teaching and learning that impose false dichotomies between the personal and the professional, the technical and the dispositional, the external and the internal, the academic and the whole student? We see evidence that many such dichotomies exist in education. We presume that the surest way forward in education for the future lies in an integrative perspective and one that honors the innate merits of all.

The time has come to illuminate the barriers between these dimensions of our lives and to strengthen the unity among all layers of the personal and professional. We are all responsible, collectively and individually, for the direction of education. We believe that core reflection provides hope for addressing at least some of the lofty questions posed throughout this chapter. The following quote from a new teacher is an example of what is possible using core reflection in a teacher preparation program:

> Core reflection became an impetus to stimulate a rebirthing of hope . . . As core qualities were introduced, I started peeling back the layers of my individualistic ideals and uncovered something buried deep within me. I discovered that I am capable of caring more about others than I initially imagined. With this realization I started to actualize that I am a compassionate person who wants to bring the joy of learning to my students. This was truly an inspiring experience, affirming my belief that I will sincerely care about my students and do everything I can to help them reach their maximum potential.
>
> (US student teacher upon completion of a teacher preparation program that emphasized core reflection)

This book is different from other books about 'self' that assume teaching and learning can be enhanced through mastering a set of techniques based on a particular theoretical model. The core reflection approach as presented here is about application and technique; it is also about a theoretical model. But, in contrast to other approaches, this book links theory and practice by highlighting the experience of the *person*. The person (teacher or student) is the central and pivotal focus in connecting the approach described here with its potential to enhance the learning process. The voices of the authors and participants represented in these chapters give life and vibrancy to their practices of teaching, modeling, and applying core reflection.

References

Intrator, S., & Kunzman, R. (2006). Starting with the soul. *Educational Leadership, 63*(6), 38–42.

Korthagen, F. A. J. (2004). In search of the essence of a good teacher: Towards a more holistic approach in teacher education. *Teaching and Teacher Education, 20,* 77–97.

Korthagen, F. A. J., & Vasalos, A. (2005). Levels in reflection: Core reflection as a means to enhance professional development. *Teachers and Teaching: Theory and Practice, 11*(1), 47–71.

Miller, J. P. (2000). *Education and the soul: Toward a spiritual curriculum.* Albany, NY: State University of New York Press.

Palmer, P. J. (1998). *The courage to teach: Exploring the inner landscape of a teacher's life.* San Francisco, CA: Jossey-Bass.

Ravitch, D. (2010). *The death and life of the great American school system: How testing and choice are undermining education.* New York: Basic Books.

2

A FOCUS ON THE HUMAN POTENTIAL

Fred A. J. Korthagen

In this chapter the basic ideas of core reflection are presented. We will explain how core reflection is grounded in a shift from an emphasis on deficiencies toward a focus on the human potential. This concurs with a new branch of psychology, called positive psychology, in which there is now much attention to people's personal strengths. We call them *core qualities*. We explain this concept, which is basic to the book, and we invite the reader by means of small activities to connect this concept with his or her own experiences. We discuss the relevance of core qualities, both for teachers and students. This leads us toward a perspective on human development in which self-understanding and interconnectedness are important principles.

Teacher 1 to a student: Peter, the problem with this piece of work of yours is that it is unclear how you got to these results. Next time you should pay more attention to explaining what you did and how you found these outcomes!

Teacher 2 to a student: Well done, John! In this piece of work I can see your creativity. I feel this is a strength of yours that you can use more often and that you can further develop.

Principal 1 to a teacher: If I take the list of teacher competencies, I think there is a problem with your classroom management. I think you should learn how to maintain more control over the classroom.

Principal 2 to a teacher: I admire your commitment to children! I feel this is a personal strength of yours that supports the learning in your classroom. How could you use this quality to further strengthen your teaching?

Mahatma Gandhi said that the real goal of education is to bring out the best in people. Wherever we go in the world, we find that educators agree on this as a pivotal goal of education. And when we speak with school principals or teacher educators, they invariably say that it is crucial to bring out the best in teachers. Yet, in spite of this general consensus around the goal of bringing out the best in others, a lot of confusion seems to exist when it comes to the question of *how* to do this. Although almost everyone in education holds the ideal of supporting others in their growth, people try to do so in many different ways, as we can see in the four examples above.

For a long time, many people have thought that the best way to 'bring out the best' was to confront people with what was not going well and then try to help them improve. This is what we call *the deficiency model*: you try to 'repair' what is weak. This model is strongly intertwined with almost every aspect of education. Look, for example, in how a teacher assesses her students after completing a test. Most teachers mark the parts that are incorrect. Very few teachers write positive remarks in the margin at places where the students have done well. Or observe an evaluative meeting between a school principal and a teacher that focuses on assessing the teacher's instructional planning and implementation. In general, most of the time in such a meeting is devoted to what could be improved in the teacher's behavior and not to an in-depth analysis of the teacher's strengths. But there are some positive exceptions. Some school principals and superintendents have discovered that professional growth among educators is strongly promoted if the evaluative emphasis is put on what goes well and how this can be extended.

Positive Psychology

The deficiency model in education is grounded in a more general view of human growth that has influenced our society as a whole, probably as a result of this dominant view in psychology. During the twentieth century, psychologists have become better and better at mapping and diagnosing abnormalities and traumas in people, at searching for causes to be found in people's life histories, and at finding and prescribing treatments. The idea was that as soon as we know what exactly is the problem with a person, we then may find a solution and 'cure' the person. Martin Seligman, who was the president of the American Psychological Association around the turn of the twenty-first century, took a brave stance against the deficit orientation that was common among almost all of his psychologist colleagues. Together with Mihaly Csikszentmihalyi, who is well known for his publications on the concept of *flow*, Seligman wrote an often quoted article stating that for too long, psychology had focused on pathology, weakness, and the damage done to people (Seligman & Csikszentmihalyi, 2000). According to these two influential psychologists, a critical review of the psychological literature showed that the deficiency model has not been very effective in enhancing people's well-being.

Seligman and Csikszentmihalyi emphasized that psychology had insufficiently acknowledged the human potential. Since the year 2000, Seligman has supported the development of a completely new direction in psychology, called *positive psychology*, which focuses on people's strengths as the fundamental basis for growth. Seligman speaks about nurturing people's *psychological capital* in order to help them develop resilience, the capacity to overcome problems and to see new opportunities in times of trouble. In the end, this makes people more happy, or, to say it in more scientific terms, it enhances people's well-being.

Seligman and Csikszentmihalyi (2000) emphasized that "treatment is not just fixing what is broken; it is nurturing what is best" (p. 7). Hence, they pointed to the importance of positive traits in individuals, which they call *character strengths*, such as creativity, courage, perseverance, kindness, and fairness (Seligman, 2002; Peterson & Seligman, 2004). Central issues in positive psychology are how such strengths can help people cope better with their lives, and enhancing resilience and well-being. These seem to be issues that are also highly relevant for education.

There have been other developments that foreshadowed the rise of positive psychology long before this new branch of the field was founded. For example, in the second half of the twentieth century, the psychologists Rogers and Maslow also focused on the human potential. Their work, grounded in extensive experiences in therapeutic relationships, became the basis for a more student-oriented approach in education that focused on the relationship between the teacher and the student and on the qualities of acceptance, respect, genuineness, and empathy as important ingredients of a teacher's attitude. Although the humanistic-based view, as it was called, created many positive changes in classrooms, for the most part it seemed not much more than just a view, or a 'belief', and little rigorous research was carried out to provide evidence that the principles of a humanistic-based education were effective or made a difference in students' learning. The strength of positive psychology is its focus on solid empirical research, which has, for example, led to evidence-based approaches for helping people identify their personal strengths and build on them.

The change that we are talking about is the change from focusing on the negative and problematic to focusing on quality, potential, and opportunities. Some people make a caricature of this 'new' view of personal growth. They say that, in this new vision, everything is possible and that you will become happy, as long as you think positively and keep smiling. Of course, this is not true, and the caricature has very little to do with positive psychology, which instead says that it helps to know and build on your own personal qualities and to be very conscious about how you do this. It is possible to deal with struggles and misfortunes in a way that makes us stronger and happier. Positive psychologist Barbara Fredrickson (2002) conducted some interesting empirical studies that showed how a focus on failures and inadequacies is counterproductive to creativity, whereas a focus on positive aspects makes people more open, creative, motivated, and effective. Together with mathematician Losada, she was able to conclude from observations of effective management teams and people in happy marriages that people need at least three times as many more positive than negative experiences in their professional or personal relationships in order to grow (Fredrickson & Losada, 2005). This conclusion may challenge the philosophy and practice of many in the field of education!

What has become clear through the work of researchers in positive psychology is that we can influence our own well-being, not by just digging into our problems and trying to 'solve' them, but by building on our strengths, our *psychological capital*. However, an important assumption underlying this book is that the positive side of things is only half the story, as we also take seriously the problems people – children or adults – encounter during their daily struggles. The approach we describe in this book is, ultimately, about connecting the negative and the positive: how can you utilize your problems to discover your qualities, and end up happier and stronger?

Exercise 2.1

1. *Think back on an inspiring situation, in your work or in your private life, in which you were interacting with one or more other people. Look back at this experience with a focus on what you did in the situation and how you did this. And how did you feel? Was a there a certain quality in you that came to the fore, a personal strength?*

2. *Now go back to a situation that was less pleasant or that was difficult, or perhaps even a situation in which you felt stuck. What was so unpleasant or difficult in this situation? What happened within you? What did you think? How did you feel?*

3. *Is there a difference in the degree to which you used your personal strengths in both situations?*

4. *Regarding the unpleasant or difficult situation, was there a possibility to use one of your personal strengths more?*

Exercise 2.1 may have helped you discover or remember some core qualities in you, and perhaps it even gave you some ideas about how you can use these more often in your work or in your private life. But perhaps it was difficult for you in this exercise to focus on your strengths. Most people are so used to dwelling on their failures and nasty experiences, instead of their successes and assets, that the negative aspects often draw all the attention.

Although we believe there are certainly benefits to understanding more about your own problems and traumas, and how they can be grounded in your personal history, this doesn't always lead to a solution for today's problems. Sometimes these problems even get worse because, for example, you start to believe that something is wrong with you. This belief system alone can create serious problems. For instance, if you think that you are not able to learn mathematics, this may rapidly become a self-fulfilling prophecy, which may create a block to ever learning how to solve quadratic equations.

Core Qualities in Teachers

We will now discuss what the view of positive psychology could mean for education. Let us first look at what we mean by teachers' strengths and their psychological capital. After that, we will turn our attention toward students.

Exercise 2.2
Think back on an inspiring teacher you have had in school or at the university level.
Write down one or two characteristics of this teacher.

At a variety of educational conferences and in professional courses, we have asked people the same question: think back on an inspiring teacher you've once had and identify a characteristic of this teacher. Most of the answers we get from this prompt name characteristics such as enthusiasm, commitment, care, humor, passion – in other words, personal qualities. Educationalists are not used to putting such qualities at the foreground of their views and theories on education. As noted above, they are rarely included in official lists of teacher competencies and assessment criteria. In such lists, often the focus lies more on technical competence or skills and not on personal qualities, whereas most of us have had the experience that personal qualities are what made the memorable difference in our teachers. As Tickle (1999, p. 123) puts it: "In policy and practice the identification and development of personal qualities, at the interface between aspects of one's personal virtues and one's professional life, between personhood and teacherhood, if you will, has had scant attention." Tickle mentions such qualities as empathy, compassion, understanding, tolerance, love, and flexibility. He says that they are essential qualities for teachers, maintaining: "The teacher as a person is the core by which education itself takes place" (p. 136). This does not mean that technical competence is not important in teaching. It surely is. What we want to emphasize, however, is that it does make a difference if teachers' professional competencies are grounded in personal qualities such as empathy, love, enthusiasm, and passion.

While positive psychologists use the term character strengths for these qualities, we prefer the term *core qualities* coined by Ofman (2000), because it refers to the 'core' of the person. The term core qualities also stresses its difference from the concept of 'core competence' (often used in the literature on competency management, for example by Prahalad & Hamel, 1990). Ofman states that core qualities are always potentially present in human beings. He maintains that the distinction between qualities and competencies lies primarily in the fact that qualities come from the inside, while competencies are acquired from the outside. Almaas (1987, p. 175) uses the term *essential aspects*, which he considers absolute in the sense that they cannot be further reduced, or dissected into simpler component parts. This is an interesting observation: indeed, technical competencies, such as the competency to maintain classroom discipline, can be further reduced into sub-competencies, whereas a core quality such as passion or care cannot be split up; they are one 'whole'.

Core Qualities in Students

Now we turn our attention to students in schools, either at the elementary or at the secondary level. But everything we will discuss is equally applicable to university students as well.

EXAMPLE 2.1

Two 9th grade students are working on an assignment to design a truck with a crane capable of hoisting up an object that a person would need both arms to lift. They have to construct a prototype at a scale of 1:5.

The assignment in Example 2.1 is a real challenge for the students. They have to use their creativity along with their analytic strength, perseverance, handiness, and so forth. These are core qualities that are not only important for the rest of their school careers, but also in the rest of their lives. This is an important reason to focus on children's core qualities: these qualities can be applied to many different situations. They are less domain-specific than many subject-specific competencies; in other words, they have a *high transfer value*.

If we want to make optimal use of the value of core qualities, it is important that teachers help children recognize such assets in themselves and use them as much as possible.

EXAMPLE 2.2

A student in elementary school has written the following answers to five problems:

$12 + 9 = 21$
$35 - 7 = 28$
$25 + 8 = 32$
$14 - 8 = 6$
$33 + 9 = 42$
$36 - 7 = 29$

Many teachers will react by saying "One mistake!" instead of "Well done, they are almost all correct." A teacher who responds "well done" may even go one step further and use his or her experiences with the student to name a core quality. For example, when a student has not been very motivated or attentive for a period of time, and now shows improvement in these areas, the teacher may say: "You have the ability to be very focused!" And it is helpful then not to talk about the period of time in which the student used that quality less.

Sometimes we ask students: "When was the last time a teacher noticed a quality of yours?" Generally these students look at us as if to say: "What on earth are you talking about?" Then we explain what we mean, but generally this only clarifies that core qualities are seldom mentioned in school. Teachers do say things like "well done," which generally leaves the student with a positive feeling but brings little specific insight into what exactly was well done. Teachers seldom say: "I see in you the quality of persistence," or, "Wow, you are creative!"

Through such interventions, children can feel truly seen as a person. This is generally not the case if teachers, in their feedback, focus on competencies. The interesting thing is that core qualities can actually be stimulated or nurtured in this way. For example, if students are seen displaying their quality of 'care' for others, as we start to recognize and name this quality as a personal strength, they become more caring, as if qualities somehow grow through giving them attention. If a teacher views a student as creative, this student will become more motivated to use her creativity in future situations. We do not believe in using this as a new 'trick' to promote children's growth. In our view, what is needed is that the teacher is whole-heartedly committed to children's growth, so that the children can feel that the feedback on core qualities is genuine and stems from the teacher's love and care for them.

Some teachers believe that you have to wait with giving feedback to children about their core qualities until the secondary school level, because only then they can understand what you mean. However, elementary school teachers have noticed that you can start at an early age, for example when children are four years old.

EXAMPLE 2.3

A teacher in a elementary school in Amsterdam discusses with her 3rd grade students what they are good at. The students react enthusiastically. The boys focus on their physical abilities: one can stand on his hands, the other can spin on his hands and feet, and a third can do push-ups with one hand. Gradually the students start to see that there are also other qualities that are important, such as: creativity, care for others, attentiveness, and so forth. Next, the students make a birthday calendar of their group. Each name on the calendar is accompanied by a core quality of the child.

Of course, you will have to find a language that children understand. This appears to be less difficult than people expect. Because children feel truly seen when their core qualities are fed back to them, they are very strong at understanding what the words mean. Some examples as used by an elementary school teacher:

Honesty: You tell exactly what has really happened. You are honest.

Curiosity: You like to understand things, and discover new things. You are curious.

Patience: You are very good at waiting and at working on something that takes time. You have much patience.

Humor: You can make nice jokes. You have humor.

Does the Emphasis on Core Qualities Work?

An interesting question is: Does it work? Does the attention given to core qualities lead to positive outcomes? And if so, what kind of outcomes? A striking experiment was carried out by Seligman and his colleagues (Seligman et al., 2005). With the aid of a questionnaire measuring people's core qualities, they helped participants in an experimental group to identify their 'top strengths' and asked them to use one top strength in a new way, every day during one week. Before and after the week, the experimental group used the questionnaire to rate their well-being, in other words, the general feeling of happiness in their lives. The remarkable outcome was that, after the week, the experimental group scored significantly higher than a control group whose assignment had been to write a short passage each day of the week on something they remembered from their past. Even more striking, however, was the finding that half a year after the experiment, the experimental group still scored significantly higher than the control group on the well-being questionnaire. The idea that people can become happier through such a small experiment, and with such a small investment of time and energy, seems to suggest that there might be an important positive impact from a focus on core qualities.

However, in these times of emphasis on academic standards and testable outcomes, one might wonder if it is sufficient that people become more happy. In this respect, other studies in positive psychology reveal outcomes that should, in our view, convince people in education of the need to focus on students' and teachers' core qualities. For example, research by Fredrickson (2002, 2009) has consistently shown that a focus on positivity leads to higher motivation, more self-efficacy, and better performance.

All this has led Dutch researcher Peter Ruit to carry out an experiment with elementary school students quite similar to the experiment done by Seligman and his team. In Ruit's experiment, described in Chapter 9 of this book, we can see that the outcomes in children at least partly concur with the results of the research in positive psychology. Ruit's study showed that by means of a short intervention, young students can be helped to become aware of their core qualities, to choose one of them, and to use this core quality consciously in new ways. After three months, more than 80% of the students still remembered the chosen core quality and 58% of the students indicated that they still used it.

In another example given in this book, we tried to promote teachers' awareness of the importance of focusing on strengths – in themselves and in their students.

Although our intervention is generally limited to a small number of workshop days for staff and the promotion of peer coaching, it seems to be highly successful according to the participants (Korthagen & Vasalos, 2008). In Chapter 8 of this book, Attema-Noordewier and her colleagues report the outcomes of their study that introduced such a staff development program into six elementary schools in the Netherlands. One important outcome was that teachers became more focused on their students' qualities instead of their weaknesses. Teachers also felt more effective in recognizing and tackling obstacles to learning and personal growth, in students and in themselves. Thus, much more potential was being liberated than before, again in teachers as well as in students. When looking at the professional development that took place in these teachers, it was evident that they became more successful in creating the conditions for optimal learning.

Through all of this, the relationships between teachers and students and among students changed fundamentally. In other words, the culture of the school changed. Participants reported back that this even expresses itself in coffee table conversations. Parents reported in their observations that their children were changing in a positive sense. Really *seeing* each other and making personal contact then became central themes in teaching. Teachers started to recognize that these form the basis for interpersonal relations supporting learning and growth (see Chapter 8 for more details). When talking about outcomes, what those involved in our workshops said is the most telling, as in the statements below.

A female teacher put it like this:

I have never felt more at home in my team than I do now. We are really talking to each other. That to me is the biggest outcome. And add to this the wonderful fact that it has already been channeled to the children. Life in the school is vibrant again. This is something I have missed for years. I think this is very precious.

Another teacher reported:

I find it something very dear to me that I can stand there in front of the class and hand this 'flow' to these children, and that they hand it on to each other. And the trust you then give them and that they gain in each other. You then really have the feeling that you are giving them something for society, and that it is not just the math lesson that matters.

The head of an elementary school said:

Teachers' progress can be observed in the student group. Even an 'old hand' tells me with a broad grin that he is doing things differently! That, too, I have been able to observe. They [the teachers] are really involved in it. I also notice that relations between teachers and students are improving.

Mutual understanding is genuinely growing. There is more openness between colleagues.

Another school principal said:

To have taken this road together as a team has tremendous added value, has triggered a lot of commitment and awareness, and is being much appreciated by the parents.

A colleague, who was a regular visitor to one of the participating schools, but had not been there for the last three months, noticed:

Something has changed here, something has happened. Earlier, there were frequent grumblings, now there is a positive atmosphere in the school and in the team room.

Adding to the examples above, we have also worked with teacher educators in the US, the Netherlands, and several other countries, sometimes with even more striking results. Here are some of the evaluative remarks of US participants following a four-day workshop on 'core reflection'.

- The biggest benefit for me has been learning new tools for refocusing problems and obstacles into strengths.
- I gained a sense of self-identity, freedom from limiting beliefs, empowerment to fulfill my life purpose.
- You would not know how much profound impact you've done to me personally and professionally. I feel so fortunate to be there at the first workshop you've given in America!
- To function from a place of strength, to affirm the qualities in self and other, and to have language that is approachable are all incredible valuable.
- Since returning, I have told colleagues and students that in my many years as an educator, I think this has been the most powerful and transformative experience I have ever had.
- The techniques of core reflection are really limitless in their application.
- This has been the most profound, influential workshop I've ever had in my life. It presented me with, no, immersed me in an ideal vision for my work, my teaching and my way of being.

In Chapter 12 of this book, Erin Wilder, Younghee Kim, and William Greene report on the significant changes in teacher preparation at Southern Oregon University resulting from two professional development programs on core reflection. Again, their study shows that the outcomes were not only important for individual teacher educators and their students, but that a remarkable cultural change took place within their School of Education.

The other chapters in this book, too, present evidence that core reflection has a strong impact on student, teachers, and teacher educators. The chapters in this book also highlight *how* and *why* core reflection works. Before ending the present chapter, we wish to focus on the deeper meaning of such outcomes for the development of identity – both as a person and as a professional.

Identity Formation

We believe that becoming aware of your own core qualities is an important ingredient in identity formation. For children, we think it is important to develop a sense of who they are as human beings and what their role in the world might be. For teachers, we connect the idea of core quality awareness to the notion of professional identity, a topic that has received much attention over the last few years.

It is clear that we live in a complex and rapidly changing society where, for many people, the traditional bonds of family and community, have eroded. As a consequence, people have less connection to the self-evident beliefs and values that were once integral to these traditional bonds. Sometimes this familial and social estrangement means that people have to discover for themselves their own direction and purpose in life. Core reflection suggests that staying in contact with their own personal *identity* and developing core qualities is a prerequisite for people to tap into their own unique potential, for directing themselves in realizing that potential, and for relating to other people. As Buber (1983, first edition 1923) helped us see, one's personal identity is formed and experienced in the company of other people. Moreover, the encounters we have with other people help us realize that we are not merely individuals but that our lives are connected with others, in fact, that we could not survive without them. In other words, it is in the relationship between oneself and other people that self-understanding and the awareness of one's *interconnectedness* with other humans becomes possible.

In our view, it is a teacher's task to guide children in these, perhaps most essential, aspects of life: the development of self-understanding and a sense of interconnectedness. This can be crucial in situations in which children struggle with their parents' divorce, or other family problems, but also of issues such as finding their place within the peer group, dealing with stress and emotions, meeting the demands of today's school system, and so forth. These challenges can direct the child toward questions such as: who am I (*self-understanding*), and how can I live the life I wish in supportive relationships with others (*interconnectedness*), amidst the challenges that I am faced with? We believe it is an important goal of education to help children find answers to these fundamental questions. This has a direct bearing on the role of schools and teachers, and thus on the development of teachers' professional identity.

References

Almaas, A. H. (1987). *Diamond heart, book 1.* Berkeley, CA: Diamond Books.

Buber, M. (1983). *Ich und Du.* [Me and you.] Heidelberg: Schneider.

Fredrickson, B. L. (2002). Positive emotions. In C. R. Snyder, & S. J. Lopez (Eds.), *Handbook of positive psychology* (pp. 120–134). Oxford: Oxford University Press.

Fredrickson, B. (2009). *Positivity: Groundbreaking research reveals how to embrace the hidden strength of positive emotions, overcome negativity, and thrive.* New York: Random House.

Fredrickson, B. L., & Losada, M. L. (2005). Positive affect and the complex dynamics of human flourishing. *American Psychologist, 60,* 678–686.

Korthagen, F. & Vasalos, A. (2008, March). *'Quality from within' as the key to professional development.* Paper presented at the Annual Meeting of the American Educational Research Association. New York.

Ofman, D. (2000). *Core qualities: A gateway to human resources.* Schiedam: Scriptum.

Peterson, C., & Seligman, M. E. P. (2004). *Character strengths and virtues: A handbook and classification.* Oxford, NY: Oxford University Press.

Prahalad, C. K., & Hamel, G. (1990). The core competence of the corporation. *Harvard Business Review, 68*(3), 79–91.

Seligman, M. E. P. (2002). Positive psychology, positive prevention, and positive therapy. In: C.R. Snyder & S. J. Lopez (Eds.), *Handbook of positive psychology* (pp. 3–9). Oxford, NY: Oxford University Press.

Seligman, M. E. P., & Csikszentmihalyi, M. (2000). Positive psychology: An introduction. *American Psychologist, 55*(1), 5–14.

Seligman, M. E. P., Steen, T., Park, N., & Peterson, C. (2005). Positive psychology progress: Empirical validation of interventions. *American Psychologist, 60*(5), 410–421.

Tickle, L. (1999). Teacher self-appraisal and appraisal of self. In R. P. Lipka & T. M. Brinthaupt (Eds.), *The role of self in teacher development* (pp. 121–141). Albany, NY: State University of New York Press.

3

THE CORE REFLECTION APPROACH

Fred A. J. Korthagen

This chapter presents the framework of core reflection. A basic idea is that the use of one's core qualities creates *flow* and a natural and rapid type of learning. This means that an inspiring process from within takes place, which contrasts with situations where external pressure is put on people. The potential for flow is present in everyone involved in education: students, teachers, school principles, teacher educators, and so on. However, in reality there is often non-flow, as outer and inner obstacles obstruct the inner potential of people. With the aid of the so-called *onion model* more clarity can be created about the inner obstacles in people, and this chapter explains how such obstacles can be overcome. This is illustrated with examples that clarify the use of core reflection in coaching. They show how the connection between thinking, feeling, and wanting is crucial in restoring flow in people. The chapter ends with a discussion of the scientific background of the core reflection approach.

Science teacher Sandra prompted her students to study their science textbook before today's lesson on genetics and to come up with interesting questions on the topic. The students asked all kinds of questions about themselves and their parents, and they had many questions about hereditary diseases. Sandra had succeeded in stimulating and engaging her students in a high-interest discussion on genetics, and this level of motivation proved exciting for Sandra. She thought: "The students have enjoyed the lesson and learned a lot." When the bell rang, the students asked, "Can we go on with this discussion in our next science lesson?"

In the situation described above, the students were actively involved and motivated. Although the topic of genetics is not simple, it created stimulating challenges for them. When students are enjoying new challenges, but feel they can deal with them, they often experience a special sensation which shows itself in a phenomenon called 'shining eyes'. Shining eyes reveal that there is a certain 'click' between the person and the situation.

In the educational literature, relatively little can be found to describe this sensation, but the psychologist Csikszentmihalyi (1990) studied a phenomenon that seems to come close to what we are talking about. He named it *flow* on the basis of his systematic research into the creative processes of artists in his search to understand what happens in these people when they create art. The artists told him that they often experienced a kind of internal 'flow', and he decided to use this as a concept that deserved further analysis. Later, Csikszentmihalyi and his team discovered that the same phenomenon happens to many people in various situations, and that the flow experience is in fact a fundamental and natural part of realizing the human potential.

In the example above, an observer would have seen through their body language that both the students and their teacher were in flow; not only did the students have shining eyes, but one would also have observed bodily gestures expressing involvement and enthusiasm. This is not only important from an affective perspective, though of course it is nice and important that the students appreciated Sandra's lesson. But it is also important for education because when people are in flow, they learn easily and rapidly. It is as if learning becomes something natural, just like in the joyful learning that we can sometimes observe in young children. When there is flow in the process, concentration on the here-and-now, enthusiasm, openness, motivation, and cognitive understanding all go together. The opening example is a situation of 'group flow'. The interesting thing about the flow experience is that it is contagious. It is hard to remain sad or cramped when you are with someone who is fully in flow. The sad thing is that non-flow is also contagious, as we can observe in many classrooms.

Flow and Core Qualities

In our example, not only were the students in flow, but teacher Sandra experienced it as well. This flow experience in grounded in her core qualities; she was creative, committed to her students and to her subject, and she was brave enough to start a classroom discussion that she could not fully predict and direct. Thus, her core quality of flexibility was also important and supported the flow experience. Also interesting is that Sandra's flow was connected with an inner ideal of hers – she wants to create student involvement and motivation in her classroom.

Flow is an important phenomenon when we speak about learning and human growth. Table 3.1 shows some features of the flow experience, based on the work of Csikszentmihalyi and others.

TABLE 3.1 Characteristics of Flow

---

1. The person experiences a pleasant challenge, one that he or she feels is not routine, but manageable.
2. While in action, the person has a feeling of 'this is the real me'.
3. There is an absorption in the here-and-now.
4. The person's core qualities are manifest in his or her actions.
5. The person feels connected with an inner ideal (a broad, general ideal or something specific aimed at in the situation).
6. The situation gives energy to the person.
7. This energy is visible in the body; there are bodily expressions of involvement and 'shining eyes'.
8. The person experiences relatively little fear.
9. Time becomes relative.
10. There is rapid learning in the person.

The flow experience is not something esoteric or something exceptional. Most people experience a certain amount of flow during their everyday lives. Exercise 3.1 is meant to help the reader reflect on such flow experiences.

Exercise 3.1

Think back on an inspiring situation in your work or in your private life, for example the same situation that you chose in Exercise 2.1, or another, recent situation. Preferably, choose a situation that made you feel really good. Now, it may be interesting to reflect on this situation and see to what degree this was a flow experience. Check the ten features in Table 3.1.

Using the Inner Potential

Characteristic #10 is especially important for education. As all good teachers know, when there is flow in a classroom or another educational situation, learning becomes a natural thing. Learning is then something that seems to happen from within the person. We call this *learning from within*, as opposed to learning that is the result of a certain degree of pressure from the outside. The latter is rather common in education. Generally, outside pressure leads to fight, flight, or freeze (F-F-F) responses that we can see happening in teachers and students almost everywhere, at various moments during their everyday lives. These F-F-F or 'survival' responses are not very supportive for enhancing learning, whereas the F of Flow is almost synonymous to natural and rapid learning. We can summarize this with two opposite figures (see Figures 3.1a and 3.1b).

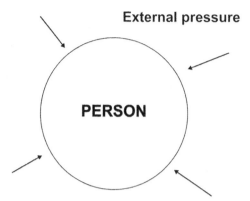

Response: FIGHT, FLIGHT or FREEZE

FIGURES 3.1A AND B Fight-flight-freeze responses versus flow

Figure 3.1b emphasizes that the flow experience is enhanced if a person is in touch with his or her core qualities and ideals. If that is the case, learning from within seems to happen almost by itself. In figure 3.1b, the person's 'inner core' is represented by a diamond and here we follow the idea of Almaas (1987) that there is *an inner diamond* in people with great potential. This seems to parallel a recent notion in psychology, namely the notion of 'psychological capital'. We consider it helpful to look at core qualities and ideals as important aspects of an individual's inner potential, a potential that promises high value for both the person and the environment.

It may be interesting to take a closer look at the relation between ideals and core qualities. It is remarkable that these two are so intertwined in people. If someone has an *ideal* such as creating more connection between people, this person generally exhibits a well-developed core quality of connection or commitment. If someone has the ideal to fully understand a mathematical topic, we may observe core qualities such as analytic understanding, curiosity, and steadfastness. Hence, when we look at a person's ideal, we usually discover that this person has important core qualities related to this ideal.

We can also start with looking at people's core qualities and see how they are connected to their ideals. For example, if a teacher has the core quality of enthusiasm for her subject, we can often observe that she has the ideal to express that enthusiasm and try to elicit enthusiasm in her students too. If someone has the quality of being supportive of others and the core quality of care, such a person generally has the ideal to make other people feel good. There seems to be an innate drive in people to bring out their full potential into the world by making full use of their core qualities.

Exercise 3.2
Identify an ideal that you have in your work or life in general and try to find two or three core qualities within yourself that are connected to this ideal.

Non-Flow

By now, the reader may start to think that all this sounds extremely positive, perhaps too positive. Isn't it the reality of everyday life that things often do not go smoothly and that we often feel stuck in situations? Indeed, our focus on the flow experience, on core qualities and ideals, is just half of the story. On many occasions, there is no flow at all, and the person experiences a problem.

EXAMPLE 3.1
Michael, age 12, wants to become a computer expert. In fact, he considers himself to be one already. A friend asks for Michael's help because he lost the internet connection on his computer. Michael fails in finding a solution. The next day, his friend tells Michael that he called a help-desk and that the problem was solved in five minutes. Michael feels frustrated.

In Example 3.1, we see a mismatch between on the one hand Michael's ideal in the situation (and also possibly his core qualities), and on the other hand what he is actually able to accomplish. This is something that regularly happens in children; they often tend to overestimate or underestimate themselves, and as a result they may encounter frustration. Thus, they have a non-flow experience. This is not completely bad, it is simply the way in which people develop a realistic self-image. A good teacher might recognize this and try to support Michael in his developing such a realistic self-image. This may be very important, as children often shift to an opposite belief about themselves, for example, "I am a failure with computers."

Our view on situations like the one in the example is that the person's core qualities (his inner potential) are potentially still present (perhaps Michael has the qualities of enthusiasm, commitment, creativity and an inquiring mind), but that these qualities are somehow blocked in the person.

Dealing with Problems

EXAMPLE 3.2

James (history teacher): Ellen, can we talk about last week's test?

Ellen (student): Yes?

James: You had this bad mark, and I strongly believe you can do better!

Ellen: I am just not good at history.

James: Well, I don't agree . . . But I want to ask you something: What would be your ideal for next week's test?

Ellen: Yeah, of course I would like to score higher, otherwise my average score for history will be really bad.

James: Great that you want to go for it. This sounds hopeful and powerful. Shall we look at this together now? How did you prepare for last week's test?

Ellen: Well, um, . . . yeah, I did try to go over the chapter again, but to be honest, I thought it would lead me nowhere.

James: How come?

Ellen: I am just not good at history.

James: This is a strong belief of yours, isn't it? How does this belief affect you when you prepare for such a test?

Ellen: ????

James: I mean, how do you feel when you're thinking 'I am not good at this'?

Ellen: Well, . . . a bit demotivated . . . I don't feel much energy then.

James: And then you really go for it? (with humor in his voice)

Ellen: Well, of course not. I find it difficult then to concentrate.

James: Mmm, . . . and then you do not succeed, and then you think: 'You see. . . I was right'?

Ellen: Uh, . . . yes, indeed.

James: What a pity . . . But let's look at something else. What is a subject you're good at?

Ellen: Math.

James: If you prepare for a math test, how do you feel then?

Ellen: Well, fine, then I work well.

James: What do you then think about yourself?

Ellen: Then I think: this is something I can do.

James: How does that affect the way in which you work?

Ellen: Uh, . . . yeah, then I can concentrate better.

James: And then you do well on the test?

Ellen: Sure.

James: Do you understand what I am aiming at? In the math case you believe you can make it. You sue your core quality of trust, and that is why you work hard and you get a good result. With history, you do not believe you can make it, you become depressed, and as a result you cannot prepare yourself well for the test.

Ellen: Yeah, you're right, there is something in this. In fact, what I do is perhaps not so smart. But, you know, I am just not good at history.

James: You keep believing this, isn't it? How would it be to no longer stick to this belief? Personally, I think you're smart enough to do better at history.

Ellen: Do you think so?

James: Yes, sure. And how do you feel when I say this?

Ellen: Um, I feel there is perhaps hope . . .

James: Yes, and how would it be to connect with this hope and with the kind of trust that you're using with math? How would you then work on the next test?

Ellen: Yeah, well, more enthusiastically.

James: And probably you will then put more energy into it?

Ellen: Yes, that is true. I wish I would have had this conversation before last week's test!

In Example 3.2, the teacher takes a different focus than is usual in education. Generally, when there is problem with a student, a teacher focuses on the problem and tries to analyze the situation in order to better understand the problem, hoping that this may lead to a solution. In practice, this often leads to 'heavy' conversations that do not give students much energy. Through the emphasis on what went wrong, the atmosphere often becomes somewhat depressed. The feelings involved block a creative approach toward the problem, as positive psychologist Fredrickson (2002, 2009) showed in her empirical studies. A focus on the negative appears to limit one's cognitive resources, whereas positive feelings promote creativity and energy. This is why the teacher in the example focuses on Ellen's ideal and on positive experiences. This helps the student to get more into touch with her inner potential.

Of course, it is important for a teacher to let her students know that their problems are taken seriously. But what appears to be most helpful as a next step is that the teacher keeps focusing on the inner potential of her students, that is, their core qualities and ideals, and that the teacher keeps believing that through this inner potential, students have the capacity to deal with their problems, knowing that this capacity is sometimes blocked by a thought-action pattern that can be overcome. This principle is visualized in Figure 3.2.

People are often in the habit of attributing their problems to *outer obstacles*, such as too high standards, too demanding others, inadequate opportunities, and

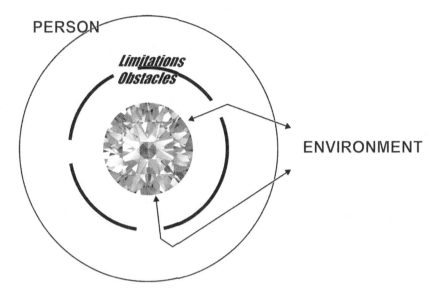

FIGURE 3.2 Core potential blocked by inner obstacles and limitations

so forth. It is important to realize that problems are often the result of limited self-concepts, or limited beliefs about the situation. These are the *inner obstacles* that hold people back from their optimal functioning.

Exercise 3.3
Identify at least one belief about yourself that often obstructs your functioning. How would your life be if you would no longer have this belief?

In fact, Figure 3.2 is not very precise: the person is drawn as a circle with a diamond inside and a ring around the diamond, representing an inner obstacle. However, in reality the personality is more complex. We can make the figure more precise by describing the inner world of the person with the aid of various 'layers'. For his purpose, we use the so-called *onion model*.

The Onion Model

The onion model is a variant of the Bateson model (Dilts, 1990 and Korthagen, 2004) and is presented in Figure 3.3. The model also shows the questions related to each of the six layers.

The onion model

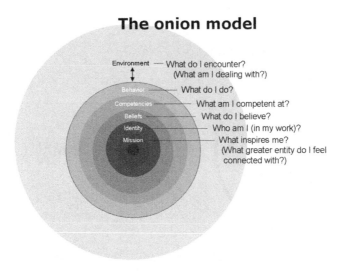

FIGURE 3.3 The onion model

We will now discuss the meaning of the six layers in the onion model.

1. *The environment*: this layer refers to everything that a person encounters outside of herself. In the case of a student, this involves the teacher, the whole classroom setting, the subject matter, the school culture with all its implicit and explicit norms, and so forth. In the above example of Ellen, a challenging part of her environment is the history tests.
2. *Behavior*: this refers to what the person does, how he or she copes with the challenges in the environment. In Ellen's case, her test preparation behavior is not very effective.
3. *Competencies*: this layer describes what a person is competent at doing. Ellen seems to have the competencies necessary to prepare well for a test, but these competencies seem blocked by the next two layers.
4. *Beliefs*: this layer refers to what a person believes about a situation. With the term 'beliefs' we refer to assumptions about the outer world, which are often unconscious. In the example, Ellen believes the test will be too difficult, and this belief then becomes a self-fulfilling prophecy.
5. *Identity*: this layer refers to people's assumptions about themselves, their self-concepts. In Ellen's case, the most important obstacle seems to be located at this layer: she does not believe she is someone who can do well at history.
6. *Mission*: this layer is concerned with what inspires us, and what gives meaning and significance to our work or our lives. Whereas the layer of identity has to do with how we experience ourselves and our self-concepts, the layer of

mission is about our ideals. Hence, for many people this is also the layer of meaning-making in a religious sense.

In the 'core of the onion' we may locate the person's core qualities. An important rule is that when these core qualities influence the outer onion layers (i.e., when there is a 'radiation' from the inside out), the person experiences flow.

EXAMPLE 3.3

Jennifer teaches in the fourth grade (environment). She sees herself (identity) as a 'guide' who supports children's development and who teaches them how to learn. In that way she feels she contributes to the world by assisting the children in becoming self-reliant and self-developing adults (mission). In order to do so, she believes it is important to help children find and assess their own answers to questions they have (belief). Therefore, she helps them develop those skills and guides them through their learning process with questions and hints (competencies), and she uses her qualities of patience and trust (core qualities).

In Example 3.3, we see that the various onion layers are in harmony with each other. This is called *alignment* of the layers. When alignment occurs, a person's behavior represents a harmonious connection between the 'inside' (the inner layers) and the 'outside' (the environment). This implies that the behavior is both an effective response to the demands of the situation and personally fulfilling. This adds an important aspect to the notion of 'adequate behavior'. For example, when a teacher interacts with a class by asking questions, building on the answers given, eliciting further questions from the pupils, and so on, technically speaking this may be adequate teacher behavior, but the interaction has a deeper impact if the teacher's behavior is fed by core qualities such as care, enthusiasm, curiosity, and goal-directedness and if this teacher is in touch with her ideal of promoting self-directed learning in students.

If a person encounters a problem, this inevitably means that there is somewhere a friction between the layers. It may then be helpful to use the onion model to locate that friction and to try and overcome the friction. In other words, the person then tries to find more inner harmony and bring the layers into alignment. We call this process *multi-level learning* (MLL), as it is about learning at all onion layers at the same time. The process of reflection on these layers (levels), including reflection on the most inner layers and one's core qualities, is called *core reflection*. In the above example, in which teacher James talks with student Ellen, we see the teacher promote core reflection. He helps Ellen to get in touch with core qualities and builds upon her ideal. He also helps her find the inner obstacle, which seems to be a negative self-image (at the identity layer), blocking her potential for flow.

Coaching Aimed at Core Reflection

EXAMPLE 3.4

Teacher Laura is strongly committed to enhancing her students' psychological capital. She feels that building self-reliance in children is crucial for their development. Last week she has discussed this subject with the class, as she wants her students to be aware of the significance of the notion of self-reliance. In this context, she has also given examples of limiting thoughts and helped the students to reflect on their own limiting thoughts. Today, the children are working on a biology assignment. What follows is an excerpt from her conversation with her student Anna.

Laura: Do you feel trust in yourself when working on this assignment?
Anna (with dim eyes): Uh, . . . no, I do not have so much trust in myself.
Laura: Do you mean when working on this subject, or in general?
Anna: Um, . . . yeah, in fact I never feel much trust in myself.
Laura: Take a moment to see whether there have been occasions in your life when you did feel trust in yourself?
Anna: Um . . . (a period of silence), yeah, when I went to town to buy Christmas presents for my family, I had some good ideas, and I also made the presents look nice. Yeah, that felt good.
Laura: Great, so then you felt trust?
Anna (with shining eyes): Yes, sure!
Laura: So you do have the quality of trust in you! How does that feel?
Anna (radiating): Yes, good!
Laura: What a pity that you're thinking you do not have trust in yourself . . .
Anna (more sad): Yeah, . . .
Laura: How does it feel inside when you think it is not possible to trust yourself?
Anna: Um, . . . not so good.
Laura: I can see that! And how does it feel when you realize there is always the potential of trust inside you?
Anna (shining again): Yeah, much better!
Laura: How would it be to work on this assignment with this feeling?
Anna: Well, I feel much more positive! Now I believe I am able to do it.
Laura: Beautiful! Do you see how you can 'think yourself down the drain'? That is what we call believing in a limiting thought. And do you see how you are able to make yourself stronger, by just realizing that you do have the quality of trust within you?
Anna (radiating): Yes! Thank you!

In Example 3.4, we see a couple of things that are characteristic for coaching aimed at core reflection:

(1) The focus is not on the problem, but on the student's potential. This creates positive feelings that help this inner potential and flow. Again, we see in Anna how an ideal (of being able to cope with challenges) and her core quality (of trust) are intertwined.

(2) The focus is also on an *inner* obstacle, in this case a limiting belief, and on the realization that such inner obstacles lead to undesirable consequences.

(3) The process does not only aim at *thinking*, but on an awareness of what the person *feels*, especially the tension between his or her inner potential and an inner obstacle, and what the person *wants*. This issue will be further elaborated in the next section.

Thinking, Feeling, and Wanting

Characteristic for flow is that thinking, feeling and wanting all go together and lead to effective behavior. If someone is stuck in his head, there cannot be flow. If someone is merely emotional and stuck in his feelings, flow is also blocked. If a person is very much focused on using his willpower without feeling what is really happening and without using some careful thinking, this does not create much flow either.

Hence, if we wish to help people get into flow, and be in touch with their inner potential, it is helpful to support them in being in touch with their thinking, feeling, and wanting. When people are in flow, there is a connection with all three dimensions. This implies that we can stimulate flow by supporting awareness of thinking, feeling, and wanting, in connection to each other. We use the image that our thinking is in the head, feeling in the heart, and the energy of wanting in the belly (an idea based on Eastern martial arts). We can then speak about moving *the elevator*; the idea is that the elevator runs smoothly along the three 'floors' of thinking, feeling, and wanting (Figure 3.4).

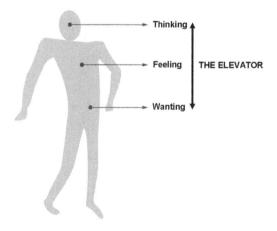

FIGURE 3.4 The elevator

Hence, if we coach someone, it may, for example, be helpful to promote awareness of feelings if the person is very much focused on thinking, and next, to ask what the person really wants.

In sum, flow and deep learning are promoted when the three dimensions of thinking, feeling, and wanting are part of the learning process. We have to state this more precisely, for in fact all three dimensions always play a role in people. Everybody always has thoughts, feelings, and needs or desires, but people are not always aware of this (Damasio, 1999). For example, we often see that if people are struggling with a personal problem, they try to find a solution through thinking. The simple question: 'what are the feelings that are involved?', or 'what would be your wish?' can be an opening to deepening the reflection process. Hence, the elevator principle means that it is helpful to promote *conscious awareness* of these dimensions, which in fact are always present in the person, but often remain unconscious.

Many teachers who use core reflection in their guidance of students report that it helps them to realize more outcomes with students and with less effort. Indeed, they help students to connect to their flow potential. We believe this is a highly important aspect of teaching, for it not only helps to remove obstacles to learning in the here-and-now, but it also has a significant meaning for these students' future lives. When children become aware of what really inspires and motivates them, of their core qualities, and of their self-created inner obstacles, this helps them to draw out the best in themselves, not only in the school, but in the whole of their lives.

Core Reflection in Collegial Coaching

We wish to emphasize that core reflection is an important ingredient for effective learning at all levels of schooling. Core reflection is not only important for student learning, but also for teachers' professional development and the professional growth of school principals. On the basis of research, Chapter 8 will show that using core reflection at all levels in the school (the *congruency principle*) is crucial to creating a stimulating and joyful culture of learning in schools.

EXAMPLE 3.5

Teacher Susan has the ideal that she wants to show respect to her pupils' uniqueness. Everyone has special qualities, and people should in her view try to see these qualities in each other, so that together they can contribute to a better world. Susan wants to prepare her students for such a world.

Two students have handed in a piece of work on volcanoes. Their text reads so well that Susan suspects that the students have simply downloaded this text from the internet. After a quick search, she finds the text on a website. She feels cheated, reacts furiously, and speaks about plagiarism. In retrospect, she regrets her reaction. She realizes she did not react respectfully at all, but she does not know how she could have handled the situation differently.

Susan decides to ask a colleague for a collegial consultation. This colleague is an experienced coach, trained in promoting core reflection. She starts with naming Susan's core qualities, such as her commitment to children, and her openness, as is obvious from the fact that she has asked for this conversation. The colleague also asks about Susan's ideal in her teaching. Susan speaks passionately about her ideal of respect for everyone's uniqueness. While talking, she becomes more aware of the influence of her belief "I was cheated." This belief makes her furious and blocks her from acting the way she really wants. Susan realizes that more often she thinks that people deal with her in an unfair way, and that this has a strong impact on her. From this insight (thinking), her colleague helps Susan to move to her feelings. She feels frustrated and sad that, as a result of her belief "I was cheated," she has let herself be drawn into a type of behavior she does not want to show. This brings her to the dimension of wanting. She wants to behave differently in situations in which she thinks "I was cheated."

Her colleague asks her how she would like to behave, what Susan's ideal is. Susan starts to reconnect with her ideal of respect for the uniqueness of people, and with her desire to promote this ideal in other people, especially her students. The colleague helps Susan to feel the strength of this ideal in herself and the power of her core qualities of care and commitment. This helps to deepen Susan's wanting; she starts to feel the strength of her ideal and core qualities even stronger, and she feels her desire to behave on the basis of this inner potential, even in difficult situations. Her eyes start to shine. Suddenly, she knows what she wants to do. She wants to go to the students and apologize for reacting too harshly. She wants to proceed with the conversation in a respectful way but also to ask her students for more respect for her need for honesty.

Do We Need the Depth of Core Reflection in Education?

One may wonder why Susan's colleague could not have given a simple solution right at the beginning of the conversation. We believe she could indeed have done so. The colleague might, for example, have given the simple advice to have an open conversation with the students. In that case, the colleague would have used what Senge et al. (2004) call a *downloading* strategy (see also Chapter 6); Susan's colleague would have 'downloaded' a solution from her memory, for example, a solution that has worked for herself before. However, it is our experience that often the person having the problem (here, Susan) may try a suggested solution, but then comes back disappointed. The reason is twofold: first, in the real world the limiting belief often comes up again and will unconsciously influence the layer of behavior. Then nothing has really changed and the problem just repeats itself. Second, what is lacking in a solution at the behavioral level is the power originating from the person's core qualities. If Susan is able to connect with this potential, and at the same time is able to recognize her limiting pattern and decides not to follow that pattern anymore, a 'solution' at a deeper level will likely surface, namely one that is connected to Susan's core. This also has another advantage; the core reflection principles involved can be used in many other situations, and thus core reflection can contribute to long-term professional development.

This view concurs with studies into the professional development of teachers. Research has shown that reflection at the behavioral level does not have a strong impact and in the long run thus not contribute much to professional development as is the case when a deeper meaning is found in the situation reflected on (Hoekstra, 2007; Mansvelder-Longayroux, Beijaard & Verloop, 2007; see also Chapter 7). This is the crux of the example; Susan develops a deeper understanding of the situation and of herself. As a result, when she goes back to her students, she may be able to deal with the situation while, at the same time, finding contact with her inner potential. We can summarize this with the aid of Table 3.2.

Still, some teachers tend to believe that it is better to keep things 'simple' and not to use notions such as core qualities, the onion model, and the elevator. We do agree that there are many everyday problems that do not require 'deep reflection'. But, this is different when students or teachers have to cope with important difficulties and struggle with challenges that really concern them. In such situations, the onion layers as well as the dimensions of thinking, feeling, and wanting all play a role, whether we like it or not. That is why it is fruitful to help people become more aware so that they are no longer directed by these aspects in an unconscious manner. By means of core reflection, we can bring thoughts, feelings, and ideals, as well as important inner frictions into our conscious awareness.

We recognize that it is not common in our society to focus our professional conversations on personal issues involving such notions as identity and mission. Even the idea of giving attention to feelings and emotions creates resistance in

TABLE 3.2 Differences between Common Strategies in Reflection and the Core
　　　　　 Reflection Approach

Common Reflection Strategies	*Core Reflection Approach*
• Reflection on problems	• Reflection on positive meaning making
• Focus on the past	• Focus on the here-and-now and on the future
• Focus on the situation	• Focus on personal strengths
• Cognitive (mental) orientation	• Focus on more awareness of thinking, feeling and wanting

some teachers. They do not feel at ease with the notion that dealing with such things may be part of their job. For example, they can have a limiting thought such as "the students may find me weird if I ask a question about how they feel." This belief sometimes changes totally when the teacher does give it a try, notices how the student reacts in a natural way, and observes that the relationship with the student suddenly improves considerably. We have heard and read impressive reports from teachers about their discoveries of the impact of the simple principles discussed in this chapter. We are not talking about just a couple of wonderful stories, but about literally dozens of revealing experiences that changed teachers' lives and the lives of their students.

Summary of Basic Principles

We will now summarize the above by identifying seven principles for promoting core reflection (described in Korthagen & Vasalos, 2005):

1. Promote awareness of ideals and core qualities in the person that are related to the situation reflected on, as a means of strengthening awareness of the layers of identity and mission.
2. Identify internal obstacles to acting out these ideals and core qualities (i.e. promoting awareness of disharmony between the onion layers).
3. Promote awareness of the cognitive, emotional and motivational aspects embedded in 1 and 2.
4. Promote a state of presence in which the person is fully aware (cognitively and emotionally) of the discrepancy or friction between 1 and 2, and the self-created nature of the internal obstacles.
5. Trust the process that takes place from within the person.
6. Support the acting out of one's inner potential within the situation under reflection.
7. Promote autonomy in using core reflection.

Scientific Background

These key principles are not only based on empirical studies in positive psychology, showing important outcomes of a focus on personal strength and positive meaning (Fredrickson, 2002; Seligman et al., 2005), but also on psychological approaches to dealing with inner obstacles in people (e.g., Epstein, 1998). Increasingly, these approaches build on the notion of *mindfulness*, being fully aware of what is happening inside and outside of oneself. The concept of mindfulness originates from Buddhism but is significantly influencing Western psychology (Kabat-Zinn, 1990; Weinstein, Brown, & Ryan, 2009) and education (Meijer, Korthagen, & Vasalos, 2009; Rodgers & Raider-Roth, 2006). Mindfulness can be understood as *full awareness* (e.g., Mingyur Rinpoche, 2007), and differs from conceptual awareness in the sense that "its mode of functioning is perceptual or pre-reflexive" (Brown & Ryan, 2003, p. 823). Mindfulness entails awareness of one's feelings, needs, and bodily reactions, and does not necessarily include conceptual awareness.

As we have seen, essential to the core reflection approach is acknowledging the interrelatedness of cognitive, emotional, and motivational aspects (see principle #3). This is based on insights from psychology (e.g., Epstein, 1998; Ortony, Clore, & Collins, 1988) showing strong connections between cognition and emotion. This concurs with neurobiological findings indicating that in the human brain cognition is interwoven with emotion (Immordano-Yang & Damasio, 2007). This has a practical significance for dealing with problems. As we all know, mere cognitive insight into our inner obstacles does in itself not always help much. We all know things that would be good to do or to refrain from, but that does not mean that we can translate this insight into effective behavior. For example, a teacher who believes "I can never deal with this class" needs more than a cognitive awareness of the constraining impact of this belief; she needs to really *feel* that because of this belief, she makes herself weak and vulnerable. On this basis, she can develop the *will* to reconnect with her strengths (at the layer of identity and mission) and to deconstruct the belief. This appears to be an effective way to promote a breakthrough toward alignment between the onion layers and to (re)create flow. Palmer (1998, p. 64) states: "Heart and mind work as one in our students and in ourselves."

Core reflection is based on a fairly radical view of how one can deal with deeply engrained inhibiting patterns in a person. Regretfully, people often associate this with 'therapy'. However, fundamental to the core reflection approach is the idea that for deep learning it is not necessary to dive into biographical issues. You can learn to rediscover your core potential if you 'unfreeze' by:

a. starting to fully feel the negative, limiting impact of a belief on your functioning in the here-and-now;
b. feeling your own presence in the here-and-now and your capacity of flow as a state prior to that belief (Almaas, 1986);
c. understanding the belief as a powerless mental construct;
d. developing the will to no longer let the belief guide you.

This means that in core reflection, 'going deep' does not mean diving into one's past or dealing with therapeutic issues, but it does refer to the power of possibilities in creating a simple yet deep connection with one's huge inner potential.

References

Almaas, A. H. (1986). *Essence: The diamond approach to inner realization.* York Beach, ME: Samuel Weiser.

Almaas, A. H. (1987). *Diamond heart, book 1.* Berkeley, CA: Diamond Books.

Brown, K. W., & Ryan, R. (2003). The benefits of being present: Mindfulness and its role in psychological well-being. *Journal of Personality and Social Psychology, 84*(4), 822–848.

Csikszentmihalyi, M. (1990). *Flow: The psychology of optimal experience.* New York: Harper & Row.

Damasio, A. (1999). *The feeling of what happens: Body and emotion in the making of consciousness.* London: Heinemann.

Dilts, R. (1990). *Changing belief systems with NLP.* Cupertino, CA: Meta Publications.

Epstein, S. (1998). *Constructive thinking: The key to emotional intelligence.* Westport, Connecticut, CT: Praeger.

Fredrickson, B. L. (2002). Positive emotions. In C. R. Snyder, & S. J. Lopez (Eds.), *Handbook of positive psychology* (pp. 120–134). Oxford: Oxford University Press.

Fredrickson, B. L. (2009). *Positivity: Groundbreaking research reveals how to embrace the hidden strength of positive emotions, overcome negativity, and thrive.* New York: Random House.

Hoekstra, A. (2007). *Experienced teachers' informal learning in the workplace.* Utrecht: IVLOS, Universiteit Utrecht.

Immordano-Yang, M. H., & Damasio, A. (2007). We feel, therefore we learn: The relevance of affective and social neuroscience to education. *Mind, Brain and Education, 1,* 3–10.

Kabat-Zinn, J. (1990). *Full catastrophe living: Using the wisdom of your body and mind to face stress, pain, and illness.* New York: Delacourt.

Korthagen, F. A. J. (2004). In search of the essence of a good teacher: Towards a more holistic approach in teacher education. *Teaching and Teacher Education, 20*(1), 77–97.

Korthagen, F. A. J., & Vasalos, A. (2005). Levels in reflection: Core reflection as a means to enhance professional development. *Teachers and Teaching: Theory and Practice, 11*(1), 47–71.

Mansvelder-Longayroux, D. D., Beijaard, D., & Verloop, N. (2007). The portfolio as a tool for stimulating reflection by student teachers. *Teaching and Teacher Education, 23,* 47–62.

Meijer, P. C., Korthagen, F. A. J., & Vasalos, A. (2009). Supporting presence in teacher education: The connection between the personal and professional aspects of teaching. *Teaching and Teacher Education, 25*(2), 297–308.

Mingyur Rinpoche, Y. (2007). *The joy of living.* New York: Harmony Books.

Ortony, A., Clore, G. L., & Collins, A. (1988). *The cognitive structure of emotions.* Cambridge: Cambridge University Press.

Palmer, P. J. (1998). *The courage to teach.* San Francisco, CA: Jossey-Bass.

Rodgers, C. R., & Raider-Roth, M. B. (2006). Presence in teaching. *Teachers and Teaching: Theory and Practice, 12*(3), 265–287.

Seligman, M. E. P., Steen, T., Park, N., & Peterson, C. (2005). Positive psychology progress: Empirical validation of interventions. *American Psychologist, 60*(5), 410–421.

Senge, P., Scharmer, C. O., Jaworski, J., & Flowers, B. S. (2004). *Presence: Exploring profound change in people, organizations and society.* London: Nicolas Brealey.

Weinstein, N., Brown, K. W., & Ryan, R. M. (2009). A multi-method examination of the effects of mindfulness on stress attribution, coping, and emotional well-being. *Journal of Research in Personality, 43,* 374–385.

PART II
Core Reflection with Teachers

Core reflection may influence many aspects of education. It can have a strong effect on students, teachers, teacher educators, school principals, and others working in education. To clarify this, the book is divided into several parts, each focusing on a specific group in education. In this second part of the book, the focus will be on the impact core reflection can have on *teachers*.

4

TEACHING FROM THE INSIDE OUT

Discovering and Developing the Self-That-Teaches

John T. King and Jo-Anne Lau-Smith

This chapter examines a multi-faceted approach to integrating core reflection across multiple dimensions of a secondary level teacher preparation program. John King and Jo-Anne Lau-Smith explore the two-year process by which teacher educators integrated core reflection within their practices, the effects this had upon student teachers' sense of mission, identity and behavior, and the tensions experienced by both. Finally, attention is paid to the reciprocal impact that the transformations experienced by student teachers had upon the personal and professional development of the teacher educators themselves.

Discovering the Disconnected Self

Today's teachers confront an ever-growing array of pressures stemming from larger class sizes, increasingly needy and diverse student populations, and escalating calls for accountability based on demonstrable evidence of teacher effectiveness. At the same time, teacher autonomy and creativity are being curtailed by ever-tightening administrative controls such as the adoption of prescribed curricula and demands to tailor instruction to preparing for high-stakes testing or other pre-determined learning goals. Faced with this convergence of factors, alarming numbers of teachers are electing to leave the profession (Darling-Hammond, 2000). For those who choose to remain, many report feelings of dissatisfaction and alienation arising from the realization that aspects of their day-to-day activities are divorced from, or even in direct conflict with, their reasons for entering the profession (Wiebke & Bardin, 2009; Tye & O'Brien, 2002; MacDonald, 1999).

connect

It is no small wonder, then, that many educators experience feelings of being disconnected from significant portions of their work or from their personal sense of meaning, inspiration, and creativity.

A pressing issue for seasoned educators, this crisis of disconnection can be particularly acute for beginning and pre-service teachers. Emerging educators confront unique situational and developmental factors that render them susceptible to adopting an external locus of control and becoming habituated to disregard their individual capacities, ideals, and beliefs about teaching and learning. Keenly aware of being constantly evaluated by others and often lacking confidence or a clear sense of their personal or professional identity, student teachers are frequently in positions where they may perceive it necessary or advantageous to conform to the expectations of those holding power over their immediate circumstances and professional futures.

Such considerations can be a powerful source of insecurity and distress. Entering the third month of her student teaching field placement in a middle school classroom, for example, Alison, a graduate student in the Master of Arts teacher preparation program at Southern Oregon University (SOU), writes about the tension between her vision for herself as an educator and the apparent expectations of her mentor teacher:

> I know I have to keep control of the classroom, but I don't want to do it by yelling at students or having them be afraid of me like they are of [my mentor teacher]. But then, when a kid speaks out of turn, that's what she is expecting me to do. She jumps in and reprimands them if I don't and that seems to show students that I'm not in charge. Then she takes me out in the hallway and lectures me on how I can't worry about "being nice" because then they'll walk all over me.

Although Alison had already completed academic coursework and developed a detailed classroom management plan aligned with her own philosophical stance, she worries that her mentor teacher expects her to abandon these plans and instead clone her more authoritarian teaching style: "I guess I just have to toe the line while I'm here because otherwise I won't get a good recommendation from her. But now I'm wondering whether I'm really cut out for this."

Within their field placements, student teachers' performance is regularly observed and evaluated according to overtly behavioral checklists of prescribed

connect

teaching competencies. More broadly, teachers at all stages of their career are increasingly tasked with developing curriculum aligned with state content standards or, in a growing number of cases, simply implementing curriculum and lessons that have been uniformly adopted at the school or district level. In each of these instances, regardless how pedagogically worthy such standards or requirements may be, the richness and complexity of the teaching process becomes easily reduced to "acting like a teacher" and teachers are conditioned to look outside themselves for direction and conform to the demands and expectations of others. Within an educational system already trending toward tightened administrative control, such conditioning diminishes the role of teachers to technical functionaries (Giroux, 2004) whose charge is limited to the efficient delivery of curriculum. This chapter describes the efforts of two teacher educators to counter these tendencies by fostering teacher autonomy and authenticity through core reflection.

Embracing Core Reflection in Teacher Education

For teachers seeking to develop or recover a sense of personal connection and meaningfulness in their work, core reflection provides a process for discerning, developing, and learning to draw upon the qualities and commitments already present within one's self. The core reflection approach invites a fundamental shift in perspective, one focusing on personal resources rather than deficits, ideals rather than problems, and on the self as well as others. Perhaps most significantly, core reflection facilitates asking new and better questions: instead of "what do you want of me?" more pressing and pertinent questions became "what do I want?" and, in order to answer that more fully, "who am I?" and "how can I integrate my 'self' more fully and authentically in practice?"

Among the faculty at the School of Education at SOU, initial engagement with these questions at a three-day introductory workshop with Fred Korthagen and Angelo Vasalos proved resonant with our own efforts to develop and adopt a more holistic and authentic approach to teacher education. For some, interest arose as well out of the recognition that much of our own teaching had gravitated away from our own personal interests and commitments, that we were teaching courses that filled programmatic needs and yet were, in many cases, divorced from our own personal source of purpose and inspiration. Subsequent to the initial training, monthly brown bag meetings provided a collective venue in which to continue sharing ideas, reflecting on our attempts to integrate core reflection within our teaching, and developing further skill and comfort in facilitating core reflection.

The brown bag meetings served also as a vehicle for introducing new faculty to the core reflection process and afforded all faculty a safe and inviting opportunity to explore and work through the tensions experienced during their everyday teaching practice:

> The first few times that I attended the brown bag meetings, I was intrigued by the openness of the conversations. Faculty members were willing to be vulnerable with the challenges that they were having with teaching. I felt reassured that I was not alone with my struggles. My natural response is to jump into discussions and provide ideas and strategies to assist my colleagues with possible solutions to their dilemmas. Instead, I made a conscious

decision to listen to the person speaking and focus my attention not just on the words being shared but on being present with the person and the core strengths revealed through their words and actions. Although initially I did not share my own teaching challenges, as I heard colleagues share their teaching experiences and have their core qualities named by other members, I made connections to my own teaching and was able to begin naming the core qualities within myself. I remember feeling energized and reconnected with my desire to build relationships with my students, to take time to get to know them as individuals, and to be transparent with my thinking so they could know me as a person. Subsequently, my teaching practices were immediately influenced and my interactions with students were driven by my intentions.

(Jo-Anne, Spring 2011)

Spurred and buoyed by these shared personal developments, program faculty joined together to integrate core reflection throughout the pre-service teacher licensure program in a more coordinated and explicit fashion. Embedding concepts such as core qualities, core reflection, and the onion model across programmatic coursework, advising and program assessments, we have sought to build a common vocabulary among students, faculty, and local teachers and administrators such that all come to identify core reflection as a distinguishing feature of the teacher preparation program at SOU. Thus far, this ongoing effort has resulted in significant changes to the content of our courses, our methods of instruction, the nature of clinical supervision, and the structure of the culminating program portfolio, and has also given rise to increased collaboration among faculty and greater transparency about our own teaching practice. Perhaps most significant has been a concerted shift in emphasis away from documenting compliance with externally defined performance indicators in favor of a more dynamic, iterative process of developing student teachers' ability to discern and draw upon their personal strengths in becoming both more authentic and effective within their classroom practice.

Integrating Core Reflection within Teacher Education

The very first courses of the program introduce students to the onion model (Figure 3.3) as a conceptual framework for helping them begin to articulate their personal sense of mission and core beliefs about the aims and purposes of education. Prior to beginning fieldwork in public school settings, these emerging educators are repeatedly confronted with questions such as: Who are you as a person and who do you hope to be as a teacher? What do you hope to achieve through your teaching for your students, your community and for the world? How do you hope your students' experience will be different because you are their teacher rather than any other well qualified person? Then, working outwards through successive layers of the onion, students are challenged to treat their answers to these questions as more than merely philosophical propositions by exploring how they might affect how they enact their role as teacher, interact with students, and plan and deliver instruction. Analyzing this portrait of their ideal classroom, students are asked to identify the knowledge and skills they themselves might need in order to bring it into being and to describe factors within the school environment that might help or hinder them in doing so.

As teacher educators, we support students in this process by being intentionally transparent about our own core qualities, commitments, and attempts to integrate these within our teaching. Already committed to modeling professional conversation by publicly reflecting upon our instructional decisions with students, we have expanded this practice to include discussing our own efforts and struggles to remain authentic within the classroom. Within a curriculum development course, for example, the concept of standards-based education is preceded by an exploration of what it would look like to build curriculum around teachers' and students' passions, interests, and questions. As students interrogate the relationship between these different approaches to curriculum development, the teacher educator names his own belief that teachers are "transformative intellectuals" (Giroux, 2004) who must maintain some responsibility for decisions about what is worth teaching, and that the desire to support their ability to do so is central to his own sense of mission as a teacher educator. Examining subsequent questions related to the tension between professional autonomy and accountability for both teachers and teacher educators serves as a recurring theme for the remainder of the course.

As the program progresses throughout the year, students are continually challenged to scrutinize the relationship between core qualities and instructional practice. Modeled first by teacher educators, this analytical perspective is gradually extended and applied to the authors of certain texts and, finally, to students' own experience in the field. In a Language and Literacy course, for example, Linda Christensen's (2000) *Reading, Writing and Rising Up* was chosen as the primary text. As students read Christensen's description and reflections about her own teaching, they are asked to name the core qualities illustrated by Christensen's choice of instructional methods, goals as a literacy teacher, and ways of interacting with students. In the discussions that ensue, students peel back the layers of the onion and consider the integral relationship between a teacher's core qualities, identity, and behavior.

When students enter into their field placements, several venues are used to help them reflect upon their classroom experiences in order to develop a deeper and more concrete understanding of their own core qualities. In addition to individual meetings with university field supervisors, students complete a year-long reflective portfolio and meet bi-weekly for the Guide Group, a seminar class that serves as a forum for attending to students' inner life as teachers and supporting their personal and professional growth. Mirroring the strength-based approach integral to core reflection, students begin this process during the first week of their field experience when they are asked to reflect upon a particular incident or interaction where they felt particularly successful or experienced satisfaction, validation or joy. After describing the incident itself in a five minute free-write, students are directed to write about the thoughts and feelings they experienced during or after the event. Then, exchanging papers in a read-around fashion, students read the descriptions written by others and are asked to identify "what qualities or values do you see in the person who wrote this?" As papers are returned to their original authors, students discuss the extent to which they resonate with what others have identified and, if so, where and how else they have manifested those particular qualities. Repeating this procedure at various points throughout the year, students are supported in developing a fuller understanding of their own core qualities and authentic selves through what they find mirrored back by others.

The focus of subsequent Guide Group meetings is scaffolded so as to spur students' development along different dimensions of core reflection (see Figure 4.1).

(low)	**Application of the Onion Model**	*(high)*
Fixate on perceived weaknesses		Identify personal strengths
Identify qualities at single or exterior levels		All levels evident and in alignment
Name core qualities in abstract terms only		Describe concrete manifestations of core qualities in practice
	Description of Ideals	
Focus on fears/problems exclusively		Describe ideal
Attribute problems to external factors		Differentiate between internal and external obstacles
Frame solutions solely in terms of external changes		Describe utilizing core qualities to achieve ideals
	Breadth of Application	
Apply core reflection only when coached by others		Initiate core reflection for self or others
Focus on students' deficits		Name & draw upon students' core qualities
	Subjective Experience When Engaging in Core Reflection	
Stuck at single level of elevator		Address thoughts, feelings and wants
Overwhelmed by fear or paralysis		Experience joy, flow and determination

FIGURE 4.1 A developmental spectrum of core reflection

In the second quarter of the program, for example, problematic situations encountered in their field experiences are moved to the forefront of the curriculum. Again employing a read-around procedure, students are asked to describe a struggle or frustration they have experienced, their thoughts and feelings experienced during that moment, and finally what they hope for in regard to that situation. Approaching the situations described by students as the basis for shared inquiry, teacher educators intentionally refrain from proffering suggested solutions and instead lead the group through a discernment process focusing on identifying the personal qualities and values apparent in how they frame these problems and ideals. Then, encouraged to treat these core qualities as internal resources to draw upon them as guideposts for making decisions and taking action, students develop a plan for responding to their problematic situation in the following weeks and eventually report back to the group about what they experience and observe when they attempt to do so.

By the third quarter, Guide Group discussions move on to examine environmental factors that students feel either support or inhibit their ability to manifest their core qualities within the classroom setting, and also turn explicit attention to the relationship between core reflection and students' teaching effectiveness. In one session, for example, students are asked to describe the behaviors of one of their own students whom they find particularly difficult to work with. They are then asked to describe their own thoughts and feelings when confronted by those behaviors. Students are prompted to include positive as well as negative responses (curiosity, compassion or determination, for example) and invited to own these as manifestations of their own core qualities. Next, they are invited to shift focus back to their own student and speculate about which of that student's own core qualities may be reflected in the problematic behaviors described earlier. Finally, the group brainstorms whether and how those qualities could be named and accessed in more productive ways to promote student engagement and learning.

One function of the Guide Group is to assist students in constructing a reflective portfolio that helps them discern, assess, and deepen their personal and professional development throughout the program. Over the last two years, the structure and focus of this culminating program assessment have been substantially revamped to align directly with the core reflection process. The restructured portfolio is composed of a series of 'snapshots' and 'synthesis essays' in which students describe and reflect upon their transformative learning process at different stages of the program. In the snapshots, students self-select events that have instigated significant learning or reflective questioning for them (these could be classroom incidents, student interactions, course assignments, or simply questions or tensions with which they have struggled). Students first describe and then reflect upon the experience, writing about what they *think* about it, what they *feel* about it and what they *want* as a result of it. Then, at the end of each quarter, students synthesize their snapshots into a narrative essay related to a guiding theme.

After the first quarter, students write to the prompt "Who am I as a person? What core qualities are reflected in my snapshots thus far?" In the second quarter, to "What am I learning and what am I struggling with? How are my core qualities shaping my identity and behavior as an emerging teacher?" And, in the third quarter, to "Who do I want to be as a teacher? How do I intend or hope to manifest my core qualities in my future classroom practice?" The final portfolio synthesis asks students to complete a self-analysis of their growth throughout the year using the developmental framework depicted in Figure 4.1. Presenting their portfolio to colleagues and faculty at the end of the program, students present evidence from within the portfolio to justify their self-analysis and discuss what they believe to have been their most meaningful areas of growth during the year.

Working in concert with the modeling of core reflection within the Guide Group, the re-oriented portfolio serves three important functions. First, it signals the programmatic commitment to a strength-based approach to teaching and learning and the value attached to cultivating the personhood of the teacher. Second, it helps focus and concretize students' learning relative to their own core qualities, strengths, beliefs, and commitments, and how these integrate within their classroom practice in an authentic and effective manner. Finally, it serves as an important source of data for helping faculty begin to track and analyze the impact of core reflection upon the burgeoning professional identity and teaching effectiveness of emerging educators.

Learning to Draw-Out and Draw-Upon the Self-that-Teaches

Now in the second year of implementing these programmatic changes, three broad themes have begun to emerge regarding areas of development observed among our student teachers: (i) greater and more concrete discernment of personal strengths; (ii) increased ability to draw upon those strengths in practice; and (iii) greater initiative in applying a core reflection approach to themselves and others. The following vignettes provide illustrations of each of these developmental shifts.

Alison

For many student teachers, the advent of field experiences in public school classrooms brings a heavy preoccupation with their perceived deficits and personal weaknesses and is accompanied by feelings of fear, anxiety, and pressure to conform to the expectations and dictates of others. For Alison, this preoccupation was reflected in her initial Guide Group reflections and portfolio snapshots, which focused exclusively upon her fears and failures related to classroom management. For much of her first quarter in the field, this student teacher wrote and talk about constantly feeling "frustrated and defeated" and her persistent anxiety manifested in personal illness and frequent absences to such an extent that she began to "wonder whether I'm cut out for this." Critically, Alison attributed the entirety of these struggles and worries to her own personal failings:

> I feel that there's this tension between who I am and who I want to be . . . Two of the biggest things I've had to confront this term are that I am afraid of confrontation and I don't like to yell. Both of these parallel the reality that I am having a difficult time maintaining authority. . . . I hear you say that we need to teach who we are, but I wonder how much I can truly do that.

Like many student teachers, Alison continued to struggle with classroom management issues throughout her first quarter in the field. However, repeatedly prompted to identify and dissect her occasional feelings of success, and buttressed by frequent engagement with the core reflection process (both through being coached herself and witnessing the process modeled with others), Alison eventually began to take greater note of her personal strengths and how these enabled her to make connections with particular students. In so doing, her written reflections began to give voice to feelings of relief, determination to continue in the program, and hope for herself and her continuing development as a teacher:

> The snapshots I wrote at the beginning of the program reflected my inner turmoil and struggles. At the time, it seemed like I was only discovering negative things about myself but, after much reflection, I've come to see that the situations I wrote about were simply helping to bring out the core values of who I am, what is truly important to me, and what I need to work on. I am passionate, witty and curious, and I care about my students both academically and personally. Although I may never be a perfect teacher, if I continue to grow and adapt and remain authentic to who I am, I will be successful.

Early in the program, students' conversations regarding their field experiences frequently center around describing environmental classroom factors and their own behaviors and interactions with students (to use core reflection terminology, upon the exterior layers of the onion). When prompted to examine or discuss the interior dimensions of their identity, mission, and core qualities as educators, their responses generally remain abstract and generalized in nature. With greater time in the field supported by ongoing engagement with core reflection through individual coaching sessions, the Guide Group, and the written portfolio, a deepening of students' self-discernment process can be found in greater attention paid to their inner life as educators (that is, to their thoughts, feelings, and wants related to what they are observing and experiencing in the classroom) and also in an ability to be more specific and concrete in describing their core qualities and how they manifest within the classroom setting.

Melissa

For one student teacher, both these paths of development are evident in the evolution of how she framed a particularly problematic situation over the course of several weeks. Midway through her first field placement, Melissa came to her field supervisor saying she was uncertain about how to maintain professional boundaries with a ninth-grade student who had revealed to her that she was using drugs and had been sexually abused by an older student. Initially, Melissa identified the issue she was struggling with as a lack of knowledge regarding her legal obligations as a mandatory reporter of suspected child abuse. Concerned also about her role as professional teacher, she asked whether she was permitted to disclose her own history with drug and sexual abuse and whether doing so would undermine her effectiveness in maintaining the respect of this student and her authority in the classroom. Prompted to explore her motivation for wanting to disclose her past history, Melissa explained that she wanted to connect with this student and let her know how much she cared about her, and that she also wanted be the type of teacher that students would feel comfortable coming to with difficult personal issues. Melissa ended by saying that she felt overwhelmed by her sadness and fear for this student: "I just go home and break down and cry when I think about her and what she's dealing with." Believing that other student teachers might be confronted with similar concerns, either now or in the future, Melissa's supervisor asked whether she would be willing to bring this issue to the wider group. Melissa said that she would.

As Melissa recounted this story in the Guide Group the following week, fellow students began sharing their own stories about students who had disclosed troubling personal issues and raising questions about their proper course of action. Others shared their own experiences with drug or sexual abuse and began proffering advice about what Melissa could and should do with respect to this particular situation. Attempting to forestall a round-robin advice giving and problem-solving dynamic, the Guide Group facilitator refocused the discussion back to Melissa and what she hoped for in relation to this situation. Asked what she wanted "for" this student, Melissa explained that she longed to let her know that "the abuse wasn't her fault and that she deserved so much better." Pressed on how sharing her own experiences might help this student, she explained that she hoped to convey that it was possible to survive these sort of experiences and eventually be happy again. Reflecting back the core qualities revealed in these explanations, the instructor and other students identified Melissa's deep well of compassion and empathy, a sense of wisdom and perspective garnered through hard experience, personal resilience, and caring coupled with responsibility for wanting to do what was best for students even at the cost of significant personal distress.

Over the following weeks, in both individual coaching sessions and through the portfolio snapshots, Melissa was invited to use the onion framework as a way of discerning how these core qualities might be reflected in the various layers of her developing self-concept as an educator. At the level of identity, Melissa explained that she had come to view herself as both a role model and a confidant for her students, that she wanted to be a "safe person" with whom students could "try out" ideas in order to gain an adult's broader perspective. At the same time, she realized that, as a teacher, she could also help students by serving as an advocate and referring them to other resources or experts when she wasn't capable of "solving all their problems" herself. Underlying this conception of her role as teacher, she articulated an abiding belief that all students are worthy of happiness, safety, and success and that, with support, it is possible to overcome even the most trying situations and become resilient, happy adults. For Melissa, all this distilled down to a personal sense of mission of feeling "called to work with at-risk, high-risk and special needs students," which she now intended to pursue through a career in alternative education.

Christina

Fundamental to the core reflection process is the belief that nurturing deeper and more strength-focused self-knowledge will contribute to individuals' ability to draw upon their core qualities as resources in practical situations. Among student teachers at SOU, this ability is reflected in increasing reference to their core qualities as guideposts when making decisions and taking action in challenging circumstances. For a student such as Christina, this involved a subtle yet powerful shift in how she framed problems and arrived at solutions. For several weeks early in her field placement, Christina voiced repeated concerns about her mentor teacher's apparent disdain for her, saying that the teacher appeared to feel that she was "just skating by doing the bare minimum and not fully committed" to the program or to doing the hard work required to become a teacher. This was particularly painful for Christina because she had always regarded herself "a hard worker who gave 100%" and felt that this teacher was jumping to conclusions unfairly. Asked to diagnose what might be causing the teacher to make this judgment, she first located the problem in the logistical nature of her placement: because she was seeking dual endorsements in both health and physical education, she was splitting her time between two different placements, a fact that she felt her mentor teacher, though aware of, was not fully taking into account. Christina arranged a meeting between her university supervisor and the mentor teacher to clarify the split nature of her placement and confirm that the time she was spending in each setting was in accordance with programmatic expectations. Two weeks later, however, she reported that little had changed in the mentor teacher's apparent disappointment and negative regard toward her. To the contrary, she felt she had been given an unfair ultimatum: "You really just need to spend more time here in order for this experience to be worthwhile."

Meeting with her field supervisor to discuss the situation, Christina was asked to describe what she wanted her relationship with her mentor teacher to be:

Christina: All I want is for her to recognize what I'm doing and all the hard work I'm putting in. What do I want for myself? I guess really just to feel valued, to be heard and to feel connected with her and with the students. That's why this is so tough, because I really care about the students and I've always been able to build good relationships and she just doesn't see that.

Supervisor: Why do you think she wants you to be in the classroom more? I see that you value feeling connected; is it possible that she values that too and just doesn't feel that she's been able to connect with you in the way she wants in just a couple of hours every other day?

Christina: I guess that's possible. She had another student last year who was only getting the health endorsement and was able to spend all her time with her. The two of them had a really good relationship. I just wish we could have that but it's just a different situation.

Supervisor: So maybe the amount of time you spend in the classroom isn't the real issue. Maybe it's that you both value relationships and being connected and that neither of you are feeling that right now. If you're not able to change the amount of time you spend in the classroom, are there other ways that you can imagine getting more connected with her?

Christina: Well, I guess it would start with just telling her that, with saying that I really do want to connect with her and that I'm trying to do that with the students even in the short time I'm in there. I could tell her about the specific students that I've built a good relationship with and show her how important that is to me. I've always given 100% and that's what I'm doing now.

Supervisor: Yes, I hear that you are very committed to building good relationships, that you are dedicated to the work you're doing and also very persistent in sticking with what I know has been a difficult and painful process for you. Knowing all that, how does it feel to you now when you picture yourself having that conversation with your mentor teacher?

Christina: It would feel like we're on the same team again. I don't know what would really change but at least I think she'd know who I really am and not think that I'm not there because I don't care. Yeah, I could do that.

Three dimensions of core development are evident in this exchange and Christina's subsequent discussion with her mentor teacher and relief at discovering that she "really wanted to know who I was as a person." First is a change in how Christina frames the situation she is dealing with, moving away from an exclusive focus upon the external dimensions of the problem: in this case, the split nature of her placement and the number of hours she was able to spend in the health class. Instead, she comes to perceive that the "root causes" of the problem lay in the internal perceptions and values of both herself and her mentor teacher, namely their shared feeling of being disconnected from one another, and that this problem was particularly acute because each regarded building close relationships as integral to their sense of personal and teacher identity.

A second, corresponding shift occurs in how Christina imagines potential solutions to this problem. Christina begins this discernment process believing that any apparent solution must either involve her conforming to the dictates of her mentor teacher by spending more hours in the health classroom or a change in that teacher's expectations as a result of her gaining greater clarity regarding programmatic requirements. The personal sense of crisis, of course, arises when Christina recognizes that she has limited ability to control the external circumstances upon which either of these solutions rests: she must spend time in her physical education classroom as well as in health while also completing a full load of academic coursework, and her mentor teacher's perceptions remain essentially unchanged even after a clarification meeting with the university supervisor. Moving beyond this apparent impasse, Christina eventually recognizes a third option that is wholly within her control: the choice to be authentic and transparent about the value she placed upon connecting and building rapport with both colleagues and students. Committing herself to communicate and demonstrate this core quality on a regular basis, Christina and her mentor teacher discovered an area of shared commitment and came to greater clarity about what each was looking for in their relationship and from each other. Moving forward in the placement, Christina later expresses relief at feeling that "we're on the same page, we're a team again."

Finally, Christina also clearly shifts from being fixated upon the problem itself, and the feelings of anxiety and frustration evoked by it, to a clear and distinct focus upon her ideal vision of what she wants and hopes for in her relationships: to feel valued, heard, and connected. Importantly, this ideal transcends the particular situation of her current placement, it is a vision of herself as a person and as a teacher that unleashes her passion and creativity in a way that not only solves the current problem but that can animate and direct her in future circumstances as well.

Sally

A third area of development observed among student teachers over the course of a year's engagement with core reflection is an increasing ownership of pertinent vocabulary, techniques, and approaches. In the Guide Group setting, students exhibited an increasing willingness and ability (in some cases, almost habitual in nature) to name core qualities in their peers and initiate the core reflection process for others. By the end of the year, the most powerful portfolio reflections and presentations centered upon student teachers describing how they had begun applying a core reflection perspective to their own students in public school settings: identifying, naming, and attempting to leverage individual students' core qualities in a conscious effort to promote their academic learning and personal development. For Sally, the entire process coalesced into her own definitive shift from an external to an internal locus of control concerning to her identity development as a teacher:

In the summer session when we began the process of identifying some of our core qualities, I felt like I should be finding the answer in a book. I would read about different philosophies of teaching and think "how can I adapt who I am to more closely match the idea presented in this textbook?" As I gain more experience in this and watch teachers that I like, I realize it is their identity and integrity which defines their qualities, philosophies and commitments. Essentially, my original concept of finding myself in the profession has reversed: now I ask "how does the person that I am translate into the kind of teacher I am, the activities I do, and the commitments I keep?" Although philosophical standpoints are interesting in the broader sense, I realize that I needn't find a neat label for myself. What a relief!

Teacher Education Turned Inside Out

Two years ago, inspired by shared experiences of personal and professional renewal arising from initial training in core reflection, faculty members from Southern Oregon University School of Education set out on a path to integrate core reflection within and across the secondary level teacher preparation program. Our intention for doing so was to help emerging teachers learn to better align their teaching practice with their personal strengths, commitments and authentic selves. As we are coming to discover, however, core reflection is a profoundly reciprocal process and the further we integrate the approach within our work with students, the more we ourselves are changed as a result.

Revisiting our own sense of mission and purpose as teacher educators through the prism of core reflection continues to have powerful impacts upon how we conceive of and enact our own role as faculty in the School of Education. Chief among these has been an enhanced commitment to operating from a strength-based model of teacher development. Our work with student teachers has come to be characterized by a constant search to seek out, reflect back, and build upon the personal resources already present within our students. Encounters with students, both in the classroom and in the field, have become, first and foremost, occasions to truly listen to our students, not primarily to diagnosis any potential deficits or misunderstandings but to ascertain what they are revealing about their own beliefs, commitments, hopes, and ideals. Perhaps, then, it would be more accurate to say that we are listening *for* our students rather than *to* them, for indications of who they are, what they value, and what they are striving to accomplish through their teaching.

Recognizing and naming core qualities is, however, but a start. As teacher educators, we have become accustomed to viewing ourselves as reservoirs of knowledge and skill whose primary role is to develop and assess student teachers' knowledge base, teaching proficiency, and professional dispositions. Within that conception, we charge ourselves with carefully observing students' performance, suggesting solutions to help them improve, and overseeing an ongoing process of self-reflection regarding their practice. Now, when students encounter difficulties or struggle with their own students or situations, our primary task becomes that of engaging them in a shared exploration of how to draw upon their core qualities and take actions to more fully and consistently integrate them within their classroom practice. Facilitating such a process requires that we, as faculty, resist the deeply ingrained urge to proffer solutions ourselves or focus on rectifying students' perceived deficits.

In other ways as well, the more deeply we internalize the nature and goals of core reflection, the more we find our own teaching scripts evolving to align with those goals and with our own personal core qualities. In our work with emerging educators, we have long recognized that the most powerful instruction we provide is in our own modeling of effective teaching practices and we frequently enlist students in meta-cognitive discourse about the teaching and learning processes within our own classrooms. While modeling good teaching certainly remains a significant focus of our work, we have become increasingly cognizant of the need to model also a commitment to being fully present and authentic as educators. As we ourselves encounter challenges in our work, in the classroom or in the field, core reflection invites us to consciously acknowledge the tensions, fears, hopes, and ideals within ourselves and to take note also of those within the students with whom we are interacting. Doing so, we become capable of re-framing the situation, less as a problem to be solved than as an occasion, a reminder even, to attend to and draw upon the whole of our personhood: not simply our knowledge and competencies, but also our deep curiosity about this particular student and our vision, our felt desire, of what we want *for* them, rather than *from* them, as a result of this moment, this circumstance.

Although the initial impetus for integrating core reflection throughout our pre-service teacher program was to nurture and deepen the personal and professional development of our students, doing so has had a transformative and renewing effect on us as well. As we coach student teachers and fellow faculty through the process, we, too, become more adept and self-directed in applying core reflection within both our personal and professional lives. And the more we urge our students to attend to and draw upon their core qualities, the more cognizant we become of our own and the more driven we become to maintain a sense of presence and authenticity in our own teaching practice.

References

Christensen, L. (2000). *Reading, writing, and rising up: Teaching about social justice and the power of the written word*. Milwaukee, WI: Rethinking Schools.

Darling-Hammond, L. (2000). The challenge of staffing our schools. *Educational Leadership, 58*(8), 12–17.

Giroux, H. (2004). Teachers as transformative intellectuals. In A. Canestrari & B. Marlowe (Eds.), *Educational foundations: An anthology of critical readings* (pp. 205–212). Thousand Oaks, CA: Sage Publications.

MacDonald, D. (1999). Teacher attrition: A review of literature. *Teaching and Teacher Education, 15*(8), 835–48.

Tye, B. & O'Brien, L. (2002). Why are experienced teachers leaving the profession? *Phi Delta Kappan, 84*(1), 24–32.

Wiebke, K. & Bardin, J. (2009). New teacher support: A comprehensive induction program can increase teacher retention and improve performance. *Journal of Staff Development, 30*(1), 34–38.

5

ACTUALIZING CORE STRENGTHS IN NEW TEACHER DEVELOPMENT[1]

Roni Adams, Younghee M. Kim, and William L. Greene

This chapter also deals with the role core reflection may play in the professional development of teachers, in this case beginning teachers. Roni Adams, Younghee Kim, and William Greene highlight their roles as facilitators of a beginning teacher group, followed by brief scenarios of six new teachers. These scenarios provide evidence of how the group's use of core reflection evolved over time. In a detailed and insightful way, they show how core reflection can influence the actualization of core strengths in beginning teachers. The authors conclude with a discussion of patterns and themes that surfaced in the scenarios and the insights they gained about the potential of core reflection for mentoring new teachers.

As professors of teacher education at a small regional university, we worked so closely with our cohort of approximately 20–30 student teachers each year that we felt both satisfaction and sadness when they graduated from our program. Curious about what our graduates were experiencing as they entered the teaching profession, we loved hearing back from them or being invited to visit them in their new classrooms. We heard from many about their sense of disillusionment over a division between what they learned from our program and what they encountered in the actual practices at their elementary schools. We were troubled to hear that they faced situations on a daily basis that challenged their core values.

---

1 The authors wish to express their deep respect for each of the teachers represented here and to thank them for allowing us to include their words in this chapter.

Realizing their frustrations, we worried that our promising new teachers would become socialized into abandoning their beliefs or quickly "burn out" and leave the profession. While discussing how we might help them re-ignite and reconnect to the ideals they embraced when they left the university, we became inspired to try core reflection as a tool to address these tensions. This chapter presents our observations of how core reflection empowered six new teachers.

After attending core reflection workshops with trainers Fred Korthagen and Angelo Vasalos, we became eager to find a way to replicate the core reflection process with a small group of beginning teachers. By using core reflection when we listened to the classroom experiences of these teachers, we hoped to inform our own practice and better prepare them with the inner resources necessary to overcome the obstacles they would face in the schools. Ultimately, we wanted to renew their inspiration for becoming teachers and their sense of purpose, even in the midst of the demands and tensions of first-year teaching.

Although our vision was to bring core reflection to these new teachers through a study, we did not begin with a formal research design. However, we wondered whether core reflection would be effective in supporting new teachers, and our group gave us the chance to explore this idea. With this goal in mind, we developed the following question as a focal point for the results reported in this chapter: What evidence do we have that core reflection helps new teachers actualize their core strengths to navigate the first critical years of teaching?

Participants, Data, and Documentation

We started with a group of our former students, first year teachers, who had been introduced to core reflection with us during their pre-service year. We invited those who had secured teaching positions in our local community back to campus in the fall to attend monthly meetings of a beginning teacher support group. The next year, we added another set of new teachers. Some teachers attended regularly; others dropped in occasionally; and a few came once or twice and, for different reasons, couldn't continue. It took a few months to settle into a core group who were interested, willing, and committed to attending regularly over what became a four-year period. Through lively two-hour meetings, nourished with refreshments we provided, our core group of 6–10 teachers gathered one evening each month during the academic year, October to June.

The evidence we collected for our study spans the four years and includes: field notes, transcriptions from audio recordings of each meeting, presentations at three professional conferences, and email communications from group members. These data became the source for our identification of key themes and patterns as well as the quotes included in this chapter, and also helped us identify six of the teachers who were dedicated to attending most sessions and continued coming to meetings beyond their first year in the classroom. These six teachers were the basis of this study. Using vignettes and scenarios, we illustrate how their experiences align with major themes we noticed in the data. We use the following pseudonyms to identify them here: Kate, Haley, Skye, Sandra, Alice, and Pat. We, the authors, were also the meeting facilitators and are identified here by our real first names: Roni, Younghee, and William.

Role of Facilitators in Introducing Core reflection

In our role as facilitators, we greeted teachers as they arrived for the evening and encouraged their stories, excitement, and eating for the first 20–30 minutes. Without having a planned structure or agenda, Roni would often transition the group to focus on a prompt, such as, "What are the challenges you are facing?" or "What makes you feel joyful in your teaching?" Teachers took turns around the table responding to the prompt. At other times, the stories or issues they came in with provided a natural transition to a more focused conversation. On occasion, teachers made it clear at the start of a meeting that they were eager to share a burning issue with the group. Even though the format was informal, we hoped to coach them by using the principles of the core reflection approach (see Chapters 2 and 3); we found our entry points instinctively, when any one of us felt moved to interrupt the flow of conversation to begin the coaching process.

Within our role as facilitators, we had to be aware of the teachers' varying levels of exposure to core reflection as graduate students; some heard the concept in class, others read an article, and others used it in their student teaching supervision groups as we implemented core reflection a little more each year. With these differences, on occasion we did more formal teaching, explaining the process and showing them the graphic illustrations of the *onion*, the *elevator*, or other images (see Chapter 3). As we listened to their stories, we looked for opportunities to name their core qualities, ask elevator questions, highlight something from the onion model, or comment when they described situations illustrating *presence* or *flow*. These opportunities arose, unplanned and informally, from the teachable moments that our group members brought to the table, giving us the chance to model core reflection using the real life examples they provided. The ways we worked with our new teachers using core reflection will be, explicitly and implicitly, embedded throughout the scenarios and transcript excerpts that follow. We continue with an expanded story of Kate in order to represent the longitudinal impact core reflection had on her development over her first four years of teaching. The example in the following vignette also illustrates how the group helped Kate navigate the challenges she faced.

Kate

Kate was a star student teacher! With her bright, positive, and bubbly personality, her warm and enthusiastic interactions with children, her creative, magical, sprite-like nature, and cheerful disposition, Kate was born to be an exemplary early childhood teacher. Her lilting, musical voice and dramatic presence entranced and engaged the students in both the academics and the arts. She exuded passion and epitomized connectedness to her core qualities. Her professors, her cooperating teachers, her school site colleagues, the students and their parents loved her. Everyone knew she was destined to be a star teacher!

No one was surprised when she landed a job in the school in which she had done her student teaching. Influenced by the glowing accolades of the interviewing committee, the new principal at her elementary school went along with the consensus of opinion and hired Kate to teach second grade. Buoyed by her educational philosophy and ideals, Kate spent the summer planning her curriculum, arranging and organizing her classroom environment, and preparing to welcome her own community of learners.

Within a month of beginning her teaching job with elation and high hopes, Kate came to our first meeting demoralized and discouraged. She described her experience as a "mourning" for the loss of her hopes, ". . . the huge transition from what we hope for, what we want . . . to what we step into." In her first few months of teaching, Kate reported that her principal had been openly critical of her teaching style, her classroom management, even her positive nature. She began to feel "belittled, unsafe, and demeaned. I drive to school nauseated; I can't sleep; I have dreams. I don't want to be there because it doesn't feel good."

Kate shared her misery at our meetings: "I feel like there's a huge weight on me going squish, squish, squish . . . the principal, socialization, 'forget your philosophy and be like us' . . . Who I am, at my core, has been questioned." Beginning at our first session, we modeled being present with her as she shared her pain. We coached her through the elevator as she confronted the conflict between her ideal of who she wanted to be as a teacher and what she was being told to do. We urged her to remember and visualize her ideals. "In my ideal, I need to believe in myself," she began, but she instantly returned to the obstacles and the limiting thoughts that interrupted her sense of flow and kept her in a state of disequilibrium and despair, "but I'm told on a daily basis that I'm not doing what I'm supposed to be doing. This year hasn't been what I hoped. No more singing, no more cooperative groups. All the things that I feel so passionate about I've been told to stop. I feel broken."

During her second year in our group, Kate described "being stuck" in her head at the *thinking* level during her first year, where she suffered "immense anxiety." She explained:

> Last year I learned how to function with such a broken *feeling* level in my elevator, with a broken heart and a broken spirit. It's exciting to experience that flow and to experience being able to move down into the *wanting* level and being able to take action and feel confident in the actions that I take and that I can trust myself and trust my philosophy and my values and my core and that those are still me. . . . I'm rediscovering that those are still me.

Throughout her second year, Kate reconnected with her core qualities and developed the confidence to take risks, to explain the rationale for her teaching decisions to her principal, and to advocate for her students.

Evidence that Kate actualized her core strengths during her third year emerged as she shared a new challenge with our group. A team of colleagues teaching the primary grades at her school met regularly in what she described as "a crazy, dysfunctional professional learning community." Although these were people she admired and respected, when they got together to collaborate, their group dynamics descended into arguments, complaints, and negativity. As a novice member, she described feeling "insecure, frustrated, anxious, and devalued" by her colleagues. Excerpts from that session demonstrate how we coached her through this dilemma by modeling the core reflection process (Meeting transcript, December 2, 2009).

Kate: My ideas aren't valid to them . . . they don't see me as having value yet.
Roni: So what are the feelings inside when those assumptions are made about you?
Kate: It makes me feel insecure and it's also very frustrating. I think those two are often tied together for me. It's like I feel like I do have something to say but it's just not being valued.
Roni: How would you like it to be for you then?
Kate: I would love for us to be able to all say our opinions and maybe disagree but have banter about it and talk about it instead of it just being, oh I know, we're all different and so we can't change anything . . .
Roni: So what core qualities do we see in Kate as she talks about this challenge?
Pat: Passion. She's very passionate.
Alice: I don't know what the right word is . . . I keep wanting to say *diplomatic* for some reason . . . but you are totally *willing*. . . you just want them to talk to you instead of ignoring you.
Skye: I'm seeing that you are, compared to two years ago . . . you are sure of yourself. You are saying, "I know what I know. I am a professional . . . let me do what I want to do."
Haley: I'm seeing quality leadership values. It sounds like you have a vision for where you would like to see your group, but you're sad that it can't get past that block.
Roni: You said the word *vision,* and I was thinking, why don't you elaborate about that vision again of how it would be in an ideal situation of collaboration with your team.
Kate: Well, I guess the part that I can take control of in changing the vision would be having the guts to just start those conversations and . . . say, "I really think we need to have conversations about this so we function as a group," . . . but be willing to butt up against a wall and accept that . . . but it is kind of disappointing. I feel let down.

Roni: How would it be for you then, Kate, having all those thoughts and having those feelings to still hold the vision of having deeper conversations?

Kate: I think that I would be honest. "This feels disappointing." Then it's not putting those feelings on anybody else. It's just saying what I'm feeling.

Roni: And how would it feel to say those words?

Kate: I think it would be really scary, but the thought of actually doing it and the possibility of having change is also really exciting and would just feel so good. And maybe if I put it out there, other people would also. I think the prospect of change and having openness would be awesome and I would be willing to put myself at risk to do that. But I guess I haven't because I do respect them so much . . . and I really value what they do. But I have to give myself some value, too . . . that my knowledge is just as important as theirs.

Roni: As you spoke about your respect for them and the genuine admiration you feel, I was imagining you finding a way to acknowledge their core qualities and the common values that you share.

Kate: I just thought of a way I could do it with something tangible. We got this great piece of Manzanita wood and made leaf cut-outs and put everyone's name on them—oh my gosh, those were core qualities written on the leaves. I could just pull our group's leaves and say, "This is what is so awesome and this is what's so alive about our group, and let's make it be alive by sharing it with each other."

Roni: Thank you for sharing that. It will be interesting to see if you decide to try something because if the group was elevated into a conversation where you, too, could shine . . . you have a depth of understanding and knowledge and talent and so much to share from your core, too – that they would be able to see you in a new light and realize more about who you are.

(Meeting transcript, December 2, 2009)

Kate participated in a conference presentation at the end of her third year, where she summed up her experience with our group:

> This group has definitely allowed me to get out of my head and all of that anxiety, down into my heart of feeling appreciated and having my strengths recognized by others, and then . . . down into my core of, what do I really want? What do I want from the world of education; what do I want from myself as a person; what do I want in my classroom . . . I've tried to take this process a further step into doing core reflection with a professional learning community of teachers at school, and then with my kids. This group has really been a lifeline.
>
> (Transcript from Pacific Circle Consortium Conference, May 2010)

In Kate's case, during her fourth year, she was grounded and centered, able to listen deeply to her peers and offer insight and encouragement. She commented to a beginning teacher during one meeting:

It's so awesome to hear you say, "I feel like I'm doing the right thing," because I know that my first year, what sunk me for a while was that I *wasn't* listening to what I felt, and I *was* listening to: "You need to do it this way." We teach who we *are* and if we aren't being us, if we're not being true to ourselves, and what we believe, then we're sunk.

At the end of four years, she was confident in her identity and aligned, better able to enact her ideals and become the star teacher we all knew she would be. With the self-efficacy and empowerment she had developed, we believed she would sustain her ideals and continue to be strong in facing the challenges she would encounter in her career.

The scenarios that follow each demonstrate a different application of core reflection as it appeared, often spontaneously, in our meetings. These aspects included: introducing the elevator model, internalizing core reflection, enacting core beliefs, advocating for philosophical ideals, and nurturing the whole person of the teacher. The scenarios contain evidence that the teachers are increasingly actualizing their core strengths.

Haley: Introducing the Elevator Model

During her first year of teaching, Haley faced deep internal struggles with how to be the best teacher for *all* of her students. Although she had high hopes at the beginning of the year, she soon realized she wasn't living her ideal. "I've had a rough year . . . a really hard class. And I've had to make some really tough decisions. And I come, and I get to talk about that." The group's process in using core reflection helped her to confront the overwhelming block she faced in one of her defining challenges. Here, we introduced the elevator concept by modeling it with Haley, as shown in the following excerpt (Meeting transcript, 21 January, 2009).

William: Yeah, if there's something where you're feeling particularly blocked, an obstacle, like you're stuck in yourself . . .

Haley: I do, actually I do . . . for the first two months of school, Ben [a pseudonym for a student in her class] was standing on desks and screaming and kicking . . . he's supposed to be in fourth grade and he's in third . . . he's reading at a first grade level and writing below kindergarten level . . . He's severely behind and behaviorally he's got a lot of issues as well . . .

William: Haley, I'm just going to stop you for a second . . . we're using Haley's situation as kind of a model for core reflection . . . one of the things that we have learned about is that it's ok to frame the problem but not go too long on the problem . . . But what we'll do now is move her to what she thinks the obstacle is, identify the problem. What is the actual obstacle for you at this moment?

Haley: Making the decision to call [child protective services]. It's really hard for me, because he's had so many obstacles and he loves his Mom so much . . .

William: How does it make you feel to talk about that? Where do you feel that in your body when you talk about that? . . . Can you describe a little of what you're feeling?

Haley: Shaky . . . my hands sweat, I feel shaky and I kind of feel like I don't know how to say it correctly because it might sound bad of me . . .

William: What would you want in this situation? What would be the ideal outcome for you in this situation?

Haley: The ideal is . . . To me, his only chance right now is to have a solid foundation . . . because he can't learn . . . without somewhere to sleep, without electricity, without food, without somebody who cares and loves him . . .

William: What would it be like for him if he had those things?

Haley: It'd be a 100 times better for him, but it's hard to make an 8-year-old understand . . .

William: What would it actually look like for him in that same school if he were to come to school . . . cared for . . . having a caring home to come from . . . what would you notice?

Haley: He'd be on time every day, he would have breakfast in the morning . . . he'd be able to focus, he'd probably be a happier kid, and he wouldn't be so nervous and scared all the time. He'd have more social skills in his toolbox to work from . . .

William: Can you describe your body right now, what you're feeling and where you're feeling it at the moment as you talk about him?

Haley: I feel like it's really heavy on me, it really is. It's something I think about all the time . . . It kills me that people would take him in and take care of him but it wouldn't be his Mom. It hurts because I know how much he cares for his Mom . . . he talks about how he worries about his Mom. It's scary; I can feel the tightness. I feel like I'm too emotionally. . . involved . . .

William: You can see another possibility for him, right? . . . You see that maybe academically, socially, emotionally, there could be some other possibilities for him . . . So, based on that, what does it feel like when you're talking about what you envision for him, what your ideal would be for him? Think about how you feel . . . do you feel that you're connected to your core qualities, or do you think that you're connected in your role as a teacher but not necessarily in your deepest essence as a person and as a teacher . . . are you feeling like that's something that's really speaking to you at your deepest level?

Haley: I think so . . . it wouldn't be so much if it didn't reach that core . . .

William: Clearly your caring is a huge example of your core qualities . . . your empathy, your sense of advocacy for the child, your tenaciousness in seeking out possible solutions, explanations, help, and you've done more than most people would do . . . You've already acted consistently with your core qualities in this case. Any observations or questions or something others want to interject or ask Haley?

Younghee: How do you feel now that you shared with us?

Haley: I feel a lot better and I kind of know more now of what I want to do, definitely. I feel like it's coming from a reassured place . . . But this feels just more reassured to me and being able to think it out in here, some reassurance . . . not necessarily exactly what my choice is going to be but where my choice is coming from is nice . . .

William: There's nothing about this process that's supposed to be a solution-giving kind of a process . . . I try to avoid giving the solution . . . the idea is that when you're in touch, if you're going to make the right decision for you at that time, it's going to be the right decision . . . you just have to make sure that you're in touch, sure that you're there . . . be assured that the decision you make, Haley, is going to be the right decision.

Younghee: Also, I noticed that when you were talking about your ideals . . . when you see him doing so well, being on time and well fed, doing the things that you want him to do . . . you looked so strong.

Pat: Your face changed when you were talking about the ideal . . . your face, your tone of voice, your eyes . . . and I felt like, wow, you could just see how that solid experience could help ground him and do so much for him . . . just emanating from you. The elevator brings you back to what you really want and being able to know how it feels to speak . . . at your core and getting back up to what I want for this child, what I wish for and hope for . . . everything about your demeanor has shifted . . . you feel so much more grounded now. . .

Younghee: Yes, . . . you're not shaking, you're not sweating . . . much calmer, solid, and . . . determined . . . you look stronger . . .

William: It's amazing the power of naming core qualities in other people . . . and when you get them to attach to their ideals . . . things that they're passionate about, they're committed to . . . then talking about it can be incredibly powerful for children, too . . .

Several things are noteworthy in the selection of this passage. First, one of the facilitators had recognized this as a teachable opportunity and made the spontaneous suggestion to use Haley's issue as a learning episode for the group. Second, Haley was able to identify a change in her state of awareness and to value the process of restoring flow, rather than just trying to solve the problem. Third, this was an early example of one of the other teachers stepping in to participate in the coaching process, which was one of the most exciting developments of this work and showed up more often during years three and four when we, as facilitators, faded into the background and our teachers naturally took over more of the coaching.

Skye: Internalizing Core Reflection

Through many sessions of hearing stories and watching us coach, our teachers began to internalize core reflection and become more autonomous in the use of it. For example, they started to name each other's core qualities, ask the elevator questions of each other, and in doing so, to help each other restore alignment and *flow*.

To illustrate, Skye brought an issue to the group that demonstrated the tension between her philosophy and the principal's that, as she put it, "took the wind out of my sails." Fifteen of her 22 students were being pulled out of the physical education and science block in the afternoons for math enrichment. While she understood the intent of wanting to raise math scores to grade level, Skye felt that her students were missing a vital and already shortchanged part of her curriculum. Bravely, and without having tenure, she brought her concerns to her principal on several occasions. Finally, as nothing was being done, she raised a significant question for our group: "How far do you take things in advocating for a student, how many times do you go to her [the principal's] office with your concerns? How do you know you're advocating enough when you don't feel like you can continue to talk about it?"

Kate spontaneously employed the elevator: "How did it feel when you talked to her?"

Skye replied, "Like there was a big rip between my values and hers . . . It made me ask, 'Am I not doing a good enough job with academics?'" As she openly questioned her own beliefs, she wondered, "Am I giving them enough academically, or am I spending too much time building community? Community is important, but are they getting the academics they need?"

As if sensing her need to restore flow, Haley unhesitatingly began to name Skye's core qualities: "Your values and your passion for doing the right things for kids just totally shine through. You are asking the questions you should be asking. You are a great teacher; it shines out of you every time you come here."

These interactions are further evidence of how the group's natural integration of core reflection into our meetings resulted in, as Skye put it, "trust in myself." In an email message to the group acknowledging the effect of core reflecting together, she wrote: "Your voices helped me move through my elevator to find peace . . . in my daily interactions!" Using core communication as a lens to understand this effect, Skye explained that recognizing the ideals and core values in others "lifts me up inside" and creates "such a real connection."

Sandra: Enacting Core Beliefs

One of the early struggles that Sandra brought to our group was the pressure she felt at her school to conform to the worksheet dominated, keep-the-students-busy approach of her grade level colleagues. But she didn't succumb; she found the courage to retain a connection and alignment to her core values and ideals. To illustrate this, she graciously thanked the 30-year veteran colleague in the classroom next door who offered to "help" her with stacks of math worksheets. Sandra then returned to her own classroom, closed the door, confidently placed the worksheets in a trash can by her desk, and took art supplies out of the sink cupboard that her students would use after recess to explore geometric shapes with charcoal and pastels. Her use of art instead of worksheets to teach a grade level math standard exemplifies a core belief that she shared in the second year of our meetings; she should "let the kids help me decide what we're going to learn about, what we're going to do next . . . but first and foremost, we're going to love school." With characteristic self-assuredness, Sandra exercised her strength by working with suggestions from others while, at the same time, resisting the pull away from deeply held commitments to herself and her students.

Sandra's thoughtful comments to the group often conveyed a concept important in core reflection: how we can use problems as opportunities to grow. "It's not easy to see your problem as a tool, but I've been really trying to focus on that," she remarked in the fall during the second year of group meetings. By year three, in grappling with the myriad of demands swirling around her about what she should be teaching and how she should be teaching it, Sandra seemed to have discovered an application of core reflection that surprised us all: "I try to look at the curriculum, like what is its core?" In year four, ideas from core reflection had clearly become internalized as a tool for looking more deeply and honestly at her students for who they were and not for what their behaviors suggested. "Sometimes I make excuses for kids rather than using their core qualities," she shared. "I feel I have let students down because I really didn't find what made them shine; instead of looking at their core, I'm just sort of bandaging up outside." Through the use of core reflection as a tool for understanding both the curriculum and her students, Sandra's commitment to her core values and ideals was exercised.

Alice: Advocating Philosophical Ideals

In her first year, Alice was placed in a school serving a low socioeconomic population and was given a large fifth grade class in which she had to have translators in 75% of her conferences to be able to communicate with the parents of her students. She knew her students had many needs, yet the school's curriculum was standardized and worksheet-driven, with very little room for creative or interactive learning opportunities. She longed to provide the enriched education she felt these children so desperately needed. It would be easy for me, she said, to jump into the system and ignore my ideals, but "I don't want to do that" (Meeting transcript, 15 October, 2008).

Alice brought up her concerns with other faculty and tried to engage them in conversations about their ideals. She reported:

> I asked a philosophy question and they looked at me like, "What are you talking about?" You know, "Why would your philosophy really have anything to do with how you're teaching?" And it's frustrating because . . . it would be so easy right now, so easy, to start printing off the worksheets and falling in [line], because that's what everybody does . . . So I finally came to the point where I don't care anymore. I realized that, yes, it's still stressful, and yes, I'm probably going to get the ax [fired] at the end of this year, but I'm going to go out there again.

By going "out there again," Alice meant she will continue to act in accordance with her beliefs, stick to her convictions, and keep trying to make a difference in the lives of the students she teaches. This scenario provides evidence of how the group supported Alice in reconnecting with her strong desire to advocate in accordance with her philosophical ideals.

As our beginning teachers gained more confidence in their abilities to do core reflection, we noticed that they began to apply the elevator, the onion model, and the recognition and naming of core qualities to their work with students at their own school sites. Alice shared another example that showed us how she was applying the elevator concept with a kindergarten student who was having a problem getting along with another teacher. She sat and talked with him, asking: What is it that's bothering you? What you do when you're so angry? What are you feeling? What are you thinking? What do you want? What would you want from the situation if it were a perfect world? "He just opened up like a book", she said. "He started talking, and it was awesome . . . the elevator." Alice related the significance of the elevator process as a coaching tool to her own ability to work through problems. "When others ask you these questions, you just start talking . . . it is hard to get to that point with yourself because you're self-critical and really, your instinctive reaction is to find the answer to a problem" (Transcript from Oregon Association of Teacher Educators Conference, February 2009). This example showed us how Alice was able to transfer core reflection from the group context to her own classroom.

Pat: Nurturing the Whole-Person of the Teacher

Pat was a bright scholar and transformative thinker in the field of early childhood education. As a kindergarten teacher, she recognized the value and importance in a holistic approach to education, for teachers and for students. She felt that core reflection provided a perspective that promoted wholeness: "It has to be a whole-person process . . . if you're not nurturing all sides of you, are you really being a good teacher?" (Transcript from Oregon Association of Teacher Educators Conference, March 2008). For Pat, core reflection offered tools for connecting the emotional, physical, and spiritual dimensions of *being* with the more traditionally accepted intellectual dimension in education. "I just came across this realization . . . that I was stuck on the top [thinking] floor of the elevator most of the time. It took me a while to get to a point where I could step back; this is what's really important for me." Pat described how she typed up a diagram of the elevator questions and posted it on the whiteboard in her classroom saying, "I trust it now" (Meeting transcript, 17 February, 2009).

Integrating the core reflection process into other aspects of her life also contributed to Pat's sense of wholeness. "It has really been a great thing for me that I've been able to apply it all across my life with all my relationships, not just with myself or with my colleagues or my kids, but with my friends and with my husband and with my sister" (Transcript from Pacific Circle Consortium, May 2010). Pat articulated that when she was having a moment of stress and anxiety, she could stop and ask, "What is it that I really want out of this situation? I don't struggle as much, and then I can do that with other people. I just feel like it has gone beyond teaching." Pat echoed a sentiment expressed by other members of the group who also commented on the value of aligning the intellectual, emotional, and spiritual parts of themselves.

Discussion

Through the four years we met with our group, we observed the pattern of grief and loss that occurred with most of our teachers during their first year evolve into a theme of reconnection to a deeper sense of purpose or mission. Our teachers entered their teaching jobs with high ideals only to have them dashed by the unexpected realities within their school settings, which created a sense of loss they described as "heartbreaking." For some of them, it was environmental factors, such as the intense workload, the school administration, their colleagues, the lack of support, and the restrictive curriculum that pushed them to the edge. For others, it was the shock of extreme student behaviors that challenged them. They found themselves in survival mode, feeling isolated and out of control. Their behavior became reactive, defensive, and most importantly, different than what they had imagined.

The wide range of feelings that emerged from these teachers during their first year of teaching included being overwhelmed and disillusioned. The emotional responses they experienced led to a sense of shame, inadequacy, and vulnerability. It seemed to us at first as though perhaps these first year tensions marked developmental characteristics that would gradually fade as experience and teaching confidence mounted in the second and third years. However, they did not. Instead, similar feelings appeared again and again. What *did* change was that through coaching with core reflection, their responses to those feelings and tensions became more grounded and less emotionally debilitating. As problems arose, our teachers more consistently summoned the awareness of their own core strengths to restore flow and to apply it to problematic situations. As Kate put it, "I feel like if I fall now, I can pull myself up." By helping our beginning teachers strengthen their inner resources for addressing the inevitable obstacles they would encounter, core reflection provided a sustainable, long-term process for personal and professional development.

When Haley came to our group for support, she left the meetings feeling trusted and lifted:

> It gives me the support to make those hard decisions and reminds me that I'm making those decisions from the person that I am, and those feelings that I have, and the caring thoughts that I have for my kids . . . that my decisions are coming from the right places. I really like how we are able to talk . . . we don't give each other the answers.

She said it [core reflection] gave her "a different way of thinking. And that's what I really enjoy. Instead of just powering through . . . the decisions that I'm making are from who I am – from my core."

We also noticed that the teachers from the original core group, who wanted to continue to participate during subsequent years, naturally transitioned into helping, mentor and guide the newcomers. In their third and fourth years, the more experienced teachers began to function as facilitators with each other and with the newcomers in naming core qualities and providing the guiding questions that moved their peers up and down the *elevator*. They felt comfortable in initiating and sharing their experiences within a group of trusted peers who understood and related to their values and philosophies. They talked about the challenges that arose in practice. By describing their thoughts, feelings, and desires, they surfaced the real issues they and their peers were struggling with, and using the onion model, identified the obstacles and limitations that blocked them. They found the core qualities and inner strengths they needed in order to gain autonomy and empowerment.

In relating our core reflection work to the wider field of mentoring, we realize that induction programs for new teachers typically emphasize the development of skills, content, and processes represented by the outer three layers or domains in the onion model: environment, behavior, and competencies. Likewise, teacher preparation programs are usually designed to meet proficiency-based state or national licensing requirements that include specific knowledge, behaviors, and competencies. The approach we took with this group was different; we focused instead on the inner layers of the onion model to help our teachers remember and manifest their beliefs, identities, and missions, which created the opportunity for a more holistic transformative process to occur. We gravitated to the onion model as a way to explain the disequilibrium our new teachers felt when the "reality" of their teaching environments, behaviors, and competencies didn't match their ideals. Summing up her experience with core reflection at an international conference recently hosted by our university, Pat explained:

It's not just about who we are as teachers; it's about who are you as a person, and those core values make you who you are, and how you reflect that in every aspect of your life, not just as a teacher. I think, as a result of that, I've seen us all really grow into better people and better teachers who will someday change the world.

(Transcript from Pacific Circle Consortium, May 2010)

Through our work with this group of inspiring and enlightened new teachers, we found validation in using core reflection as the starting point for supporting new teachers and as a process for empowering them in those first critical years.

We, as a university faculty, had experienced core reflection in our training as a one-on-one coaching process. One of the unexpected but significant outcomes of having group sessions was the power of those relationships to enhance the coaching process. This chapter contributes to our understanding of how core reflection can be integral to a group's process of forming supportive relationships among its members. After reading an earlier draft of this manuscript, these teachers confirmed what we suspected – that the shared experiences of group membership may have added to the effectiveness of the core reflection process, but in a reciprocal way, the core reflection process may have deepened the nature and quality of the connections among the teachers. We agree with Kate's affirmation of the value of the group, the relationships within it, and the process of core reflection: "The gift of this group is that we have had shared experiences . . . I believe you when you tell me my core qualities . . . we built our philosophies together . . . and you help me put the mortar back into the cracks of the bricks."

6

COACHING BASED ON CORE REFLECTION

A Case Study On Supporting Presence in Teacher Education[2]

Paulien C. Meijer, Fred A. J. Korthagen, and Angelo Vasalos

This chapter describes a study of one student teacher who was supported in developing 'presence' while teaching through the use of core reflection. Based on analyses of audio-taped coaching sessions, Paulien Meijer, Fred Korthagen, and Angelo Vasalos identify six stages in the teacher's development. These stages are described related to the elements of the core reflection approach. The coaching interventions leading to the transitions between the stages were identified, analyzed, and related to key principles of core reflection. In this chapter, both the teacher's growth and the coaching interventions are described in detail and illustrated using quotations from coaching sessions, logbooks, and interviews.

Introduction

In this chapter, we will focus on the way core reflection can be used in the coaching of teachers. In teacher education, we currently witness an emphasis on standardization and on the grounding of teaching in lists of competencies. This creates much criticism from people advocating a more personal perspective to teacher development. For example, Allender (2001), Bullough (1997), Kelchtermans and

---

2   This chapter is an adapted, shortened and updated version of Meijer, P.C., Korthagen, F., & Vasalos, A. (2009). Supporting presence in teacher education: The connection between the personal and professional aspects of teaching. *Teaching and Teacher Education*, 25(2), 297–308.

Vandenberghe (1994), and Loughran (2006) have all emphasized the personal element in teaching and the importance of learning to know oneself better as a prerequisite to being a good teacher. McLean (1999) concludes that after decades in which 'the person' was largely absent from the theory on how best to educate teachers, we have witnessed a surge of interest in the question of how beginning teachers think about themselves and how they cope with the substantial personal transformations they pass through in the process of becoming teachers. The aim, then, is to promote student teachers' reflection on such questions as "who am I?," "what kind of a teacher do I want to be?," and "how do I see my role as a teacher?", with the purpose of developing a professional identity.

In our view, the ongoing debate about an emphasis on personal growth versus developing competencies creates too much of a contrast. We believe that there are strengths in both perspectives, and that core reflection combines both sides of the coin as it focuses on developing teaching competencies *in line with* who people are and what motivates them to become teachers. This means that we agree with Senge et al. (2004) and Scharmer (2007) who stated that high quality performance implies more than simply 'choosing' a routine type of behavior matching a specific type of teaching situation (see Figure 6.1).

Senge et al. (2004) and Scharmer (2007) argued that such a form of behavior is often ineffective and they stated that finding professional behavior of high quality requires a deep kind of learning that they described with a so-called 'U' (see Figure 6.2 for an adaptation of their figure to the area of teaching).

At the bottom of the U, the practitioner is in a state of being that Senge and his colleagues called 'presence.' We believe that *core reflection* is an approach suited for supporting presence and helping people use this state for arriving at high quality behavior, concurring with who they are (see Chapters 2 and 3; cf. Meijer, Korthagen, & Vasalos, 2009).

This chapter describes a research study aimed at an in-depth analysis of the learning process of a teacher who was coached using core reflection. We will present a detailed description of the coaching interventions that promoted important transitions in her development. This research study shows how the teacher starts integrating her capacity for *presence* or, in her own words, develops a sense of 'being-while-teaching' during her lessons, which strengthens the development of her professional behavior. The aim of this chapter is to illustrate how this kind of coaching bridges the gap between the more professionally and the more personally oriented perspectives on teacher development.

Certain type of teaching situation   **Standard teaching behavior**

FIGURE 6.1 Routine behavior

Certain type of teaching situation   **Teaching behavior**

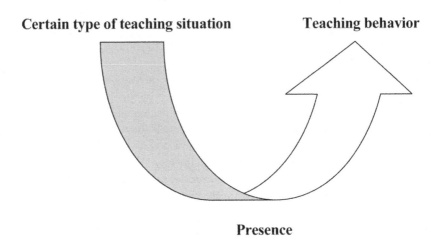

Presence

FIGURE 6.2 Deep learning according to the U-theory

Presence and Core Reflection

Rodgers and Raider-Roth (2006) drew on various sources when elaborating the concept of presence within the context of teaching. They offer the following definition: "Presence from the teacher's point of view is the experience of bringing one's whole self to full attention so as to perceive what is happening in the moment" (p. 267). Greene (1973, p. 162) called it "wide-awakeness." Presence is related to the concept of mindfulness (Brown & Ryan, 2003; Germer et al., 2005) and to what in Buddhist traditions is called "full awareness" (see e.g., Mingyur Rinpoche, 2007). In line with this, Palmer (1998) stated that "good teaching cannot be reduced to technique; good teaching comes from the identity and integrity of the teacher" (p. 10). Rodgers and Raider-Roth (2006) elaborated on this and noted that 'integrity' here means an integration of the self and the subsequent strengths that result.

The idea of presence is central to the core reflection approach. This approach not only aims at integrating the self and its strengths in teaching, but also at an optimal integration with the demands of the specific situation, which introduces the professional aspect. This means that the full awareness of the here-and-now, which is what presence is all about, encompasses and connects both the teacher's self and the environment. The starting point of the core reflection approach is the assumption that professional behavior becomes more effective and also more fulfilling if connected with the deeper layers within a person. As described in Chapter 3, the so-called *onion model* distinguishes six of such layers: (1) environment; (2) behavior; (3) competencies; (4) beliefs; (5) identity; and (6) personal mission. The ideas underlying core reflection concur with the essence of the 'U-theory,' namely that the process in which the connection with the 'inside' is made adds an important aspect to technically adequate behavior.

In this study, we followed the key principles of the core reflection approach, as described in Chapter 3 (see for more details Meijer et al., 2009):

1. Promoting awareness of ideals and core qualities in the person that are related to the situation reflected on, as a means of strengthening awareness of the layers of identity and mission.
2. Identifying internal obstacles to acting out these ideals and core qualities (i.e. promoting awareness of disharmony between the onion layers).
3. Promoting awareness of the cognitive, emotional and motivational aspects embedded in a and b.
4. Promoting a state of presence in which the person is fully aware (cognitively and emotionally) of the discrepancy or friction between a and b, and the self-created nature of the internal obstacles.
5. Trust in the process that takes place from within the person.
6. Support for acting out one's inner potential within the situation under reflection.
7. Promoting autonomy in using core reflection.

Research Method

Aim, Research Questions, and Design

The incentive for the present study was our desire to arrive at an in-depth analysis of the way the core reflection approach to coaching works out in practice. We aimed at answering the following research questions:

1. What stages occur in a one-year process of a student teacher's professional development, guided by a coach promoting core reflection?
2. What coaching strategies promote presence?
3. How does the connection between the personal and the professional aspects of teaching come about during the teacher's development?

We conducted a case study of one female teacher's developmental process in the first year of secondary school teaching, and analyzed this process to determine the stages that subsequently evolved. We also analyzed the coaching strategies that guided her in this process in order to understand their impact. In the description of the results, we will pay specific attention to describing the principles identified in the core reflection approach as outlined in the previous section.

The teacher, Paulien, was followed during one school year in which she taught social studies to three groups of 15- and 16-year old students and was also enrolled in a teacher education program. Paulien did have teaching experience in higher education, even in teacher education, but she had never before taught at the secondary level. During this period, Paulien had seven one-hour sessions with a coach, Angelo Vasalos, who is also one of the developers of the core reflection approach. Angelo did not attend the lessons with Paulien's students.

Data Collection and Analysis

We used the following instruments for data collection:

1. All coaching sessions were audio taped and transcribed verbatim.
2. The teacher kept a journal to record day-to-day events and reflections.
3. Around the middle and near the end of the school year, a researcher not involved in the process held semi-structured interviews with both the coach and the teacher. The questions in these four interviews focused on two main categories: the teacher (learning process and learning results) and the coach (types of interventions and the overall coaching process). Audio recordings of these interviews were transcribed verbatim.

The data analysis started from the teacher's and coach's answers in the final interviews to the question of what, to them, was the essence of the teacher's development. From that, we worked backwards: from the transcripts of the coaching sessions or from her journal, the teacher chose a number of instances that she saw as crucial in her developmental process and that had most contributed to what she in retrospect had described as the essence in her development as a teacher. She selected eleven fragments.

Next, the coach analyzed these and the parts immediately preceding and following them, and (a) wrote down his opinion on what happened to the teacher in these episodes (in terms of the theory on the process of core reflection) and (b) identified what coaching strategies were related to this. The result, consisting of the eleven 'deep learning episodes' and the coach's comments on each of these, was discussed in a meeting between the researcher who had not been involved in the rest of the process, the coach, and the teacher. The goal of this meeting was to identify the distinct stages in the process of Paulien's development (research question 1), and the crucial interventions that brought about stage transitions (research question 2). The procedure revealed a path of successive stages, which were labeled with the help of elements from the theory on core reflection. In the following *Findings* section, these stages will be described and illustrated with excerpts from the coaching sessions, the journals, and the interviews. We will also illustrate how the principles, identified as being essential to the core reflection approach, contributed to the teacher's development, especially to the teacher's growing presence.

Findings

The Essence of Paulien's Development as a Teacher

According to Paulien, the central issue in her development as a teacher was the fact that she learned to 'feel herself' during teaching. In an email at the end of the whole process, this 'feeling herself' seemed to have deepened further, and Paulien's description concurred with the ways in which authors writing on the issue of 'presence' phrase it. She wrote: "This sense of *being-while-teaching* was what I felt to be the most crucial aspect of my process of becoming a teacher."

In the closing interview, Angelo's answer to the question of the essence of the teacher's developmental process was in line with this, although it was stated in more theoretical terms:

> She has made a big shift from someone who tried to avoid feeling her feelings towards someone who is more present, based on her growing confidence in feeling her feelings and, most of all, feeling *herself* (. . .) She is also much more in contact with the layer of mission, since she realizes the importance of focusing on her ideals and core values. (. . .) In sum, I feel that there has been a significant development of professional identity.

We will now describe our findings concerning research questions 1 and 2 in connection with each other. We will do so by labeling the stages we distinguished in the teacher's development. We will illustrate the stages using excerpts from the teacher's journal as well as transcripts of the coaching sessions (see for more details Meijer et al., 2009). These transcripts also illustrate the interventions that brought about this development.

Stage 1: Chaos and a Fixation on Problems

At the beginning of the process, the teacher states:

> So many things happen.[. . .], I just can't seem to figure out the time things take in a lesson (always more than I had expected), and I just can't seem to focus on the essence of a lesson. It's too chaotic: in class as well as in my head.

During the first coaching session, Paulien describes a lesson that had been a real challenge to her. She tends to focus on the negative aspects in this lesson, and seems not very satisfied. The coach, Angelo, notices her tendency to ignore the value of her successes in this lesson and her personal influence in these successes, and to focus all of her attention on problems and the related negative feelings:

Angelo: . . . I notice that at the moment I give you positive feedback, you seem not to receive this, you seem not to let it get through to you. You seem to back away from it . . .

[. . .] I find it interesting to address your essential qualities or core qualities here: I see a lot of playfulness, excitement in you as you are talking about the students and how you stimulate them, and I see how you enjoy their motivation at that very moment. These are some of the qualities that I notice. And as we are talking about what exactly happens at that moment in that classroom, then I see you provoke humor in these students, that's an important core quality. I also see the quality of involvement: everybody is extremely involved in the task, the assignments you give them. So now I'm curious: what does it do to you to see these qualities in you and in your students? So, in the lesson you give, you know how to evoke and activate these qualities, in yourself as well as in your students. [. . .]

Paulien: Well, yes, now you mention this, I knew of course, as I said earlier, that the lesson just went well, and I was thinking how can I hold on to this. And the fact that you now label this, I think, well, it seems to become a bit more tangible or understandable. [. . .] Apparently, I've done something that made it go that way, but what? I understand that a bit better now. It also reassures me a bit, apparently it's not a coincidence if it should happen again. Maybe I can even prepare myself for it.

At this stage, we can see an important shift in Paulien's perception of the events that happened in the classroom. In the coaching dialogue, the resourceful aspects of problematic situations and Paulien's core qualities are deliberately being highlighted (key principle 1). This challenges Paulien's tendency of fixating all of her attention on the problematic aspects of the situation toward a focus that also includes what went well.

Stage 2: Deepened Awareness, but Also Confusion and Fears

Another issue arose in the first coaching session: Paulien's tendency to focus almost exclusively on thinking. Angelo decides to focus on balancing Paulien's thinking, feeling, and wanting (key principle 3) to counteract this tendency. He does so by building on one of her core qualities that surfaced: her respect for students. Cognitively, she recognized this quality in herself, but it did not seem to touch her emotionally. She took it for granted but did not realize the effect of it in her teaching. Angelo helps her feel the effect of such a quality and the strength of this effect by using the here-and-now of the relationship between the coach and the teacher:

Angelo: [. . .] I respect you a lot, as well as the process you're going through. But suppose I would NOT show respect, would that make a difference?

Paulien: O yes! Then I would not give my best as I do now. . . yes, that's true.
Angelo: Ah, so it IS important. I would say so too.
Paulien: Yes, you're right, that's true indeed. [*awareness of thinking*]
    [. . .]
Angelo: [. . .] So now you aim to be [*awareness of wanting*] explicitly aware of certain
    core qualities you express, and their meaning in a specific situation. [. . .]
    How does this make you feel, being aware of this and seeing the effects of
    being conscious of qualities in yourself? [*awareness of feeling*]
Paulien: A feeling of YES, this is indeed what it's all about.

Paulien has now become more aware of the importance of recognizing and
appreciating her core qualities and its effects on her students. She can recognize
some of the qualities after teaching, but the coach helps her realize she does not
feel them consciously while teaching. Analyzing this in her journal, she asks herself
if she *dares* to feel at all.

[. . .] So, what kind of qualities do I recognize? Enthusiasm, humor, respecting
    people, courage. [. . .] These are very important, not just for me, but I would
    also like to encourage these in students. But I "know" them, now I have to
    learn to "feel" them. How can I do this? And not just afterwards, but also
    right while I'm teaching. . .
[. . .] One way or another I seem not to be in the center of my teaching, I wait
    what's going to happen, let it happen to me as it were. Why do I do it like
    this? [. . .] I seem to more or less "protect" myself, apparently I don't have
    the guts to be completely *in* my lesson?

Stated in theoretical terms, Paulien seems to become more aware of her *not*
being fully present. She starts 'to move down the U'; she becomes more aware
of herself, of her core qualities and her feelings, but this also creates confusion
and anxieties: "If I start to feel more, can I still function well?" In the second
session with the coach, this becomes a central focus. Much of this session is devoted
to 'feeling the feelings,' as Damasio (1999, p. 279) calls it, which also means
negative feelings. During the meeting, the constructive meaning of negative
feelings is explored. The session ends like this:

Paulien: Well, I think that at least I realize better – and I want to keep that in
    mind – that, well, that negative feelings, too, have a function and that I don't
    have to be afraid of them.

Although Paulien selected this insight as an important learning episode, this
does not automatically appear to lead to fully embracing this insight and acting upon
it during her teaching. In a journal entry, she describes the confusion and fears
connected to extending one's comfort zone. Angelo's main strategy in this process

is being fully present with Paulien's reflective processes, focusing on her core qualities and using empathy. This is why a focus on qualities as well as trust and empathy from the coach are so important to support the process: this counterbalances the feelings of fear that trigger the teacher's closing up. In the final interview, Paulien answers the question of what worked well in Angelo's approach:

[. . .] specifically the unconditional acceptance of everything I encountered, and that I felt that everything I said really mattered, I found that . . . I mean it gives so much space to telling just everything you want. It caused me to feel that I could elaborate the things I said and felt, and I found that very important.

Stage 3: Reflection at the Identity Layer and Confrontation with an Existential Tension

In the third session, Paulien and Angelo reach the identity layer. A limiting core belief becomes more specific: Paulien believes about herself that if she opens herself fully to feelings, she might not know how to cope with these when they are negative. Elaborating on this existential fear for negative feelings, Angelo helps Paulien become aware that she tends to *think why* she has certain negative feelings, and helps her discover that she can *just feel* such feelings. They discuss that accepting such feelings is part of accepting yourself.

Angelo: So what would it be like if you would not believe this thought of "I might faint" anymore? But instead see the thought just as it is: an assumption that is definitely wrong, a misconception. The whole idea that you might faint because of certain feelings is just . . . a misconception, which only has an effect if you believe in it.
[. . .]
Paulien: It would mean that I would have confidence in . . . just in me. That I would know I wouldn't faint in those kind of moments. That I would manage. That it would be okay.
Angelo: If you just stick to that. How would *that* be like? What do you feel?
Paulien: Yes, that's an extremely happy feeling. That's really . . . it really makes me happy.
Angelo: What exactly triggers that happy feeling?
Paulien: The idea that I do not have to be afraid.
Angelo: Okay. Let's go one step further in your understanding. Why exactly don't you need to be afraid of those kind of feelings anymore?
Paulien: (silence) Yes, confidence. Having confidence in me. And in the students. And . . . well especially self-confidence.
Angelo: Self-confidence. But why, how can self-confidence help you at the moment you encounter such negative feelings? Because that's what you're actually saying, isn't it?

Paulien: (silence) It gives a kind of peace of mind. To have confidence in yourself means, I think, that whenever you're faced with something negative, that you can deal with it. That it would not *really* matter. That you will manage nonetheless.

In retrospect, during the final interview, Angelo explained how important he considers feeling the feelings during a lesson to be, and why he focused on this issue:

> The deeper significance is that only on the basis of awareness of her feelings, Paulien will get sufficient direction *from within herself* for immediate adaptation of her lesson plan while teaching.

In terms of the core reflection theory, Paulien has gotten in touch with a core belief about herself (If I start to feel, I will faint), so a belief at the identity layer. This might be a 'frozen belief,' perhaps developed earlier in life when there was insufficient internal and external support to 'survive' amidst strong negative feelings. Angelo helps Paulien identify an internal obstacle (key principle 2) by focusing on feelings surrounding the core belief and her motivation (will) to deal with the belief (key principle 3).

Stage 4: Discovering Presence and Deconstructing Core Beliefs

Immediately after the previous transcript, the conversation proceeds to the next stage, in which the core belief is further deconstructed. Angelo combines a focus on the core quality of trust (key principles 1 and 3), and a focus on feeling the feelings:

Angelo: Just stick to that insight for a moment. If you do have this confidence that everything would be okay, then you say you would manage. What does it do to you if you just stick to that, if you concentrate on that?
Paulien: Oh, it gives such a peace of mind!
Angelo: Aha. Now keep feeling that peace of mind and observe what it is that evokes that peace of mind in you. [. . .] Concentrate on this and see, what is it, what do I realize that makes me start to feel that peace of mind?
Paulien: Well, yes, here's that self-confidence again.

Paulien starts to differentiate herself from her feelings: She experiences that she *has* feelings, but she also experiences that she *is more* than her feelings (a principle formulated by Assagioli, 1965), because she starts to feel and recognize her presence as being more fundamental than her mental constructs and the emotional effects of these constructs. Through this awareness, her capacity to stay in the here-and-now, while feeling the feelings, is growing. In other words, her capacity for presence starts to develop. All Angelo has to do is to support and label this (key principle 4).

Paulien: And I could elaborate upon why that's the case, why I get a feeling of "not being there," and that even if they [the pupils] don't do anything, I still feel they seem to draw on me . . . But I don't need to do that: I just don't like that feeling. Full stop! And that's okay! I don't know, I feel kind of pleased that I allow myself . . . I AM allowed to not like certain things!

Angelo: That sounds very accepting! "I AM allowed to not like certain things."

Paulien: Yes!! [. . .] It's allowed! It's part of the deal. In fact, it would be rather strange if I didn't feel it that way!

Angelo: Great! You're beaming with joy!

Paulien: I'm really happy, yes! (laughs) Yes, you know, when I think this over, and feeling like this, it's not just me for which it's much more pleasant, but also for my students.

This session appears to be a breakthrough. Afterwards, Paulien is totally overwhelmed and can only write down a couple of words in her journal such as "self-acceptance" and "I am not my feelings." This kind of joy is typical for the core reflection process at the stage that teachers start to discover the powerful sense of their own state of presence in the midst of their professional functioning, and because of that, feel a deep fulfillment as well as a feeling of relief, which is the effect of seeing mental constructs in a more objective way.

Stage 5: Deepening Presence

We cannot be certain about Paulien's process during the next days, but her journal shows that a week later she starts daring to "be herself" while teaching:

I notice on all fronts that I'm feeling more "me" among the students. [. . .] I felt great and totally "present." [. . .] I was aware that I felt relaxed. And that precisely this relaxed feeling made me feel really "free" in my actions in class. I noticed that this felt relaxed and "natural."

Theoretically, we see that Paulien starts to rediscover her natural potential for presence.

I feel stronger every minute, it feels like I'm more and more the manager of what we are doing in class. I'm more and more in charge, while on the other hand I feel I'm more and more letting students take charge as well. So what am I taking charge of? Maybe at first I tried to take charge of the students, while at the moment I'm taking charge of "the lesson." I know the latter has to be 'the students' learning process.' So the lesson went well, but the students' learning is still not very obvious. I know, I cannot be satisfied until that's taken care of, but that moment will come, I can feel it.

This journal entry illustrates how Paulien's personal learning process starts to enhance her capacity for 'professional reflection' and the integration with effective professional behavior, enabling her to remain in a state of presence. Thus, Paulien seems to gradually become more autonomous in her own learning and reflecting (key principle 7). For example, she seems to have gained trust in herself ("that moment will come, I can feel it") (compare key principle 5), and in her reflection, she makes use of her inner potential, that is, her core qualities and an ideal (thus applying key principles 1 and 2 autonomously).

Stage 6: Autonomy in Core Reflection and Maintaining Presence

Now that Paulien is learning to be herself, in a next session, Angelo tries to make the process of core reflection she is going through explicit as an important step toward enhancing her autonomy in using core reflection (key principle 7). In fact, together they explore the effects of the strategies used by Angelo. They focus on what Paulien really wants (to do or feel), how she obstructs or limits herself (by creating disempowering beliefs), and what she might do to deconstruct such obstacles. This appears to further deepen Paulien's insights into herself. At the end of the session the conversation goes as follows:

Paulien: So in the situation I just described, then I'm sitting there feeling stressed [because I only have one hour to prepare lessons], and then it comes: the moment that I recognize; now I'm doing it again, creating my own stress.

Angelo: Yes, you're creating your own stress.

Paulien: Yes [. . .] and then I think; well, this is NOT what I want. What I do want is peace and quiet. The feeling of oh, I actually have one whole hour, let me think, what kind of interesting things I can do in one hour!

Angelo: Great!

Paulien: Yes, this is what I want . . . Oh, I'm going to use this immediately! Because this is something I do quite often. Creating my own stress.

Angelo: Hm.

Paulien: Yes, I know, yes, I recognize this so much. Terrible, isn't it?

Angelo: So what are you going to do?

Paulien: Well, I'm not going to create my own stress. Never again! Here and now decided!

And shortly after the session, Paulien writes in her journal:

> Now I understand why "peace and quiet" are so important to me [to aim for]: I need that to be creative. What a terrific insight this is. So true!

In a following session, Paulien and Angelo further elaborate Paulien's new insights, based on her growing capacity for presence. They discuss how this relates to directly experiencing herself, her students and her teaching. Paulien describes how this implies awareness of her feelings and she states that this results in clearer thinking about (mechanisms in) herself. Important is that Paulien becomes aware of how she frustrates 'being herself' by a tendency to detach herself from the here-and-now, and that she is developing the capacity to alter this tendency. Angelo's strategies are (1) promoting reflection on the *meaning* of presence; (2) stimulating Paulien to *imagine* always to be fully present; (3) helping her to *deconstruct* limiting beliefs that suppress the experience of presence; and (4) *explaining* the core reflection theory.

Angelo: [. . .] And what does this mean to you, when you teach from this sense of being, or, being a teacher who's able to teach from her inner sense of being? Imagine you would always be able to teach from your sense of being, your inner self? What would this mean?

Paulien: Well, it would save so much of your energy. If you're really yourself – I know it's strange, but it's really hard to be yourself – but if you finally succeed in being yourself, everything just comes naturally. [. . .] But this I find very difficult, when I lose touch with myself, to reconnect with myself.

Angelo: [. . .] So it's just an imaginary construction in your mind. At such a moment, first you have to recognize it, then you have to name it, reflect on it, and then you have to connect to it. *Then* the process will start from the inside, from yourself.

Paulien: So, what you're actually saying is that this feeling that nothing really touches me, so this dissociating that I'm doing, that this is just something I created myself?!

Angelo: Yes, you were not born that way, you acquired it.

Paulien: O well, then I *immediately* want to get rid of it, it's so irritating! It's very annoying.

Angelo: It's very annoying indeed. And you don't want it.

Paulien: No!

After this session, all journal entrances as well as the final coaching sessions are of a much lighter tone. Paulien describes and analyzes her lessons in a much calmer way that is more aligned with the goals she has with her lessons. Also, the focus is on integrating Paulien's new insights into her analyses of her teaching practice and on her own capacity to do so while teaching (reflection-in-action). In the final interview, Paulien describes how she tries to maintain her presence while teaching.

Interviewer: So how do you do this now, core reflection without Angelo?

Paulien: Well yes, for example, during a lesson in which I forget to be myself so to speak, I notice this during the lesson, and I can do something about it.

Interviewer: Could you describe this? I find that interesting. How do you notice this? What is this "noticing"?

Paulien: Well, that I *hear* myself talking. I hear myself and then I think something like "how would she finish this sentence?" Like I'm thinking about myself in the third person, something like that.

Interviewer: So you notice that this is happening, and what happens then?

Paulien: Then I don't panic like I used to.

Interviewer: You don't panic.

Paulien: No, then I'm thinking "oh, here I'm doing it again." And then I immediately think "well, I don't want this, and I don't need to, it's nonsense." And then I turn around as it were . . . then I start focusing on the fact that I don't want this, and sometimes I need some time to do so, but that's okay, I do take that time now. Earlier, I felt "well, I need to finish this sentence no matter what, or I need to finish my story," a very stressful feeling, but now I will think "okay, I need some rest now." And then I can call this 'being present' to the fore really easily. It just comes. In the beginning I needed some deep breaths to do so, and to focus on my stomach . . . I know this sounds strange, but that's how it goes for me.

In the final interview with Angelo, he indicates the following changes in Paulien:

> Now Paulien even finds it pleasant and interesting to deal with her feelings. She also considers feelings as being very practical, useful, and she is much more familiar with her feelings. [. . .] Even more importantly, she is very interested in being totally present. This has touched her deeply. It has led to an increased capacity for steering, for determining what she wants.

Conclusions and Discussion

Above, we have described how, through the core reflection approach, the concept of presence can be made operational in the coaching of (beginning) teachers. The data analysis showed how the connection between the personal and the professional in teaching took place during the learning process of one teacher. Our study revealed a path of successive stages in her development that concur with the theoretical framework and at the same time sharpen it. Table 6.1 relates the coaching interventions to the seven key principles of the core reflection theory.

The integration between the personal and the professional appeared to take place through a shift in awareness. The teacher's reflection moved from a focus on the many problems she encountered toward more awareness of her strengths,

TABLE 6.1 Relations Between Stages in the Teacher's Development, Key principles of the Core Reflection Approach, and the Coaching Interventions

Stages in the teacher's development	Key principles of the core reflection approach	Coaching interventions
Stage 1 *Chaos and a fixation on problems*	Promoting awareness of ideals and core qualities (principle 1)	• Focusing on acceptance of problems and empathic understanding • Focusing on positive experiences and strengths
Stage 2 *Deepened awareness; confusion and fears*	Promoting awareness of cognitive, emotional and motivational aspects (principle 3)	• Focusing on balanced attention for feeling, wanting and thinking • Self-exposure • Being present
Stage 3 *Reflection at the identity layer and confrontation with an existential tension*	Identifying internal obstacles to act out ideals and core qualities (principle 2), and promoting a state of presence in which the person is fully aware of this (principle 4)	• Explaining focusing on feelings • Exploring the core belief • Focus on staying present with the core belief • Empowerment by focusing on emerging core qualities
Stage 4 *Discovering presence and deconstructing core beliefs*	Trust in the process that takes place from within the person (principle 5)	• Focus on core qualities; focus on feeling the feelings • Support for the state of presence
Stage 5 *Deepening presence*	Promoting a state of presence in which the person is fully aware (cognitively and emotionally) of the discrepancy or friction between 1 and 2 and the self-created nature of the internal obstacles (principle 4). Trust in the process that takes place from within the person (principle 5)	• Support of acting out the inner potential within the situation under reflection (principle 6) • Expressing trust • Modeling presence
Stage 6 *Autonomy in core reflection and maintaining presence*	Promoting autonomy in using core reflection (principle 7)	• Explaining the process of core reflection • Use of imagination • Listening and accepting

her presence and her view of how she wanted to teach. This represents a movement to the more inner layers of the onion model, the layers of identity and mission. Based on this deeper awareness, the teacher develops professional behavior that is both appropriate to managing her classes and matches who she is. This leads to her experience of "being-while-teaching," as she expressed it at the end of the process. In terms of the U-theory of Senge et al. (2004), the teacher's consciousness expanded from the surface of the onion toward the 'bottom' of the U (presence) through a deliberate focus of attention (mindfulness) and from this again 'upward' to effective behavior in concrete professional situations.

Looking at the coaching interventions, some readers may feel Angelo was rather directive. For a long time, many educators have been influenced by the Rogerian notion that coaching should always be non-directive. We do not believe so. On the contrary, it is our experience that a coaching in which (empathic) following and (empowering) directiveness are well balanced seems to be much more effective. It is important to emphasize, however, that the direction the coach gives is not so much oriented toward a kind of teaching he thinks the teacher should demonstrate. A coach who applies core reflection should, in our view, give directions with regard to the *reflection process* rather than the teaching behavior. Direction in the reflection process is necessary to break ineffective reflection patterns such as thinking without feeling or emotional ways of thinking.

Was the teacher's developmental process completed? We do not think so. It may take her much longer to really become autonomous in using core reflection. Perhaps individual coaching is also not the most effective way to promote such autonomy. From core reflection workshops given to a large number of teachers, we have reasons to believe that learning how to use core reflection in the coaching of a colleague seems to be more effective for learning how to apply the approach to oneself. Perhaps this is an example of the well-known principle that the best way to learn something is to teach it to someone else.

Core reflection can inevitably have consequences beyond the process of teaching. For example, it may make people aware of their level of "presence" in non-teaching situations as well. In the final interview, the teacher being studied confirmed that in her private life she also used to think rather than to feel (and her journal provides some examples of this), and that she had also profited from making the connection to self in non-teaching situations. As Korthagen and Vasalos (2005) wrote:

> [. . .] no neat and watertight boundary can be drawn between professional core issues and personal biographical material. On the other hand, it is not difficult for coaches to make a deliberate choice to stick to the professional domain, and leave other areas out of the reflective conversation, something that we advocate in our courses for teacher educators.

> (p. 65)

The transcripts of the coaching process as presented above show that the coach did indeed make that choice. In his book *A hidden wholeness,* Palmer (2004) elaborates on the risks of "living divided" as a teacher, and ends this book by pointing toward the benefits of "living divided no more." In this respect, paying attention to the integration of the personal and the professional in teaching through coaching based on core reflection may contribute to educational goals that go far beyond the development of the individual teacher.

References

Allender, J. S. (2001). *Teacher self: The practice of humanistic education.* Lanham, MD: Rowman & Littlefield.

Assagioli, R. (1965). *Psychosynthesis: A manual of principles and techniques.* New York: Penguin.

Brown, K. W., & Ryan, R. M. (2003). The benefit of being present: Mindfulness and its role in psychological well-being. *Journal of Personality and Social Psychology, 84,* 822–848.

Bullough, R.V. (1997). Practicing theory and theorizing practice in teacher education. In J. Loughran, & T. Russell (Eds.), *Purpose, passion and pedagogy in teacher education* (pp. 13–31). London/Washington, DC: Falmer Press.

Damasio, A. (1999). *The feeling of what happens: Body and emotion in the making of consciousness.* London: Heinemann.

Germer, C. K. Siegel, R. D., & Fulton, P. R. (2005). *Mindfulness and psychotherapy.* New York: Guilford Press.

Greene, M. (1973). *Teacher as stranger.* Belmont, CA: Wadsworth.

Kelchtermans, G., & Vandenberghe, R. (1994). Teachers' professional development: A biographical perspective. *Journal of Curriculum Studies, 26,* 45–62.

Korthagen, F., & Vasalos, A. (2005). Levels in reflection: Core reflection as a means to enhance professional development. *Teachers and Teaching: Theory and Practice, 11*(1), 47–71.

Loughran, J. (2006). *Developing a pedagogy of teacher education: Understanding teaching and learning about teaching.* London: Routledge.

McLean, S. V. (1999). Becoming a teacher: The person in the process. In R. P. Lipka & T. M. Brinthaupt (Eds.), *The role of self in teacher development* (pp. 55–91). Albany, NY: State University of New York Press.

Meijer, P. C., Korthagen, F., & Vasalos, A. (2009). Supporting presence in teacher education: The connection between the personal and professional aspects of teaching. *Teaching and Teacher Education, 25*(2), 297–308.

Mingyur Rinpoche, Y. (2007). *The joy of living.* New York: Harmony Books.

Palmer, P. J. (1998). *The courage to teach.* San Francisco, CA: Jossey-Bass.

Palmer, P. J. (2004). *A hidden wholeness: The journey toward an undivided life.* San Francisco: Jossey-Bass.

Rodgers, C. R., & Raider-Roth, M. B. (2006). Presence in teaching. *Teachers and Teaching: Theory and Practice, 12*(3), 265–287.

Scharmer, C. O. (2007). *Theory U: Leading from the future as it emerges.* Cambridge, Mass: Society for Organizational learning.

Senge, P., Scharmer, C. O., Jaworski, J., & Flowers, B. S. (2004). *Presence: Exploring profound change in people, organizations and society.* London: Nicolas Brealey.

7

COACHING BASED ON CORE REFLECTION MAKES A DIFFERENCE[3]

Annemarieke Hoekstra and
Fred A. J. Korthagen

Annemarieke Hoekstra and Fred Korthagen describe Nicole, a veteran teacher, who struggled with implementing a new pedagogy requiring her to teach in a more student-oriented way. Coaching based on core reflection helped Nicole realize her ideals, as a detailed analysis of her learning process reveals. A shift took place in Nicole, both in terms of her beliefs and her behavior, and in her way of learning. Detailed descriptions of the coaching interaction illustrate its power. The conclusion section concentrates on the importance of reflection, awareness, modeling, and a focus on the teacher as a whole person.

Introduction

First, after the first two coaching sessions, I realized it is this manner in which Fred asks questions that allows one to learn. I want to stress that I learned from him that by asking the students questions and inviting them to answer, they themselves realize where they get stuck and what kind of behavior it is that brings them to where they do not want to be. I value greatly Fred asking me such questions. He basically kept asking questions and confirming what I said. That is how I obtained insights I previously did not have.

(Nicole, 2006)

---

3   This chapter is based on: Hoekstra, A. & Korthagen. F. A. J. (2011). Teacher learning in a context of educational change: Informal learning versus systematic support. *Journal of Teacher Education, 62*(1), 76–92.

This chapter, based on a previously published article (Hoekstra & Korthagen, 2011), describes how the learning process of a teacher, Nicole,[4] thoroughly transformed through her participation in seven coaching sessions based on the core reflection approach. In the 1990s, Nicole and her fellow secondary school teachers in the Netherlands were encouraged to adopt a new pedagogy, requiring teachers to support students in taking more responsibility for their learning and actively engaging in their learning process. Yet, for Nicole, a 22-years of teaching veteran teacher, and for many other teachers at the time, this new pedagogy required a profound shift in their thinking about teaching and learning, as well as their teaching practices. However, there was limited support to make this profound shift.

Initially, knowledge about the new pedagogy was disseminated through publications, workshops, and staff meetings. Some schools offered their teachers support for learning through professional development trajectories such as coaching by an expert or peer coaching. However, the majority of teachers had to rely on their own initiative to learn. To find out more about how this unsupported learning at work took place, we documented the learning processes of 32 teachers, including Nicole, over a 14-month period (Hoekstra et al., 2009). Our data on Nicole showed that she embraced the new pedagogy enthusiastically and wanted to implement new teaching strategies. Nicole had high expectations of the effectiveness of the active learning strategies she wanted to employ in the classroom. The school administration applauded her innovative attitude. Nicole believed, and still does, that students have an innate curiosity that teachers can invoke during class, which will motivate them to actively engage with the subject matter. However, despite her willingness to learn and her tireless efforts to improve her practice, Nicole felt frustrated in her ability to draw out the innate motivation of her students. Toward the end of the data collection period, Nicole reflected on a lesson Annemarieke video recorded:

> It appears as though they [the students] are not even using their study planning document. (. . .) 70% of them reflect far too little on their process. They have some sort of passive approach to what to do next, and then come to me with a far too general request. I hate that. I find that very disappointing. Anyway, if their motivation is not triggered from the very first year in secondary school, this current situation can be expected. That is the way it is. I am ready to get some help. Again, I'm a lone voice in the dessert. How do I turn this to my advantage so that it does actually work, despite the fact that nobody [here at school] co-operates? I do not want to lose my vision. So how do I do this? I just want some help!

---

4 Nicole is a pseudonym.

Fred, who had been involved in the data analysis, anticipated that with greater awareness of her feelings and negative thinking patterns, Nicole would be able to overcome a number of barriers in her own learning process. He offered Nicole seven coaching sessions based on core reflection, in exchange for her participation in a follow-up study of her learning process. We compared her learning activities and outcomes in the year prior to coaching with the learning activities and outcomes in the year she received coaching.

In this chapter we describe the story of Nicole, focusing on the difference between Nicole's unsupported and supported learning. The story shows that as a result of coaching, a strong shift took place in Nicole, both in terms of her beliefs and behavior, as well as the way she learned. We will also highlight the coaching interaction that contributed to this shift, as we believe it illustrates the power of coaching based on core reflection.

Investigating Teachers' Professional Learning Processes

We studied 32 teachers' unsupported learning in the workplace for over a year (Hoekstra et al., 2009). During this time none of these teachers were involved in a structured professional development trajectory. Both at the start and conclusion of the period, all 32 teachers filled out a questionnaire regarding their beliefs of students' active and self-regulated learning. Examples of questions about the importance of students taking responsibility for their own learning included:

- students learn better if they themselves assess whether the learning process evolves according to plan;
- it is important that I as a teacher ask the students how they plan to address a task effectively; and
- students learn better if they are aware of their emotions.

Examples of questions about students' active and collaborative learning included:

- students learn better if they themselves create links between components of the subject matter;
- it is important that I stimulate students to underpin their own opinion; and
- students learn better if they think about their tasks together with their peers.

The participants' students also filled out a questionnaire at the beginning and conclusion of the 14 months. The student questionnaire measured student perceptions of their teachers' behaviors helping them to be active learners who take responsibility for their own learning. The students chose responses to statements about their teachers' behavior, ranging from (1) *This teacher hardly ever does this* to (5) *This teacher almost always does this.* Examples of these statements included:

- my teacher asks me how I think to address a task effectively; and
- my teacher stimulates me to provide arguments that support my opinion.

Every six weeks throughout the year, the teachers sent us reports of their workplace learning experiences by email. Four teachers, including Nicole, were also video-recorded during six of their lessons and interviewed after each recorded lesson (Hoekstra et al., 2007).

The Story of Nicole

When we first met Nicole, she was a 55-year-old biology teacher with 22 years of teaching experience. She taught at a school located in a suburb of a large city in the Netherlands. The school called itself an open Christian school, meaning that respect and solidarity were core values. Most students in the school were from white, middle-class families, and from both urban and rural areas.

At the end of the 14-month period we had the following types of information about Nicole: data from the questionnaires on beliefs and behavior at the beginning and end of the year, six video-recorded lessons and consecutive interviews, and nine emails containing reports on learning experiences. We also audio-recorded an interview about current concerns about teaching and one about the school context.

Unsupported Learning

During the 14 months in which we gathered data about the teachers, Nicole tried out many active learning strategies. She regularly let her students work in groups, something she had learned fits with the new pedagogy. She talked passionately about her vision of the ideal classroom, where students' intrinsic motivation is evoked. However, Nicole was troubled by what she perceived as her lack of control over what her students were learning when working in groups. When this happened, Nicole had a tendency to fall back on her old teaching behavior of concisely presenting the content matter to the students and providing them with the right structure, especially when students appeared to be uncertain. During the second lesson, Nicole interfered in students' own attempts to make sense of the subject matter by taking the floor and concisely presenting the topic:

> I felt some undetermined uncertainty. . . So I thought I needed to present an overview of this theory quickly and strongly, because they said they did not see the structure anymore. I was consciously aware of my thoughts. I wanted to put the subject matter back on track, so that they'd leave the

classroom with a good feeling, like "oh is that what we're doing." That was my intention . . . [I thought] now I have to make sure that they know exactly what to expect.

Note the combination of thinking, wanting, and feeling in this situation. Nicole thought about the students losing overview of the topic. She felt somewhat uncertain and wanted to reduce students' sense of uncertainty so that they could leave the class with a good feeling. However, by taking over the floor, Nicole prevented the students from learning how to make sense of the topic themselves.

Comforting the students when they felt uncertain made Nicole feel good. In the third lesson, she told the students that she would repeat the most important subject matter of the last months. She reported:

> I noticed that they liked it that I put them back on track. I gave them a feeling of certainty about the exams next week, because they really don't look forward to that . . . That is nice. It strokes my ego, that I know what they want and that I meet their needs . . . It was exactly how I wanted it to be and I enjoyed it.

Nicole seemed to have the implicit belief that students should not feel uncertain and did not seem to realize that uncertainty is a natural part of the learning process.

Nicole repeatedly emphasized that envisioning the ideal classroom helped her persevere. However, she felt frustrated when she found that her strategies did not motivate the students as much as she had hoped. Nicole didn't realize that by taking over the sense-making of the subject matter from the students, she in fact inhibited her attempts to foster students' own sense-making. This could be due to the way she reflected on her work. When Nicole sensed that a strategy worked, she felt very happy and it reinforced her belief that she was on the right track. However, when she noticed that some of her strategies did not work, she seemed to retreat into somber feelings of powerlessness. This type of reflection did not help Nicole to really transform her teaching practice. Not surprisingly, the questionnaires showed that after a year of unsupported learning, Nicole's beliefs and behavior regarding students' active and self-directed learning had not changed.

Coaching

Nicole was then offered seven coaching sessions from Fred, which were recorded on video. After the final session, Nicole once again filled out the questionnaires on her beliefs, and her students filled out the questionnaire on her behavior in the classroom. Both halfway and at the end of the coaching trajectory, Annemarieke interviewed Nicole regarding her learning activities and outcomes. A detailed description of the data collection and analysis procedure can be found in Hoekstra and Korthagen (2011). In the remainder of this chapter, we will summarize the coaching process and the outcomes.

Session 1: Identifying Ineffective Patterns

After introductions, Fred provided Nicole with feedback about her core qualities, such as her strong commitment to her work and her enthusiasm. By doing this, he worked according to core reflection principle 1 (see Chapter 3, in this book), which stresses the importance of promoting awareness of personal qualities. Next, Fred explained why he had become interested in supervising Nicole, namely because he had seen her potential in the initial study but felt she needed more support in order to actualize this potential. Fred communicated his trust in the process (core reflection principle 5). During this dialogue, it looked like Nicole *felt seen* as a person, for the video-recording of the session shows Nicole's strong emotional involvement. She spontaneously started talking about her struggle with teaching:

> I always want to be innovative in my teaching. But my underlying premise is that students need to want to learn, and need to discover things by themselves. (. . .) But I have to be careful that I'm not too ambitious. Sometimes students just really don't feel like doing anything.

Upon scrutiny, it became clear that Nicole often started her classes with deliberate enthusiasm about the subject matter, hoping that the students would then become enthusiastic, too. However, as soon as she sensed she was not connecting with her students, she would be disappointed and enter into a negative thinking cycle. Fred helped Nicole identify the thought processes she engaged in during classroom teaching and the inner obstacles involved: her tendency to give up, her habit of reflecting on what went wrong, and what to do next time. Nicole realized that by engaging in these thought processes *during* her classroom teaching, she obstructed herself in showing the behavior necessary to reach her ideal teaching practice where students become self-motivated, self-directed learners. Hence, this was an example of making an unconscious pattern explicit and through which Nicole developed more knowledge about herself.

Following up on Nicole's ideal, Fred asked Nicole how it would be if the students were able to become aware of what happened *inside them* at such a moment, as part of the process of becoming self-motivated, self-directed learners. Fred said:

> In moments that students seem to give up, you have the tendency to solve this for them, by encouraging them to keep working. . . Would it be possible that students themselves learn to see within themselves what is happening

to them? And that they think about whether they want to continue like this? You may explain to them that if they don't learn how to do this and motivate themselves, they may fail at school. That way you would be coaching them in how to be self-directed learners.

Nicole instantly became enthusiastic and talked excitedly about a classroom situation in which she had challenged a student to consider that her lack of motivation for a task was related to her coming to school unprepared. Together, Fred and Nicole explored the distinction between thinking, feeling, and wanting as well as the notion that people do not change by thinking alone. Nicole: "So, actually, I would have to say to them: 'When I am saying this to you, how do you feel?'" Whereas in the past, Nicole had been quick to label a situation as a 'failure,' she now began to view seemingly compromised learning activities as 'teachable moments' in which the students could learn to regulate their own emotions and motivation, under her guidance. She exclaimed excitedly: "Okay, okay! Yeah, I really like this!" We hypothesize that this was an important phase in her development toward a new professional identity.

Looking back in the final interview, Nicole explained:

> My enthusiasm itself also inhibited me. My enthusiasm was aimed at creating new assignments to promote active learning, rather than on whether the students would like different methods . . . Instead, I learned that I can shape my enthusiasm for the subject matter in several ways, for instance, the way I do it now, aided by Fred's strategies, is also a form of enthusiasm which is more aimed at how to generate processes within the students, while I used to preoccupy myself with the active learning strategy I could create around the subject matter.

Fred also helped Nicole see that through her former behavior of taking over from the students, she herself had hampered the very process she wanted to support in the students. The coach thus helped Nicole to identify internal obstacles to enacting her ideal (core reflection principle 2). To heighten Nicole's awareness of the conflict between her ideal and her tendency to give up as soon as she experienced failure, Fred used the metaphor of building a house. He asked her, "If one brick falls down, do you go on building, or do you start to reflect on this failure and stop building, based on a negative evaluation of the situation?" Nicole quietly acknowledged her tendency to give up too quickly, her voice demonstrating that this insight touched her emotionally. This strongly motivated her to deal with her own ineffective patterns (core reflection principle 3). In other words, Nicole became acutely aware, both through thinking and feeling, of the self-created nature of the process that obstructed her in trying to reach her ideal (core reflection principle 4).

Session 2: From Problems to Ideals

In the second session, Fred began by asking Nicole to reflect on her learning process during and after the first session. Again, it became clear that Nicole's primary focus was on problematic experiences, not on successes. The coach showed empathy with her feelings and underlined that in her stories he observed two core qualities in her: clarity and creativity. Nicole brought up two classroom situations, in which she tried to stimulate students' self-reflection. In both cases, Nicole had tried to get the students to reflect.

Nicole: "I am becoming more and more aware that I am not succeeding and that is terrible."

Fred summarized the situation for Nicole: "So you engaged in a conversation with them. You were aware that you fell back into your tendency to tell them how you feel and what they need to do. But in the beginning you had started to ask them the right kind of questions."

Fred urged Nicole to summarize things she *did well* in the situations she brought forward and what was *good* about them. He observed again that Nicole primarily tended to *think* about her experiences and did not reflect much on her feelings and on what she wanted: her ideal. He asked Nicole about how she felt in the interaction with the students, and he pointed out how these feelings influenced her behavior toward the students. Using the principle of focusing on positive meanings, Fred asked what an ideal situation would have looked like, but, more than once, she did not really answer the question.

Finally, Nicole explained: "In an ideal situation, the students would have returned to their work and changed their behavior. And one student, Jack, actually said that."

Fred exclaimed: "Oh?" and continued: "So in this situation, Jack acts in the ideal way, but you are also faced with a problem, and you choose to focus on that problem."

Following core reflection principle 4, Fred helped Nicole to realize and *feel* the friction between her ideal and her actual behavior, which is another example of promoting her self-knowledge. He said: "How could you have strengthened further reflection in Jack?"

When Nicole did not respond, Fred explained that what he was doing was fostering reflection in Nicole by asking her about her ideal. He stressed that Nicole could have similarly asked the students about their ideal situation. Nicole put her forehead in her hands resting on the table. At this moment, Fred asked: "What is happening? I see you do this." He mirrored her behavior.

Nicole sighed and said: "Oh how stupid, this makes so much sense."

Fred: "We are all, especially in education, so used to looking at problems, not at strengths and opportunities. You could have asked Jack to explain himself, and the other students would have heard the opinion from a peer."

Nicole clapped her hands, raised them, laughed, and said: "What a lost opportunity!" Then: "I am indeed inclined to look at the problem areas and treat them as problems." This sentence reflects that Nicole is developing more self-knowledge. Her face showed a somber expression.

After being quiet for a few moments, she explained her somber expression: "I am now starting to see all those moments that have triggered me to address problems, instead of focusing on what goes well."

Nicole showed emotion as she began to realize that she was obstructing not only her own, but also her students' potential (core reflection principle 4). In the final interview, Nicole said about this part of the supervision: "I remember clearly we did that, and it was very confrontational." This learning experience deeply impressed Nicole and contributed to a profound and lasting shift in the way she approached students in the classroom. The following excerpt from the final interview describes this change:

Nicole: I notice that I do not preach so much anymore, because that kills the process.
Interviewer: What does preaching mean for you?
Nicole: When I tell them how they have to behave. When I tell them what they are doing is wrong.
Interviewer: Why does that kill the process?
Nicole: Because it doesn't work. They withdraw within themselves . . . I noticed that instead I could ask them something like 'I see you do this . . . I do not like that' . . . Then, I ask them whether they would like to change that behavior and how they could change it, concretely. What they would like to do about it. Then I see them starting to think.

Gradually, Fred shifted the attention to supporting behavioral changes in Nicole, such as focusing on students' core qualities instead of on problems, sharing her ideals with her students, and supporting them in the systematic development of becoming self-directed learners. He helped her to formulate her new insights and her new view of her role and mission as a teacher, thus aiming at a fundamental identity change. Nicole: "I will concentrate on what a student can do, and not on what he or she does or cannot do. Students will then better recognize their own strengths and focus on them." In the final coaching session she reported:

As soon as you show students their strengths, they become more aware of them. And that is a positive energy I give them (. . .) and as soon as you do that, you see their eyes light up, and you see streams of positive energy. I never did that before.

Sessions 3 to 7: Toward Self-directed Learning

The issues discussed in the remainder of the sessions were similar to those in the first two sessions, but more in-depth. Much attention was devoted to Nicole's present behavior and to specific, possible new actions. During this process, the coach explicitly modeled interventions such as focusing on thinking, feeling, and wanting, focusing on successes rather than problems, and sharing an ideal with the learner. He thus supported the actualization of Nicole's inner potential (core reflection principle 6). Regularly, Nicole and Fred reflected on these interventions, their influence on Nicole's learning process, and their possible translation to situations in Nicole's classes. Nicole was able to apply the same strategy Fred applied to the conversation in her classroom, as she reported in the final interview:

> I learned that if you point out their feelings when you see how the student is doing [emotionally], and when you point that out, that part of her [the student's] frustration disappears, because I acknowledge those feelings. I learned that from Fred when he sometimes said: "that must have been depressing for you" . . . He acknowledged my feeling, that is so extremely important, I learned that. And when you do that with students, then they feel that their emotions are acknowledged, which happens much too little at school.

Fred and Nicole did several role-plays in order to promote the transfer to practice and to stimulate Nicole's self-directed professional learning. He continued to express his faith in Nicole's potential to change (core reflection principle 5). In the reflection on concrete classroom situations and role-plays, Fred emphasized the importance of a long-term strategy for promoting self-directed learning, and he introduced the idea of making small steps. He stressed that Nicole should not expect immediate, amazing strides and encouraged her to be happy with small successes, regardless of their size. In the final interview Nicole reported that she had learned new behaviors that could help her realize her vision:

> My vision is very much alive in my head, and it is what keeps me going. It already did before meeting Fred . . . I used to have the hope or idea that there was flow and that my behavior conformed to my vision, and I realized that that wasn't true. And now I realize that it does start to flow from my vision to my behavior. I notice that each moment in the classroom when I say "I do not see you do anything, what are you doing?" or "why aren't you doing anything?" or "what could you be doing right now?" or "how come you are not doing anything?" that I find all these are related to my vision. And also, that this will have its effect in the long run, instead of [what I used to think] expecting an immediate effect in the student.

Learning Outcomes

Through sessions 3–7, Nicole gradually learned to develop the kind of classroom behavior that was more in line with her ideals and her new insights. More specifically, an important new insight for Nicole was that students need to learn how to reflect on their own learning processes, and that learning should be considered a long-term process. In terms of teaching behavior, she learned to invite students to reflect on their own learning processes by asking them open-ended questions. In addition, Nicole learned how to recognize and deal with students' emotions – and students' strengths. These important learning outcomes were also evident in the questionnaire data, which showed that Nicole's beliefs regarding students' self-regulated learning had indeed changed significantly (p < 0.05). This change was particularly evident in questions that related to students' dealing with emotions and motivation:

• the need for students to understand their own emotions in order to learn better;
• the discussion of students' feelings of anxiety; and
• the discussion of the importance of content and assignments.

According to the student questionnaire, Nicole's behavior in the classroom changed significantly as well, particularly the kind of behavior that fosters students' own reflection (p < 0.05) and their active involvement in their learning (p < 0.05) (Hoekstra & Korthagen, 2011). Examples of items that scored significantly higher are:

• this teacher asks us to connect several different aspects of the subject matter with each other; and
• this teacher makes us think about how we can address feelings of anxiety and uncertainty.

Learning How to Learn

An important aspect of the final sessions was that Fred helped Nicole to take responsibility for and organize her own learning (core reflection principle 7). He encouraged her to reflect much like she wanted the students to reflect with the aid of the core reflection guidelines. As a result, Nicole changed her superficial *does work/does not work* evaluation of teaching strategies into a more meaningful reflection by looking at what her students were doing. She learned that students' responses provided a rich source of information:

> When a student didn't do what I wanted, I quit . . . I thought like: "it doesn't work." The whole strategy doesn't work, it is clear, they don't feel

like it. I looked at a student from the perspective of "he doesn't do anything, and that is wrong." Now I see: "he is doing something else." Now I look at what they are doing instead, when it's not what I want them to be doing. That opens a world of possibilities to start a conversation with them. When you ask them the right questions, they will be more open, and will start doing their work.

In addition, Nicole had become aware of a number of barriers to learning, which she managed to overcome. These barriers included:

- the belief that change can happen immediately;
- her tendency to take control of classroom interactions; and
- too high expectations of the abilities of students.

Finally, Nicole learned that openness toward students' perspectives involves emotions in herself that she needed to deal with, and that required patience. Nicole reflected, "I find it very scary to reflect with a group [of students] on the process. I used to avoid this type of confrontation." She also recognized that learning takes time:

[If it doesn't happen immediately] it will succeed in the long run. I started a process that I know will succeed sometime. I do not always ask the right questions, I cannot expect myself to do that, because I am still learning. I know I am going in the right direction, I know how I want it, and how it will work, only, I still need to practice. I am on my way . . .

Two Years Later

Nicole not only learned how to keep learning herself; she also successfully managed to transform her workplace as a learning environment. Two years after the final coaching session, she told us that she had continued to use her newly acquired skills and insights: "I also keep working on new ideas to support students to become more responsible and active learners and I achieve great results with minor interventions." In addition, Nicole had also started to make changes within the school: "After I became aware of how I wanted to enact my vision, I realized that there was little support for this kind of learning within my school . . . I started my own teacher team." She had taken courses in core reflection and had begun to use her new insights and skills to coach the student teachers who were doing their practicum in her classes. Looking over our first research paper about her learning process, she exclaimed: "My God, I learned a lot. It hit the core of my being, and I am glad that this is visible in this research paper."

Conclusion

The story of Nicole is the story of a committed, determined, and passionate teacher who wants to be the best for her students. She generously provided us with a window into her deepest ideals, fears, and struggles related to her teaching. It was an honor to witness and support her in her struggle to overcome the barriers she had unwittingly created for her own and her students' development – a struggle she approached with honesty, persistence, patience, and above all courage.

In comparing Nicole's unsupported learning process with her learning process during coaching, we can see a formidable change. Not only did Nicole change her teaching behavior and her ideas about teaching, she also changed in the way she approached her own learning process. Would Nicole have changed so profoundly without Fred's support? Possibly. Would she have made the shift without Fred's support *in only five months*? Most likely not, as she did not change much in a year of unsupported learning. Fred's use of the core reflection approach to coaching was most effective in supporting Nicole to break through and abandon the persistent patterns in thinking and behaving that she had developed over the years, and that ultimately inhibited her from reaching her ideal. The story of Nicole shows us that core reflection has the potential to profoundly and permanently transform a teacher's knowledge, behavior, and attitude in a relatively short period of time. In addition, the approach supported Nicole in accepting herself as a learner as part of her own professional identity.

The concrete descriptions of the coaching sessions presented above illustrates the fundamentals of core reflection, as described in Chapters 2 and 3, and especially Figures 3.1 and 3.2. Through a constant focus on Nicole's strengths, her core qualities, and on her ideals, the coach created a climate in which Nicole's inner potential started to flow. Exactly because of that, the obstacles that Nicole encountered also became very obvious. They appeared to be mostly inner obstacles, for example the deeply ingrained pattern of focusing more on problematic issues than on successes and opportunities. As a result of this pattern, Nicole's potential used to be blocked. Through deep reflection, in which the 'elevator movement' (see Chapter 3) was used over and over again, Nicole's awareness of both her own potential and her inner obstacles grew. As the story shows, it is the tension between these two 'poles,' the pole of the inner potential and the pole of the obstacles and limitations, that is brought into full awareness through coaching based on core reflection. Similar to what happens between electric poles, this creates a 'spark' leading to sparkling new insights and new behavior. This is a springboard for a transformative learning process. Nicole even learned how to use the types of interventions that Fred modeled in her own teaching.

Will core reflection always be so successful in supporting transformative change in teachers? Many other chapters in this book can attest to that. Regarding the success of the approach in the life of Nicole, we need to keep in mind that

(a) Nicole was an exceptionally motivated learner, who was (b) acutely aware of the fact that she had gotten stuck in her own learning. She was (c) open to receive support, and (d) willing to take a hard look at herself.

Nicole's story shows four basic features of the coaching and learning process that we would like to conclude with, namely: *reflection, awareness, modeling,* and *the need to address the whole person of the learner.* We elaborate on these features, since we believe they are essential to any fundamental learning process and hence also important in other contexts than only those in which core reflection is applied.

Reflection

Through the coaching sessions, Nicole changed from a works/doesn't work type evaluation (action-oriented reflection) by herself, to a more meaningful reflection in which she involved the students. Focusing her attention on the students' learning process, rather than on whether or not the students liked her teaching strategy, opened Nicole's eyes to the myriad of variations in students' emotions, motivation, and learning patterns. Our previous study and Mansvelder-Longayroux et al. (2007) have shown that meaning-oriented reflection has more potential than action-oriented reflection to contribute to transformative teacher change.

Awareness

During the coaching, Nicole became aware of her own thought patterns that obstructed her in working toward her ideal. This awareness did not come about during the previous year, in which Nicole did not receive support for learning. In fact, Nicole felt rather alone in school in her ambition to change. Day (1999) has pointed us toward the limitations of individual reflection and has stressed the need for input from others into the reflection process. The story of Nicole suggests that in order for deep change to occur, this input from another person needs to include: a focus on the learner's strengths, a recognition that becoming aware of inhibiting processes can be painful, a display of compassion and trust in the learner's ability to succeed, and a keen eye to pointing out contradictions and frictions in layers of the onion (Chapter 3). Such input from others may not naturally exist in the workplace of teachers, and when profound change is required, teachers would profit from receiving the type of support that promotes awareness.

Modeling

During the coaching process, Fred explicitly modeled some of the behaviors that Nicole wanted to show in the classroom. In the interviews, Nicole referred several times to the fact that she herself had experienced the impact of Fred's coaching behavior and explained how she had made the transfer to her own classroom teaching. For teacher learning in general, this means that teachers profit from a positive learning climate in which excellent teachers and coaches can act as role models (Putnam & Borko, 1997).

Addressing the Whole Person

The story of Nicole shows the need to address the whole person of the teacher in efforts to bring about change. The transformation would not have occurred if Nicole's feelings of uncertainty had been ignored or if she had not been encouraged to motivate herself to change by focusing on her ideal. The story shows how teacher learning can be successfully supported by addressing all layers of the onion, in conjunction with clear guidance in reframing beliefs and practicing new behavior. In our view, the crucial step for supervisors and teacher educators is to acknowledge that professional development initiatives should not separate the personal from the professional.

References

Day, C. (1999). *Developing teachers: The challenges of lifelong learning*. London: Falmer Press.

Hoekstra, A., Beijaard, D., Brekelmans, M., & Korthagen, F. A. J. (2007). Experienced teachers' informal learning from classroom teaching. *Teachers and Teaching: Theory and Practice, 13,* 129–206.

Hoekstra, A., Brekelmans, M., Beijaard, D., & Korthagen, F. A. J. (2009). Experienced teachers' informal learning: Learning activities and changes in behavior and cognition. *Teaching and Teacher Education, 25,* 363–373.

Hoekstra, A., & Korthagen, F. A. J. (2011). Teacher learning in a context of educational change: Informal learning versus systematically supported learning. *Journal of Teacher Education, 62,* 76–92.

Mansvelder-Longayroux, D. D., Beijaard, D., & Verloop, N. (2007). The portfolio as a tool for stimulating reflection by student teachers. *Teaching and Teacher Education, 23,* 47–62.

Putnam, R. T., & Borko, H. (1997). Teacher learning: Implications of new views of cognition. In B. J. Biddle, T. L. Good, & I. F. Goodson (Eds.), *International handbook of teachers and teaching* (pp. 1223–1296). Dordrecht: Kluwer Academic Publishers.

PART III
Core Reflection with Students and Schools

Part III of this book contains three chapters focusing on the use of core reflection with *students* and *schools as a whole*. First, Chapter 8 shows how a school-wide change can take place if it is grounded in core reflection. The following two chapters describe the impact of core reflection on students. In Chapter 9, the focus is on students in the elementary grades; while Chapter 10 discusses the beneficial influence of core reflection on university students.

8

CORE REFLECTION IN PRIMARY SCHOOLS

A New Approach to Educational Innovation

Saskia Attema-Noordewier,
Fred A. J. Korthagen, and
Rosanne C. Zwart

Saskia Attema-Noordewier, Fred Korthagen, and Rosanne Zwart describe an innovative approach for professional development – called Quality from Within – based on the principles of core reflection. This approach is essentially bottom-up; teachers' qualities and inspiration are taken as a starting point for the innovation. In this study of six primary schools, quantitative and qualitative instruments were used for analyzing the outcomes of the approach for teachers, students, school principals, and for the school culture as a whole. Moreover, the authors analyzed which specific aspects of the approach stimulated or hindered these effects.

I now have tools for looking completely differently at myself and a situation . . . more positively. That can give a complete shift. Instead of thinking "ah, I am so busy" and feeling irritated, I now decide consciously to get in touch with my quality of care, and I decide to look at the positive side of the situation. In this way I see much more, and I feel a much lighter kind of energy.

(Primary school teacher after a core reflection training at her school)

Introduction

Much of this book is devoted to individual learning and personal growth based on core reflection. This chapter describes how core reflection can be used for changing whole schools. An intervention called *Quality from Within* was implemented in six primary schools to improve the quality of the school by using core reflection. The aim was to provide professional development to teachers by promoting awareness of their qualities, potential, and inspiration and to support them further in applying this awareness to their work.

Projects like this one were already organized by the Institute of Multi-level Learning (IML) at other schools and educational institutions in the Netherlands and other countries (e.g. Belgium, the US, the UK). Although the projects were limited to a small number of group meetings for staff and applied to peer coaching, they seemed to be highly successful according to the participants (Korthagen & Vasalos, 2008). The study reported here systematically explores the impact of the *Quality from Within* approach on the professional development of participating teachers and on school culture. It also deals with the question: What specific aspects of the approach stimulate or hinder the outcomes? We expect that insights from this study may be useful for other schools when designing interventions for professional learning.

The study was guided by the following research questions:

1. What do the participants in the *Quality from Within* projects perceive as the outcomes of the project (for themselves, their students and the school as a whole) and how do these outcomes – according to the participants – become realized in daily practice?
2. Do the participants perceive themselves as better facilitators of student and colleague learning as a result of the *Quality from Within* projects?
3. What aspects of the project, of their schools, or of themselves do the participants perceive as:

    *   promoting the learning process and the outcomes?
    *   hindering or limiting the learning process and the outcomes?

Theoretical Background

The Failure of Most Educational Innovations

Despite all the time and effort being put into educational innovation, most innovations fail (Holmes, 1998). One reason for this is that often the organizational structure and policy of the school are not taken into account (Fullan, 2001). Therefore, the innovation takes place in an isolated way and the effects are likely to fade out after the intervention is over (Van Veen et al., 2010).

Another important reason for failure is ineffective leadership with top-down approaches (Fullan, 2001). Teachers in these situations do not feel they are taken seriously or treated as professionals (Elliot, 1991). In addition, fixed goals are often pre-established without consulting the teachers (Korthagen, 2007). A top-down approach to innovation often creates a feeling of external pressure in the teachers, especially when the innovation is not in line with their needs and views.

As a result, teachers often respond by showing patterns of fight (active resistance), flight (attempts to escape from the pressure), or freeze (becoming tensed). For example, a common flight or fight response of teachers is to put innovations away as being useless or impractical and to speak negatively of educational innovators (Elliot, 1991).

In sum, the overall picture is rather hopeless: educational experts and teachers do not really take each other seriously and teachers reject potential innovations, regardless of their potential benefits for practice. Even though the top-down approach to educational innovation is often not very successful, it is still very much part of the educational culture (Korthagen & Vasalos, 2008). Education seems to be in need of a fundamental solution to this widespread phenomenon. The *Quality from Within* approach could be part of this solution as it is essentially a bottom-up instead of a top-down model. More detailed information about the approach is given on pages 114–116.

Deficiency Model versus Growth Model

Another reason why innovations fail is that there is often a focus on problematic and troublesome issues with respect to the quality of the schools and the teachers teaching in those schools. This implies an emphasis on what should be improved. This is called the *deficiency model* (see Chapter 2). This negative focus generates little enthusiasm in teachers and is rather ineffective. A different approach to innovation, the *growth model*, is grounded in positive psychology (Seligman & Csikszentmihalyi, 2000; see Chapter 2). Its basic assumption is that we should emphasize the inner potential of people, that is, their core qualities. Acknowledging and focusing on core qualities instead of emphasizing deficiencies does not only value the individual's irreplaceable contribution to their own and colleagues' professional growth, but it also promotes a more holistic approach to students while creating room for alternative ways of approaching problems in work and life.

Self-Determination Theory

In the literature, insights from positive psychology have been connected to the self-determination theory (SDT), in which three basic human psychological needs are distinguished: the need for autonomy, for competence, and for relatedness (Deci & Ryan, 2000; Ryan & Deci, 2002; Evelein, 2005). According to Deci and Ryan (2000), fulfillment of these basic psychological needs is essential to psychological health and growth, to intrinsic motivation, to the experiencing of well-being, optimal functioning, and self-actualization. Evelein (2005) showed that teachers who are encouraged to identify and use their core qualities will experience fulfillment of their basic needs, which in turn correlates with more effective teaching behavior.

In this study, we focus on the basic need of autonomy, as the assumption underlying the *Quality from Within* approach is that enhancing the fulfillment of this need is crucial to successful learning processes. Autonomy refers to the need to experience the self as the source of one's own behavior and the need to express one's authentic self (Ryan & Deci, 2002). The personal will and clear decision-making based on personal values are central in experiencing autonomy (Hodgins, Koestner, & Duncan, 1996).

Quality from Within and Core Reflection

The *Quality from Within* approach is based on the above analysis of the causes of failure of educational innovations, the principles of core reflection and positive psychology, and the basic need of autonomy. Teachers' qualities, inspiration, and existing knowledge are taken as the starting point for further development. Fredrickson (2002) calls this the *broaden-and-build model*, which means broadening and extending on the basis of what is already there. Furthermore, alignment of the different layers in the onion model is promoted (see Chapter 3 for a description of core reflection and the onion model) based on the assumption that professional behavior becomes more effective and fulfilling (in the sense of fulfillment of the three basic psychological needs) when behavior is connected with the deeper layers in a person and when the different layers are in harmony with each other. The essence of the approach is to make teachers aware of their core qualities, potential, and inspiration, and to support them in putting these into action and in dealing with obstacles. In addition, it supports teachers in doing the same with their students.

Different from most innovations, the *Quality from Within* approach does not aim at a specific outcome in terms of how teaching should be. If teachers connect with their inner strengths and inspiration as well as those of their students, they may start to find their own approaches to effective education.

Context of the Study

In this study, we examined the implementation of the *Quality from Within* approach in six primary schools between June 2008 and June 2009. The teachers learned to use the (self-) reflection and coaching method of core reflection, which starts with acknowledging their own core qualities, potential, and inspiration and those of their students and promotes development from there. Moreover, they reflected on their pedagogical views, based on their experiences with this new method. It was assumed that, by using this method, the teachers would become better facilitators of learning for their students and their colleagues. An intervention was implemented at each school, with the following characteristics. (For more details, see Attema-Noordewier, Korthagen, & Zwart, 2011.)

1. Building on the Needs and Concerns of the Participants

The three one-day group meetings centered on a pedagogical approach that was based on the concept of 'realistic teacher education' (Korthagen et al., 2001). Concerns that participants encountered in their work were taken as the starting point of the learning process and were approached according to the principles of core reflection.

2. Practicing in Authentic Situations

Authentic situations in teachers' daily practice and during meetings were used as a starting point for core reflection. Moreover, teachers practiced the methods of core reflection in their real work situations with students. This included some coaching by the trainers through coaching-on-the-job in the classroom or by working with students in the group meetings.

3. Promoting Individual Reflection

Personal reflection by the participants was constantly encouraged in order to realize deep learning. This reflection was about several topics: for example, recent situations in their work, their ideals and beliefs, their core qualities, the obstacles they encountered, and so forth (see the key principles of core reflection in Chapter 3).

4. Enhancing Transfer

Transfer was enhanced by encouraging participants to continuously apply what they learned to practice, both in their work with their students, as well as with each other (see also characteristic 2). Moreover, participants practiced inter-collegial coaching in pairs, kept logbooks for reflecting on their experiences – sharing them with the trainers and their colleagues, and they read a few Dutch articles on the core reflection method. In addition, a developmental group was formed that monitored, guided, and supported the development within the school. The group size varied from two to five teachers.

5. Promoting Reflection on the Team and School Level

Besides learning at the individual level, a learning process of the school as a whole was promoted by letting everyone in the school (teachers, school principals, remedial teachers, and student-teachers) participate together. Participants were stimulated to reflect on and discuss the educational identity and mission of the school. The development of a common language was essential in this process, a language that supported the teams' discussions on the relationship among theory, vision, and practice at the school level, and it also deepened individual reflections.

Moreover, the participants were stimulated to make the innovation that was taking place public, for example by organizing an informative afternoon for parents, other schools, the educational inspectorate, and so forth. This helped them to formulate a sharper definition of the educational identity of the school and to critically reflect on what had been achieved and what remained to be accomplished.

In sum, what made the difference was not just three course meetings, but the whole ongoing process that included meetings of the developmental group, inter-collegial coaching, and so on. Finally, in order to fully realize these characteristics of the intervention, it is important to mention that the trainers were experienced teacher trainers who were specifically trained for several years in guiding the learning process using core reflection. For more details on the implementation of the core reflection approach in this project, see Korthagen and Vasalos (2008).

Method

In this study, the six primary schools implementing the *Quality from Within* approach were followed over a period of 17 months. All were state-funded schools, typical for the Dutch context. They ranged from small schools with only five teachers up to large schools with 30 teachers. The teachers taught in grades from kindergarten to grade six and had a variable amount of teaching experience. We used a design with both quantitative and qualitative data, which was described in detail in Attema-Noordewier et al. (2011). Questionnaires were filled out by 61 teachers, of whom a subset coming from four of the schools was also interviewed (24 at stage 1, 20 at stage 2, and 14 at stage 3). At the second stage, we also interviewed the four school principals.

The questionnaire was filled out right before the project started and immediately after it ended. It measured what the teachers perceived as the outcome of the project regarding their fulfillment of the basic need for autonomy and their self-efficacy concerning core reflection coaching, for example, whether they perceived themselves as better facilitators of student and colleague. Examples of items are: "In my work, I feel free to come up with my ideas and opinions"; and, "I can help people to express their personal qualities." Answers could be scored on a seven-point Likert scale, ranging from (1) *not true at all* to (7) *very true*. (See Appendix A for the complete questionnaire.)

We also conducted semi-structured interviews to study the teachers' experiences in depth. These interviews focused on the outcomes of the project for the participants and what they perceived as stimulating or hindering aspects concerning these outcomes. (See Appendix B for the complete set of interview questions.) Some examples are:

- What are personal outcomes for you as a result of your participation in this project?

- Do you notice something has changed in the students?
- What do you think were aspects that stimulated the outcomes of the project?

At four schools we interviewed a sub-sample of six teachers per school. We held the interviews: (1) halfway through the workshop period; (2) within three weeks after it had ended; and (3) approximately seven to eight months after it had ended. At each school, we chose two or three teachers who were enthusiastic about the project and seemed to learn a lot, one or two teachers who were not enthusiastic about the project and seemed to learn little, and one or two teachers who were neutral.

Findings

Outcomes of the Quality from Within Project at the Individual Level

Teachers' fulfillment of their basic need for autonomy and their self-efficacy in coaching increased after the trajectory (see Table 8.1). Their scores on the fulfillment of the basic need for autonomy increased from 5.11 to 5.39 and on their self-efficacy in coaching from 4.74 to 4.96. These are small, but statistically significant effects.

In Table 8.2, teachers' perceptions of personal outcomes reported in the interviews are summarized through percentages of teachers who mentioned these outcomes. Table 8.2 displays only the outcomes mentioned by more than 50% of the participants in at least one of the interview stages. This was done to condense the data into the most important results. Often, in research on teacher professional development, the analysis of the outcomes ends when the project ends (Desimone, 2009). We interviewed at T3 to take the more long-term effects of the intervention into account. Unfortunately, not all teachers could still participate in the study by that time. Hence, with respect to the longitudinal outcomes of the project, we report on the data of 14 teachers.

The data in Table 8.2 are categorized in order to reduce the data into meaningful units. Therefore, we condensed the six layers of the onion model into three layers, by combining adjacent levels into one category (Figure 8.1).

TABLE 8.1 Means and Standard Deviation (SD) on the Pre-Test and Post-Test ($\star\star$ p $<$ 0.01)

	Pre-test		Post-test		
Sub scale	Mean	SD	Mean	SD	P
Autonomy	5.11	.87	5.39	.71	.001$\star\star$
Self-efficacy in coaching	4.74	.89	4.96	.78	.006$\star\star$

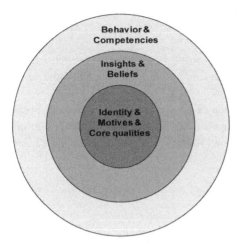

FIGURE 8.1   The simplified onion model (Attema-Noordewier et al., 2011)

In order to find illustrative examples, we checked the data to look for examples that were representative for all three stages.

Table 8.2 demonstrates that a perceived increase in coaching skills was mentioned most in the interviews as an important outcome of the project. It also shows that the reported outcomes were rather similar for the first and second measurement stages and still remained true seven to eight months after the end of the project. An exception was the category *increased awareness of one's own motives*, which was reported significantly less at T2. Furthermore, one outcome that was remarkably less mentioned at T3, is *increased awareness of certain coaching skills*. One explanation could be that when teachers were participating in the project longer, they were not only aware of these coaching skills, but were also feeling more competent regarding these skills and mention just this latter fact. For example, at T1 teachers reported things like, *I know now that I can give feedback on core qualities, but I find it hard to practice it in the classroom.* At T2 and T3 they reported that they were actually doing this more in the classroom and therefore it might be that there was no need to report that they were aware of it.

An important feature of core reflection is that it promotes learning that takes place at all levels of the onion model. To see whether participants were really experiencing learning at all levels, we checked how the outcomes of the 14 participants we interviewed three times were distributed across the levels of the simplified onion model (see Figure 8.1). We noticed that all but one (93%) mentioned individual outcomes at three levels in at least one interview stage. Seven to eight months after the project ended, most outcomes that the teachers reported were still connected to all three levels of the onion model. As it concurs with the intent of multi-level learning, this seems a promising result with respect to the long-term effects of the *Quality from Within* approach.

TABLE 8.2 Teachers' Perceptions of Individual Outcomes of the Project

Perceived outcomes	Illustrative example	T1 (N=24)	T2 (N=20)	T3 (N=14)
Behavior and competencies				
Increased coaching skills (regarding coaching of students and colleagues): stronger focus on the emotional and motivational side of learning; let the other person find the solution; more structured coaching	"I ask the children more about how they feel, and what they think. I have noticed that the children are then able to come up with their own solutions." "In conversations with my student teacher, I ask her to describe her experiences and ideas about the situation, instead of telling her myself what went right, and what went wrong, and how she should solve this."	75%	85%	79%
Feedback on core qualities (to students, colleagues, parents)	"I give more and more conscious feedback on core qualities."	63%	55%	71%
Increased awareness of certain coaching skills	"I became aware of the difference between giving a compliment and giving feedback on core qualities."	58%	45%	29%
Insights and beliefs				
New and/or renewed insights and ideas about learning	"One learns from positive feedback" "It is better to focus on strengths than on problems."	75%	80%	64%
Identity, motives and core qualities				
Increased awareness of one's own motives	"I want to contribute to the well-being of the children" "I now know better why I do what I do."	71%	30%	64%
Increased awareness of one's own professional identity	"I feel there is more appreciation for me, that my experience really matters."	54%	55%	57%
Increased awareness of one's own core qualities, like commitment, care, calmness, enthusiasm, honesty	"I now have tools for looking completely differently at myself and a situation (. . .) I now decide consciously to get in touch with my quality of care, and to look at the positive side of the situation. In this way I see much more, and I feel a much lighter kind of energy."	63%	70%	50%

When analyzing the data at the several levels reported above, we found striking differences between enthusiastic and less enthusiastic teachers, which seemed to be related to their learning attitude. If they had an open, learning-oriented attitude, they were more enthusiastic about the project and seemed to learn more from it. Those who had a less open attitude seemed to 'close up' already at the beginning, although the positive experiences of colleagues and their enthusiasm almost always started to influence those less enthusiastic teachers after a while.

Outcomes Regarding Others: The Students, the Team and the School Principals

Table 8.3 shows the most important perceived outcomes of the project regarding the students, the team, and the school principals mentioned by more than half of the teachers at least at one interview stage.

TABLE 8.3 Outcomes of the Project Regarding the Students, the Team and the School Principals

Perceived outcomes	Illustrative example	T1 (N=24)	T2 (N=20)	T3 (N=14)
Increased working and communicating skills and attitude of the students: better attitude toward working and learning, better group work, more independent in solving problems, more understanding of each other's feelings, giving more positive feedback to each other	"At days that I use it [CR], I notice that the children are working quite well and that their attitude is much better, and their concentration as well." "I believe that this positive approach will lead to better learning outcomes, because if they get this trust they will also use it."	67%	60%	71%
Teachers experience more openness, safety and a deeper connectedness in school	"The barrier to be open to each other really diminished." "We grew closer together."	75%	65%	64%
Better management and coaching skills of the school principals	"When I had a problem and talked to the principal about it, she immediately worked it out with me through CR. (. . .) After five minutes I was ready and knew how to solve it. That was nice!" "The principal is much more decisive."	50%	45%	57%

Table 8.3 demonstrates that, similar to the personal outcomes, the reported outcomes with respect to 'others' do not vary much between the measurement stages and still remain true seven to eight months after the project ended.

Aspects that Promoted the Outcomes

In Table 8.4, we summarize those aspects of the project, with regard to content, context, and the individual teachers, mentioned by more than half of the teachers at least at one interview stage as promoting the learning process and the outcomes.

TABLE 8.4 Aspects that Stimulated the Process and Outcomes

Perceived outcomes	Illustrative example	T1 (N=24)	T2 (N=20)	T3 (N=14)
Fitting in with the school (its development, culture, methods)	"We are together as a team for two years now, and are ready for reformulating our educational identity and mission. This project can help with this."	96%	25%	36%
Paying attention to the project during the school weeks: during staff meetings, active developmental group, peer coaching, sharing of successes, integrating what is learned in standard structures, inspiring conversations with the school principal	"The installation of a developmental group, that is active and feels responsible, helps." "Practicing giving each other feedback on core qualities within staff meetings really helps."	71%	55%	86%
Inspiring experiences during and after the workshop	"When we practiced [with CR], I solved my biggest problem." "Two teachers that always have problems communicating with each other, started to understand each other."	71%	60%	64%
Open and active attitude toward the project and your own learning	"I think about the project and what I want with it. And I plan conversations [with the students] in order to practice and become competent at it."	63%	25%	14%
Quality of the trainer	"The trainer is inspiring." "The trainer is very positive."	33%	50%	14%

Table 8.4 demonstrates some aspects that stimulated the process and outcomes of the project. One of them is that the project should be in line with a school's development and culture, especially at the start of the project. The developmental group can play an important role in this alignment. This group is also very important in paying attention to the project during the implementation period. Within the teachers themselves, an open attitude is an important promoting aspect, especially at the start of the project.

Aspects that Hindered the Process and Outcomes

In Table 8.5, we summarize those aspects of the project with regard to content, context, and the individual teachers that hindered an optimal process and positive outcomes; these aspects were mentioned by at least a third of the respondents. As we had selected a relatively high percentage of less enthusiastic teachers for the interviews, it helped us to get good insight into the reasons why a small number of teachers responded less positively to the project.

Most often mentioned was lack of time and being busy. The fact that the workshop was not practical enough was mentioned considerably less at T3, which seemed to indicate that the usefulness of the workshop for practice increased during the project, although another explanation could be that most of the participants could not remember the pedagogical approach in the project well.

Conclusion and Discussion

This chapter presents the outcomes of the *Quality from Within* approach at six primary schools in the Netherlands. It also describes what aspects of the approach the school and the individual teachers promoted or hindered these outcomes. In this final section we will formulate our main conclusions.

TABLE 8.5 Aspects that Hindered the Process and Outcomes

Hindering aspects	Illustrative example	T1 (N=24)	T2 (N=20)	T3 (N=14)
Lack of time and busyness during work	"We are so busy with many things that I have no time to practice this."	58%	45%	57%
Workshop was not practical enough	"The workshop was different from how it is in the class room."	42%	30%	7%
Resistance (to the focus on personal aspects of learning and to the focus on emotions)	"I felt a lot of resistance at the start" "I don't want to ask in each conversation 'What do you feel?' I find that not normal."	21%	30%	36%

Main Outcomes

We found statistically significant increases in feelings of autonomy and in self-efficacy regarding the coaching of students and colleagues. In the interviews, a large number of the teachers reported important individual outcomes that were mainly consistent over a longer time period, for example: increased coaching skills, (re)new(ed) insights and ideas about learning, and increased awareness of one's core qualities. For most participants, a real process of multi-level learning took place in the sense that they reported outcomes at all layers of the condensed onion model. These outcomes seemed remarkable, especially because of the relatively short intervention period and the well-known problems of educational innovation.

Suggestions for Designing Educational Innovations

We also looked at which aspects regarding the content of the program, the context, and the participating teachers were promoting or hindering these outcomes. The characteristics of the *Quality from Within* approach, described earlier, appeared to be important and helpful to the outcomes. We believe that these aspects could lead to guidelines for enhancing the effectiveness of any educational innovation. In this respect, the most important characteristics seem to be:

1. Make sure the innovation fits in with the school.

On the basis of our research outcomes and the literature (e.g. Elliot, 1991; Van Veen et al., 2010), we believe that in educational innovations much more attention should be given to the existing developments and the culture within the schools. In addition, the content of the trajectory could be connected to subject matter content, for example, in language learning. At the start of the trajectory, almost all respondents mentioned the *fit with the school* as a helping aspect. Later on, they mentioned it remarkably less often. This could be because they then took it for granted, or perhaps the minor initial flaws in the 'fit' were solved. Of course, this does not mean that, after starting, the innovation can suddenly change its design and not fit in with the school any longer.

2. Keep the innovation continuously alive at school.

One effective way of doing this is to create an active 'developmental group' that monitors and supports the innovation within the school. Such a group may consist of two to five teachers and ideally contains one of the informal leaders of the school, a teacher who may be very enthusiastic about the approach, and one who may be not so enthusiastic. The group helps to keep the things learned in the project alive during the practical, daily work of the school. One way to do this is by paying attention to the innovation in staff meetings, for example, through sharing successes, discussing a 'difficult' student from the core reflection view, and doing exercises with the teachers that they can do with the students as well. Other ways in which the group can stimulate the innovation is by having informal conversations and by organizing a meeting to inform the parents about the project. Keeping the project alive is also supported by peer coaching in between the workshop days, (a) by providing the teachers with specific exercises to practice aspects of core reflection in their own classroom; (b) by an active and supportive attitude of the school principal; and (c) by actively looking for the connection of ideas from the project with other developments in school.

3. Use the quality and inspiration that is already there in teachers and stimulate their development on this basis.

This aspect of the *Quality from Within* approach concurs with Fredrickson's (2002) broaden-and-build model. Attention should be given to the qualities that teachers, school principals, and students already have. As this intervention shows, learning processes at the individual and the organizational level start to 'flow' much more smoothly as soon as people feel that their strengths are valued and taken seriously in further developments.

4. Stimulate an open and active learning attitude in the teachers.

Those teachers who have little 'willingness to learn' can be stimulated by creating 'problem sensitivity' (Van Eekelen, 2005). The *Quality from Within* approach requires teachers to have a certain awareness, not only of their core qualities, but also of situations in their practices that could be improved. Perhaps for the 'less sensitive' teachers a more gradual approach is needed in which they get more time to reflect on their daily practices and to identify issues they might want to work on. Besides, for teachers with a lack of self-confidence, an even safer learning environment might be needed, for example, by giving them the opportunity to show their colleagues first what they are good at.

   Another explanation for some teachers' lack of willingness to learn could be their lack of familiarity with the specific approach, specifically with the focus on inter-human aspects and the language used, in our project, for example: *core qualities, flow, ideals*, and *core reflection*. In order to overcome this obstacle, we believe the trainers should pay more attention to the language used and could, together with the teachers, develop a common language that everybody feels familiar with. On the other hand, as discussed above, we also found evidence that even those teachers who were skeptical at the beginning of our project (about 20% of the participants) became much more positive and open toward the *Quality from Within* approach after several months. It seemed as if they changed under the influence of the general development that took place in their team. They saw that other teachers applied what they had learned successfully and with interesting results, and that the whole culture in the school changed. This seems to show that it is hard for an individual to remain resistant when the whole environment changes in a positive way.

5. Stimulate a development at all levels of the onion model (i.e. stimulate multi-level learning).

Individual outcomes of the intervention were reported on all levels of the onion model. This might be an important promoting aspect for the long-term effects of the *Quality from Within* approach. Hence, in order to make an innovation successful, it might be important to not only pay attention to the participants' skills and behavior, but also to underlying beliefs, motives, identity, and core qualities.

6. Make deliberate use of modeling.

We believe that a strong feature of the *Quality from Within* approach is that the trainers were role models for the behavior and attitudes they tried to develop in the teachers. Expert knowledge about change and theoretical notions underlying their own behavior were also made explicit by the trainers during the workshop. This is called *explicit modeling* (Lunenberg, Korthagen, & Swennen, 2007).

Summary

In sum, our study gave an answer to the research question of what the participants in the *Quality from Within* projects perceive as the short- and long-term outcomes of the project. At the teacher level, we found, for example, increased feelings of autonomy, increased self-efficacy regarding coaching of students and colleagues, increased coaching skills, new or renewed insights and ideas about learning, and increased awareness of one's core qualities. For most teachers, a real process of multi-level learning took place. At the student level, the teachers reported an increase in the students' working and communication skills and attitude. At the level of the school principals, the teachers reported that they experienced them as having better management and coaching skills. Finally, at the level of the school as a whole, the teachers experienced more openness, safety, and a deeper connection with others.

Important aspects that were found to stimulate these outcomes were that the project should be in line with the school development and culture and that attention should be paid to the project during the implementation period. Important aspects that hindered the outcomes were *lack of time* and *being busy*.

In conclusion, our study indicates that the *Quality from Within* approach is an effective model of professional development. This shows that core reflection not only has a potential for individual learning in students and teachers, but it can have a strong impact on the development of schools as a whole. Moreover, our study on the *Quality from Within* approach has yielded a set of relevant suggestions for shaping educational innovations in general.

Acknowledgments

The research reported on in this chapter has been made possible thanks to external funding from the marCanT Foundation.

The authors wish to thank all the participants of the *Quality from Within* project for their contributions to this study, Mart Haitjema (marCanT Foundation) for his generous support of our research and Judith Schoonenboom, Jolijn Serto, and Lumine van Uden for supporting in the data analysis.

Appendix 8.A: Questionnaire on Perception of Work

After a brief instruction on how to fill out the questionnaire, some basic questions were asked about gender, age, and teaching and coaching experience. Next, the teachers scored the following items on a seven-point Likert scale (1 = not true at all, 7 = very true), which in the questionnaire were mixed in a random order.

Need for autonomy

1. I have the feeling I can decide how I do my work.
2. I feel under pressure in my work.★
3. In my work, I feel free to come up with my ideas and opinions.
4. In my work I have to do what I am told.★
5. In my work, my feelings concerning the work are taken into account.
6. I can be myself at my work.
7. I experience little space to decide myself how to do my work.★

Competency in coaching

1. I find it hard to deal with personal obstacles in the learning process of others.★
2. I feel competent in in-depth coaching.
3. When I coach people, I am able to tune in with personal elements in the other.

★ = negative item

4. I can support people in dealing with their problems.
5. I manage to tap into the inspiration of others.
6. I can help people to express their personal qualities.
7. I have a clear view of how I can do a coaching conversation.
8. I have a grip on my own way of coaching.
9. I find myself a good coach.
10. I can deal well with emotions of other people.

Appendix 8.B: Interview Outline

In the three interviews that were held over time (T1 = halfway through the trajectory, T2 = within three weeks after it had ended, and T3 = seven to eight months after it had ended), the questions below were asked after a brief introduction. Complementary questions were asked when necessary to concretize the answers.

Question	T1	T2	T3
General questions			
What's the first thing that comes to your mind when you think of the Quality from Within project?	X	X	
Does the project match your expectations about it?	X	X	
How did your school come to join this project?	X		
Do you feel you had a voice in the design of the project?	X		
When we will evaluate the project, what do you think are important aspects to evaluate?	X	X	
Individual learning outcomes			
What are personal outcomes of your participation in this trajectory?	X	X	X
Did you recognize them in your reflective reports when you read these reports again?		X	
Behavior: Are there things you do differently now?	X	X	X
Competencies: Do you now have more skills/ competencies?	X	X	X
Competencies: Did the program influence your coaching competence?	X	X	X

continued

. . . continued

Question	T1	T2	T3
Beliefs: Did you get new insights? Have things become more important to you?	X	X	X
Identity: Did you change your opinion about yourself or your role in your work?	X	X	X
Core/Mission: Are there certain personal qualities that you are showing more often now?	X	X	X
Core/Mission: Are you more aware of your deeper motives in your work?	X	X	X
Are the things you have learned significant? To whom/what?	X	X	X
What aspects of CR/Quality from Within fascinate you now/do you still find difficult?		X	
Learning outcomes of others			
Do you notice something has changed in your: • students? • colleagues? • school principal?	X	X	X
The interviewer compares all outcomes mentioned during the interviews at T1 and T2 with the outcomes at T3, and asks if the outcomes not yet mentioned at T3 are still valid.			X
Professional development			
How would you describe your own development?		X	
How would you describe the development of your team?		X	
Now that the project has finished, are you confident that the process will continue?		X	
Stimulating and obstructing aspects			
What do you think has contributed to these outcomes?	X	X	X
Are there things that have obstructed your learning process or outcomes?	X	X	X
What should be done to get you to learn more/better?	X	X	X
Did you take part in the intercollegial coaching? If yes, how did you do that and with what results? If no, what made you not do it?		X	

continued

. . . continued

Question	T1	T2	T3
Vision and school context			
Are there any other courses/projects at your school that influence your development?	X		
Can you describe how your school is dealing with the professional development of teachers?	X		
Has the vision of the school on learning, teaching and/or coaching (of both students and colleagues) changed?	X	X	
Other outcomes based on the reflection form			
If the reflection form has been filled out: How did you feel about working with the reflection form?	X		
If it has not been filled out: What made you not fill out the form? If the form and its use would change, would you then work with it?	X		

References

Attema-Noordewier, S., Korthagen, F. A. J., & Zwart, R. C. (2011). Promoting quality from within: A new perspective on professional development in schools. In M. Kooy, & K. Van Veen (Eds.), *Teacher learning that matters: International perspectives* (pp. 115–142). London/New York: Routledge.

Deci, E. L., & Ryan, R. M. (2000). The "what" and "why" of goal pursuits: Human needs and the self-determination of behavior. *Psychological Inquiry, 11*(4), 227–268.

Desimone, L. M. (2009). Improving impact studies of teachers' professional development: Toward better conceptualizations and measures. *Educational Researcher, 38*(3), 181–199.

Elliot, J. (1991). *Action research for educational change.* Buckingham: Open University Press.

Evelein, F. G. (2005). *Psychologische basisbehoeften van docenten in opleiding.* [Basic psychological needs of student teachers]. Ph.D. Thesis. Utrecht: IVLOS.

Fredrickson, B. L. (2002). Positive emotions. In C. R. Snyder, & S. J. Lopez (Eds.), *Handbook of positive psychology* (pp. 120–134). Oxford: Oxford University Press.

Fullan, M. (2001). *The New Meaning of Educational Change* (3rd edn). New York/London: Teachers College Press/RoutledgeFalmer.

Hodgins, H. S., Koestner, R., & Duncan, N. (1996). On the compatibility of autonomy and relatedness. *Personality and Social Psychology Bulletin, 22*(3), 227–237.

Holmes, M. (1998). Change and tradition in education: The loss of community. In A. Hargreaves, A. Lieberman, M. Fullan, & D. Hopkins (Eds.), *International handbook of educational change* (pp. 558–575). Dordrecht/Boston/London: Kluwer.

Korthagen, F. A. J. (2007). The gap between research and practice revisited. *Educational Research and Evaluation, 13*(3), 303–310.

Korthagen, F. A. J., & Vasalos, A. (2008). *Quality from within as the key to professional development*. Paper presented at the Annual Meeting of the American Educational Research Association, New York.

Korthagen, F. A. J., Kessels, J., Koster, B., Lagerwerf, B., & Wubbels, T. (2001). *Linking practice and theory: The pedagogy of realistic teacher education*. Mahwah, NJ: Lawrence Erlbaum Associates.

Lunenberg, M., Korthagen, F. A. J., & Swennen, A. (2007). The teacher educator as a role model. *Teaching and Teacher Education, 23*(5), 586–601.

Ryan, R. M., & Deci, E. L. (2002). Overview of self-determination theory: An organismic dialectical perspective. In E. L. Deci & R. M. Ryan (Eds.), *Handbook of self-determination research* (pp. 3–33). Rochester: The University of Rochester Press.

Seligman, M. E. P., & Csikszentmihalyi, M. (2000). Positive psychology: An introduction. *American Psychologist, 55*(1), 5–14.

Van Eekelen, I. M. (2005), *Teachers' will and way to learn: Studies on how teachers learn and their willingness to do so*. Ph.D. Thesis. Maastricht: Universiteit Maastricht.

Van Veen, K., Zwart, R. C., Meirink, J., & Verloop, N. (2010). *Professionele ontwikkeling van leraren*. [Professional development of teachers]. Leiden: ICLON/Expertisecentrum Leren van Docenten.

9

DEVELOPING CORE QUALITIES IN YOUNG STUDENTS

Peter Ruit and Fred A. J. Korthagen

In this study, Peter Ruit and Fred Korthagen explore the impact of stimulating younger students in the Netherlands (ages 7–12 years-old) to consciously use their personal qualities. What are the effects of a relatively simple intervention focusing on the personal qualities of these students? Apparently, students are capable of recognizing their own core qualities and in linking these with their actions after a relatively short intervention by their teachers. Through this research, it became clear that it is possible to influence the personal growth of children through a relatively short and simple intervention by building on their core qualities.

Introduction

This chapter reports an experiment in which elementary school students were supported in becoming aware of and using their core qualities. In the experiment, we integrated notions from core reflection and positive psychology. The core reflection approach helps students to discover their core qualities and to make use of them. Research shows that the level of one's well-being can be permanently affected by doing simple exercises that address core qualities (Seligman et al., 2005). An example of this can be found in Seligman et al.'s experiment in which individuals consciously used one of their personal qualities in a new way. This simple activity seems to produce, even half a year later, a significant increase in reported well-being. This line of research has led us to investigate what happens in education when students are stimulated to become more aware of their core qualities and to make conscious use of them. On this topic, there has been much research done with adults but not with young students in the elementary grades.

Our research is based on the work of Seligman and other researchers who studied the processes that contribute to the psychological growth and optimal development of individuals (e.g. Gable & Haidt, 2005). On the basis of his research, Seligman put forward the important question of whether or not students in schools are able to discover their strong personal qualities (also one goal of the core reflection approach), to link them with their actions, and to realize what this means to them. We believe that these processes are often overlooked in education. This led to the central research question in our study: *What are the effects of an intervention focused on increasing awareness and developing core qualities among students in elementary school?* The main idea behind our experiment was that we expected the students in elementary school to become aware of their personal qualities and the possibility of developing them optimally.

Theoretical Framework

Positive psychology emphasizes expanding personal strength through positive activities. In this field, strong personal qualities and positive experiences are the most important focal points (Park, Peterson, & Seligman, 2004). Positive psychology states that emphasizing so-called "character strengths" in individuals generates positive emotions, which yields more creative thinking and higher motivation. In this context, Fredrickson (2004) speaks about the *broaden-and-build model* "because positive emotions appear to broaden peoples' momentary thought-action repertoires and build their enduring personal resources" (p. 1369).

Happiness, or well-being – both terms are used interchangeably here – is an important concept in positive psychology. Seligman (2002) and Seligman et al. (2005) argue against a material approach to happiness. Seligman approaches happiness from three immaterial perspectives: positive emotion (the pleasant life); engagement (the engaged life); and meaning (the meaningful life). According to Seligman, by approaching happiness from these immaterial perspectives, the level of life satisfaction rises.

As discussed in Chapter 2, we use the term *core qualities* for character strengths in order to emphasize a distinction from competencies. According to Korthagen and Lagerwerf (2008), core qualities strengthen competencies. Core qualities give a personal color to the execution of competencies, and an integration of core qualities with competencies is important. Ofman (2000) calls core qualities our most personal properties. They constitute the potential of personal possibilities we have at our disposal and of which we make use or not. In principle, core qualities are always present and they can be tapped and developed.

Every person possesses core qualities which, if nurtured, can produce a guard against problems that may get in the way of creating, enhancing, and maintaining a healthy psychological state (Peterson & Seligman, 2004; Seligman, 2002).

In a further elaboration of core qualities, Peterson (2006) states that they are universal, provide moral value, and are clearly recognizable.

Seligman and Peterson (2003) emphasize that an important consequence of activating core qualities is the experience of fulfillment. Experiencing fulfillment influences a person's performance and the environment will respond to this. When one is able to use and develop one's potential in using core qualities to interact with the environment, this can lead to an overall happier state. By using core qualities, an abundance of satisfaction results in the main areas of life; this forms the path to a meaningful life (Seligman, 2002). Seligman et al. (2005) focused on psychological interventions that increase individual happiness. In a placebo-controlled internet study, the authors tested five purported happiness interventions and one plausible control exercise. They found that three of the interventions increased long-term happiness and decreased depressive symptoms. As Seligman's research has shown remarkable positive results for adults who used their core qualities, we wanted to investigate the effects of the conscious use of core qualities by students in primary schools.

Method

Our study was carried out among 781 students from grades 4–8, with 33 teachers from 15 Christian schools. Table 9.1 shows data about the gender and age of the students in our study. The choice for students from grade 4 (age 7) and up was based on neurophysiological data. According to Frith and Frith (2003), children from 6 years old and up appear capable of *mentalizing*. They state: "It is only from 6 years of age onwards that we can safely attribute to a normally developing child a full and explicit awareness of mental states and their role in the explanation and prediction of other people's behavior" (p. 462). Deben-Mager (2005) defines mentalization as being able to reflect on our thinking, ideas, desires, fantasies, and on the mental states of others.

TABLE 9.1 Number of Participants and Their Gender and Age

	N boys	N girls	Average age	Minimum age	Maximum age	Standard deviation	Total
Experimental group	330	277	9.5	6	13	1.44	607
Control group 1	36	39	9.6	8	12	1.53	75
Control group 2	48	51	9.4	7	11	0.87	99
Total	**414**	**367**					**781**

The experiment was conducted in three different conditions:

1. The Experimental Condition

The students in the experimental group were asked to perform the following activity during a school week: use your core quality, which you have chosen on the basis of the questionnaire, every day for one week, and use it again in a different way. Write down a situation in which you used your core quality and which you are satisfied with at the end of the school day. With this activity we wanted to increase the awareness of what students think to be the most positive quality in themselves. During the week, the students evaluated in a logbook at the end of each day how they experienced the activity that day. We used "The Children's Strengths Survey" of Dahlsgaard (Seligman, 2002, p. 232), which contains 24 core qualities to help the students in the experimental group discover their dominant core qualities. Finally, the students chose, out of the five remaining major core qualities (from a total of 24 core qualities), one core quality that they would use again for one week and that they would also use in a different way. An example of the items in this questionnaire is the statement, "If I participate in a game or competition, then the other children want me to be the leader." This item refers to the core quality leadership (other core qualities in this questionnaire can be found in Table 9.2). The items were scored on a five-point Likert scale (1= completely true for me; 5 = not at all true for me). Descriptions of the character strengths of this survey are consistent with what we have previously written about core qualities. Examples are integrity, valor, kindness, honesty, prudence, loving, and optimism.

First of all, the activity was tested on its usability. Four primary teachers tried out the activity in a group by explaining the activity and by letting the students perform it; this included an evaluation at the end of the day. In response to the results of this try-out, a manual was written for the implementation of the questionnaires and the activity. The manual with the explanation and instructions given to the teachers and students helped ensure that the experiment would be performed in a uniform manner.

2. The First Control Condition

Among a group of 75 students, only the questionnaires were used in order to be able to evaluate whether there exists any unintended effect of just filling in the questionnaires.

3. The Second Control Condition

A placebo control group of 99 students was given a simple assignment, which was:

during one week, at the end of the school day, write down something you remember from the past when you were younger.

To avoid influencing the research, no special pedagogical measures were taken by the teachers to influence students' responses to the questionnaires.

Of course, teachers gave their usual degree of care and attention to the students. To ensure confidentiality at various stages of data collection, data analysis, and reporting, it was described beforehand where and to whom results would be reported. When informed about the study, about 15 parents did not allow their child to participate in the experiment. These students joined in the activities but did not fill in the questionnaires.

Elaboration of the Research Question

The research question was: What are the effects of an intervention focused on increasing awareness and developing core qualities among students in primary education? This question led to four sub questions:

1. What is the effect on the students of filling out the questionnaires?
2. What is the effect on the students of performing the activity?
3. Do the students remember their core quality after three months, and do they still use it?
4. Is there a significant increase in the scores for well-being on the question-naires?

Data Collection

For measurements of the variables indicating well-being and the use of core qualities, we made use of existing questionnaires, logbooks especially developed for this study, interviews, and reports of teachers. The questionnaires were chosen on account of their validity and reliability in other studies. These questionnaires were adjusted to the Dutch school situation and the age of the target group. The questionnaires were used four times: (1) in the week before the experiment; (2) in the week after the experiment; (3) one month after the experiment; and (4) three months after the experiment.

The Questionnaires

1. Fordyce Emotions Questionnaire (Seligman, 2002, p. 15)

This questionnaire was created by Fordyce and used by Seligman in his book *Authentic Happiness*. It consists of one question ("How happy or unhappy do you feel?") to be scored on one out of 11 options. In this manner, the respondent indicates how happy he or she feels. By this method we can measure the level of well-being (happiness). The statements were adapted to the age of the target group. Because the questionnaire contains only one question, Cronbach's alpha could not be calculated.

2. General Happiness Scale (Seligman, 2002, p. 46)

This questionnaire was developed by Lyubomirsky and Lepper (1999) and measures the general happiness level. This instrument consists of four statements in which respondents can indicate, on a seven-point scale, to what degree the statement corresponds to their own situation. In this instrument, we replaced the word "person" with "student." Again, statements were adapted to the target group. Both questionnaires 1 and 2 provide an insight into feelings of happiness (well-being) and were chosen to measure the impact of the activity on the level of well-being. The reliability of questionnaire 2 appeared to be good (Cronbach's alpha = .78).

3. The Reflection Questionnaire

This questionnaire was only used at the fourth measurement moment. The following questions were asked:

a. Which core quality did you choose?
b. Do you still use your core quality? YES/NO (select the word that fits you)
c. If you still use your core quality, what do you think about it? Can you describe your feelings?
d. If you still use your core quality, can you give an example of a situation in which you did so?

The Logbook

Students in the experimental group used logbooks to write down at which moment and in what way they used their core quality during the week of the experiment. Questions in the logbook were:

1. Were you able to perform the exercise (using your core quality)?
2. Did you use your core quality outside school yesterday? (For example, at home or at the sports club.) Can you give an example?
3. How many times did you use your core quality today?
4. How do you feel when you use your core quality?
5. Write down an example of an exercise you are satisfied about.
6. Did you like doing this exercise?

The Interviews

During the week in which the activity was performed, 20 randomly chosen students were briefly interviewed about how they experienced using their core quality, what feelings this gave, and if they could recall any examples of using their core quality. After seven weeks, the same interview was repeated with the same 20 students.

Teacher Reports

After the different measurement stages, the teachers were asked if they had noted any special things regarding filling out of the questionnaires by the students. Also, the teachers reported special cases during the week in which the students were carrying out the experiment.

Data Analysis

In the qualitative part of the data analysis, we looked for meaningful categories in the reflection questionnaires, logbooks, interviews and reports of the teachers. We also scored the frequencies with which these categories occurred in the data. To check the validity and reliability of the research results, we used the following methods.

First, we used a *member check* (Merriam, 1998). The study has been prepared and performed in cooperation with four teachers (who also participated in the study) from different elementary schools. They were asked to read the raw data, to read the data-analysis afterwards, and to check this analysis with the collected data and their own knowledge and experiences. With this member check, the reliability of the results was evaluated and verified by the teachers. Second, we made use of a *critical friend*. An independent colleague and teacher educator, who has participated in many core reflection courses, was asked to read all data and the results with the following questions in mind: Can you agree with what was concluded from the data? Do you think something completely different? Can you perhaps find examples of an opposite conclusion? This method was also used to determine the credibility of the results. Both the teachers and the critical friends confirmed our analysis almost completely. Where they had minor comments, we used these to improve the report of the findings.

Using a one-way ANOVA, we also analyzed the increase or decrease in the scores on the questionnaires between the measurement moment 1 on the one hand and measurement moments 2, 3, and 4 on the other.

Findings

Below, the results are presented on the basis of our four sub-questions.

What is the Effect on the Students of Filling in the Questionnaires?

The first time the questionnaires were completed, the students were interested in filling in the questionnaires. Teachers who performed the research reported that many students indicated they liked becoming aware of a core quality; it made them feel proud. Becoming conscious of their core quality sometimes led to surprising discoveries for the students, like: "I didn't know I was kind." One teacher wrote, with reference to the Children's Strengths Survey:

> Two students discovered their core quality *love for learning*. Spontaneously they came to me at the end of the school day and asked if they could copy some math exercises, because they did not fully understand them that morning. In this way they could practice at home. Magnificent! The past year, there was not a single student asking for that!

The Children's Strength Survey, the questionnaire by which students find out which core quality is important to them, produced a positive effect in the example mentioned above. This questionnaire paid much attention to getting ready to choose just one core quality. One teacher said about this: "Children find it hard to choose just one core quality and to think about a fitting story. They need quite a lot of guidance in this." Students were not used to thinking about their core quality. It was not always easy to separate core qualities from skills, which was illustrated by the following question from a student: "If you are good at singing, is this also a core quality?" (We consider singing as a skill, and you need a core quality like *love of learning* or *perseverance* to learn how to sing well.)

That the effect of filling in the questionnaires was also noticed at home is illustrated by the following reaction of a teacher: "One of my students came home with his core quality: humor. His father replied: 'Harry really likes to go on with this. It has influenced him in a positive way'." Students appeared proud of their core quality, which they wrote down on a card that they placed on their table.

The motivation for completing the questionnaire was experienced differently at the second, third, and fourth measurement points. A number of students were enthusiastic, while others were less motivated. According to the teachers, the overall trend was a decrease in motivation, especially in the higher grades. In a few cases, the completion of the questionnaire appeared to provoke conflicting thoughts. An example of a student's remark illustrating this was: "Then I have to think deeply about myself, but then a lot of unpleasant things come up into my mind."

During one week, students in the 26 experimental groups wrote down in logbooks when and how they used their core quality. Of these 26 groups, there were four teachers who, by accident, gave the logbook to the students at the end of the week in which they had performed the experiment. The logbooks of those four groups were thus excluded from the final data analysis. Eventually, we had 22 groups left for which we could analyze the logbooks.

Table 9.2 shows that the core qualities kindness (83) and valor (77) are the most chosen ones.

Sometimes the students chose in a socially desirable way. When the students had to choose five or more core qualities with a score of ten points, they sometimes chose what their friend had already chosen, or they chose a core quality they thought would be appreciated by others. This explains why there was one quality that was dominantly chosen in one group, namely, valor.

TABLE 9.2 Core Qualities chosen by 485 Students from 22 Groups. The Right Hand Column Shows the Number of Students Who Chose the Core Quality

Core quality	#
Kindness	83
Valor	77
Humor	53
Love of learning	40
Zest	33
Gratitude	23
Citizenship	23
Self-control	22
Perseverance	19
Fairness	19
Loving	17
Humility	14
Hope	10
Integrity	9
Curiosity	9
Social intelligence	9
Prudence	5
Ingenuity	5
Appreciation of beauty	4
Spirituality	3
Forgiveness	3
Judgment	2
Leadership	2
Perspective	1

What is the Effect on the Students of Performing the Activity?

The experiences of the students while performing the activity (conscious use of their core quality), according to the teachers.

One teacher reported: "The children were very enthusiastic about using their core qualities. They really enjoyed it. Some of them had a lot of examples every day. A girl had filled in all the boxes with examples for two days, but the next day she had nothing. She said: 'I want to use my quality in another way, but I can't'." That the students were having trouble in using their core quality became clear from the following comment of a teacher:

> I notice that it is very hard for the students to use their core qualities concretely. For example, Integrity . . . What can you do with that? . . . How do you use it? One boy from group 5 had chosen *humor* as his core quality. On Wednesday he burst out in tears and said: "I don't even know what humor is!"

The teachers discovered that making use of core qualities was beneficial. To give an example, one mentor teacher said to us: "My colleagues agree with me that using core qualities is really valuable."

The experiences of the students while performing the activity (the conscious use of their core quality), according to the students.

With the help of the students' logbooks and the interviews with them, we analyzed their experiences. Approximately 75% of the students wrote down examples in their logbook of when they used their core quality; the other 25% did not write down any example. Several comments of students about how they experienced the use of their core quality are listed in the following:

- "It's fun to do, because you learn something of it."
- "Super fun. I hope we'll do this again."
- "It's nice to do, because you keep thinking about it and learn of it."
- "Boring."
- "Not really fun, because it is hard to me to say something about myself."
- "A bit exciting."
- "Good, because you get to know more about yourself."

A student noticed at the end of the week in which the activity was done, that she had become far more kind. The feeling while using her core quality was, most of the time, described as nice, pleasant, fine, glad, good, or cheerful. Three quarters of the students indicated that they liked to use their core qualities. Situations in which they used their core qualities were at school, at home, and at a hobby club. About one-third of the students indicated that they thought it was useful to become aware of their core quality; this can be seen in the following interview excerpt: "I like it very much and it might be useful for later. You already learn a lot from it now, and when I will have developed my core quality later on, I might never have been aware of it."

Approximately 75% of the students described in their logbook one or more examples of using their core qualities. These students thus connected their actions with their core quality. We give several examples:

- Core quality kindness: "Someone didn't understand his math exercises, so I helped him. Now he knows that he can trust me."
- Core quality social intelligence: "I have spoken with Lisa about her little brother, which passed away a long time ago."
- Core quality loving: "I helped an old man with a walker cross the street."

This indicates that becoming conscious of having a core quality influenced behavior. From conversations with teachers who participated in the study with their group, it became clear that when a student did not report the use of a core quality in the logbook, it did not necessarily mean that he or she had not used it. Some students were hardly able to describe things. Students really did show their core qualities, according to the teachers, but they did not always seem to be aware of it. They became aware of it when the teacher acknowledged the use of their core quality.

When the use of a core quality was experienced as a positive activity, it evoked a positive emotion in almost all cases. This appeared from the following examples:

- Core quality zest: "When I was doing math, I was just so cheerful and satisfied with everything and I was glad also."
- Core quality kindness: "When I helped a fellow student at gym, I felt really fine." "I've spoken to a handicapped girl. She went home hopping. It gave me a good feeling."
- Core quality spirituality: "I trusted that God gave me strength. The whole day I think of that everyone is valuable and that they have a purpose here." "It's nice to do so, because I become more sure of myself and do my own thing and I don't feel ashamed anymore."
- Core quality hope: "I knew it was possible, that I could do so, that's how I got to task 4. Really I only succeeded because of my self-confidence." "At the club I hoped I wouldn't be made fun of, and it didn't happen. When you hope for something, then it is like you don't have to worry about it anymore."

From an interview with the following student, it became clear that at first it felt a bit strange to use his core quality, but when he was used to it, it gave him a positive emotional response.

Interviewer: What was your core quality?
Student: Zest.
Interviewer: So you've felt zest today. Did you also use it?
Student: Yes.
Interviewer: Yes? Tell something more about it?
Student: Well, eh, at first I wasn't really in for it, but afterwards we went to work and I really enjoyed it. Then I've written down several things really quickly.
Interviewer: How does it feel when you suddenly feel that? How did it feel?
Student: A bit strange.
Interviewer: Try to explain that. Why was it strange?
Student: Well, at first you feel nothing, and suddenly you feel that you enjoy it.

Based on the answers in the student logbooks and the question of how they felt about using core qualities, we concluded that less than 25% experienced negative feelings. Sometimes the words "boring" or "stupid" were mentioned. Approximately a quarter of the students reported that they started to pay more attention to others by consciously using their core qualities. This appeared in the following examples.

- There was a girl in my class and she was supposed to be the tagger in the tagger game because she never had been it before. When she was the tagger I let myself be tagged, because I thought it wasn't fair. I liked it because I made someone else happy with it.
- I hoped for my mother that she could continue her study, and she liked that very much.
- I said that Brian could run very hard. It gave me a good feeling.
- I did my best the whole week (using the core quality) and I enjoyed it very much, and I've learned a lot from it. I also think the others used their core quality well. You get to know each other better.

It appeared that generally the students who reported about the use of their core quality were good at interpreting their chosen core quality in the right way. However, the logbooks showed that sometimes students did not always interpret their core quality correctly. Several examples follow:

- Core quality valor: "Father got mad and then I started to laugh." "When Bas was being beaten by dad I had to laugh." "I've ignored the red light, I was brave."

- Core quality humor: "At school I used Jan as a floor and as a staircase and he liked it."

Especially regarding the core qualities humor and valor, we see that in approximately 15% of the reported examples a wrong interpretation is made of the core quality.

Do the Students Remember Their Core Quality After Three Months and Do They Still Use It?

At the final measurement moment, we not only used the questionnaires mentioned above, but also another reflection questionnaire was completed in which we asked: Which core quality did you choose? From the experimental group there were 483 students (80.7%) who still remembered their chosen core quality, while 124 students (19.3%) of the 607 students of the experimental group indicated that they did not remember their core quality.

Do You Still Use Your Core Quality?

Out of the students of the experimental group, 350 students (58%) indicated that they still used their core quality, against 224 (37%) who indicated that they did not use their core quality (of 33 students – i.e. 5% – the answer is not clear or missing).

a. If you still use your core quality, what do you think about it? Can you describe your feeling?

Many times the words "nice," "glad," and "fine" are used. A few times the words "exciting," "cheerful," and "proud" are used. Only a few students indicated "boring" or "stupid."

b. If you still use your core quality, can you give an example of a situation in which you did so?

More than half of the students described with an example how they used their core quality. A few examples are below.

- Core quality perseverance: "If my autistic brother is really wild, it is hard to hold back but then you have to continue."
- Core quality integrity: "A little while ago I had to keep a secret I did so until I was allowed to tell."
- Core quality spirituality: "Well, I pray every day because it makes me feel fine and it gives me rest. I sing when I'm sad, that makes me happy."

- Core quality social intelligence: "If someone is sad, I walk towards him and try to make him happy again."

It was remarkable that a few students indicated that they did not remember their core quality, whereas these students actually wrote down an example of how they used their core quality:

- "I helped Eve when she didn't feel so well, she said I helped her really good."
- "I feel that I am nice when I help children if they have pain or feel ill."

From the examples that the students wrote down in the reflection questionnaire, it appeared that a quarter of the students used their core quality more or less automatically – that is, many times they were not aware of using them. Examples are:

- "When I use it [appreciation of beauty], I don't do it on purpose but it just happens. It just feels normally, pretty good."
- "When I use it [zest], I don't even think about it because I do it automatically."
- "When I use my core quality, I sometimes think: "Yes! I used my core quality" [kindness].

Is There a Significant Increase in the Scores For Well-being on the Questionnaire?

Using an ANOVA, we looked at whether there was a stronger increase in the scores on the questionnaires in the experimental group as compared to both control groups. The measurements showed that the scores on the questionnaires of the experimental group kept increasing, except on the second questionnaire at the fourth measurement. It appeared that one group had a big influence on this. In this group the scores decreased fast. We have not been able to find out the reason why. If we omit this group from the analysis, we see an increase of all scores of the experimental group at all measurement points. The differences in the increase of scores of the experimental group in comparison with the control groups were, however, not significant. Also, there were no significant differences found when we limited the analysis to students who indicated that they still thought about and used their core quality. Neither did we find significant differences for boys or girls on any of the questionnaires. We found only that older students scored higher on happiness than younger students ($p = .02$).

Conclusion and Discussion

In our study, the central research question was: What are the effects of an intervention focused on increasing awareness and developing core qualities among students in elementary school?

Our study showed that by means of a short intervention young students can be helped to become aware of their core qualities, and that this often leads to a certain pride. In particular, kindness and valor appeared to be important core qualities. Many students enthusiastically embraced the exercise to use a core quality again and in new ways. Approximately 75% of the students appeared to be good at independently doing so in different contexts, not only at school, but also at home or at a club. In addition, the students were quite capable of translating the core quality into an action, but the core qualities were not always interpreted in the right way. The conscious use of a core quality was experienced positively by approximately three-quarters of the students and stimulated a positive emotion in almost all cases.

Words such as "nice," "glad," "cheerful," and "fine" are used by students. This concurs with Seligman (2011, p. 11), who states that "you need to deploy your highest strengths and talents to meet the world in flow." It could mean that becoming conscious of and using the core quality was experienced as a source of well-being. Our study showed that in some cases, it may be important that the teacher names the core quality in order for the student to become aware of it. After three months, more than 80% of the students remembered their chosen core quality and 58% of the students indicated that they still used it without the teacher paying extra attention to it. Apparently, for many students, there was a long-term effect. Approximately a quarter of the students reported a positive image of themselves, but also that they started to pay more attention to others, especially their fellow students. This could mean that the conscious use of core qualities can lead to a positive influence on the pedagogical climate in the group. From the examples that the students have written down or mentioned in the interview, it appeared that core qualities such as social intelligence, citizenship, and kindness stimulated them to pay more attention to each other.

A quarter of the students reported that the use of a core quality was a matter of course, which happened automatically and was not something they were aware of. It was remarkable that a few students indicated they did not remember their core quality, but nevertheless they gave several examples of when they used their core quality. This concurs with Damasio (1999), who states that emotion works independently from our conscious awareness. Although students could not consciously remember which core quality they had chosen, they seemed to remember the related positive emotion that helped them to report an example.

To avoid an uncontrolled influence on the experiment, the teachers gave no special attention to the experiment after they had explained how to perform the activity, so that the students executed the activity as much as possible by themselves. This approach was taken to avoid further support by the 33 teachers as much as possible and to be able to measure the influence of carrying out the simple activity. The activity was carried out for only five days. It may be assumed that over a longer period the effect will be stronger than we found. We also think the results may be more powerful when there is more intense support by the teacher. However, teachers who did not have substantive knowledge and experience of working with core qualities indicated that they needed more knowledge and training to be able to support the activity of the students in the right way. This forms an argument for training teachers who want to use core qualities to improve the psychological growth and well-being of their students. Moreover, it is important to realize that completing the questionnaires appeared to be confusing for a few students. This suggests that careful guidance by the teacher in completing the questionnaires is important.

As we reported earlier, it appears that the core qualities of valor and humor were not always interpreted correctly. This could have been prevented by letting the students discuss the interpretation of the core qualities in a group. Then, the activity could have been further supported by having daily group reflections and by reflecting on how the experiences with using core qualities went and which positive emotions were activated.

It is striking that, different from the experiment of Seligman (see the Introduction), we found no significant increase in the student scores on well-being. We think we have several explanations for this. Seligman did his study with adults who were motivated to cooperate, and many adults took the opportunity to get rid of their depression. Seligman worked with two detailed questionnaires that measured well-being and depression, while we used two simple questionnaires that both measured well-being. We conducted our research among students of 6–12 years old, in which the students had no choice but to participate (after parental consent). In follow-up research, we plan to do a longer and more comprehensive experiment, and we would then also pay more attention to supporting the students with regard to the meaning of core qualities.

We carried out our study at traditional Christian schools. Perhaps this also affected the results of our study, because it is less common to focus on earthly luck and happiness for students with a traditional Christian belief. Therefore, it would be interesting for further research to perform this at schools with a different philosophy of life.

In summary, the interesting aspect of working with students in this way is that it stimulates 'learning from within' (see Chapters 2 and 3). Through our research, it became clear that through a relatively short and simple intervention, it is possible to influence the personal growth of students by building on the human capital of their core qualities.

Acknowledgments

We thank Rens Rottier, Bram de Muynck, and Petronelle Baarda of the *Driestar University for Teacher Education* for supporting the research described in this paper. We are grateful to Lennart Visser for being our critical friend, and to Judith Schooneboom, William den Braber, and Nico Broer for their methodological support. Last but not least, we thank all teachers and their students, who participated in our study. Without their dedication our research study would have been impossible.

References

Damasio, A. (1999). *The feeling of what happens: Body and emotion in the making of consciousness.* London: Heinemann.

Deben-Mager, M. (2005). Gehechtheid en mentaliseren. [Attachment and mentalizing.] *Psychoanalytische Perspectieven, 23*(1), 31–48.

Fredrickson, B. (2004). The broaden-and-build theory of positive emotions. *The Royal Society, 359*, 1367–1377.

Frith, U., & Frith, C. D. (2003). Development and neurophysiology of mentalizing. *The Royal Society, 358*, 459–473.

Gable, S., & Haidt, J. (2005). What (and why) is positive psychology? *Review of General Psychology, 9*(2), 103–110.

Korthagen, F. A. J., & Lagerwerf, B. (2008). Leren van binnenuit. [Learning from within.] Soest: Nelissen.

Lyubomirsky, S., &. Lepper, H. (1999). A measure of subjective happiness: Preliminary reliability and construct validation. *Social Indicators Research, 46*, 137–155.

Merriam, S. B. (1998). *Qualitative research and case study applications in education.* San Francisco, CA: Jossey-Bass.

Ofman, D. (2000). *Core qualities: A gateway to human resources.* Schiedam: Scriptum.

Park, N., Peterson, C., & Seligman, M. E. P. (2004). Strengths of character and well-being. *Journal of Social and Clinical Psychology, 23*(5), 603-619.

Peterson, C., & Seligman, M. E. P. (2004). *Character strengths and virtues. A handbook and classification.* Washington, DC: APA Press and Oxford University Press.

Peterson, C. (2006). *A primer in positive psychology.* New York: Oxford University Press.

Seligman, M. E. P. (2002). *Authentic happiness: Using the new positive psychology to realize your potential for lasting fulfillment.* New York: Free Press.

Seligman, M. E. P. (2011). *Flourish: A visionary new understanding of happiness and well-being.* New York: Free Press.

Seligman, M. E. P., & Peterson, C. (2003). Positive clinical psychology. In L. G. Aspinwall, & U. M. Staudinger (Eds.). *A psychology of human strengths: Fundamental questions and future directions for a positive psychology* (pp. 305–317). Washington, DC: American Psychological Association.

Seligman, M. E. P., Steen, T., Park, N., & Peterson, C. (2005). Positive psychology progress: Empirical validation of interventions. *American Psychologist, 60*(5), 410–421.

10

A CORE REFLECTION APPROACH TO REDUCING STUDY PROCRASTINATION

*Marjan E. Ossebaard, Fred A. J. Korthagen,
Heinze Oost, Jan Stavenga-De Jong,
and Angelo Vasalos*

This chapter illustrates a study on the use of core reflection in reducing study procrastination among university students. Marjan Ossebaard, Fred Korthagen, Heinze Oost, Jan Stavenga-De Jong, and Angelo Vasalos developed and tested the effect of a course based on the core reflection approach for the treatment of study-procrastination. Using a process-oriented research design, they investigated the experiences of the participants regarding: (1) What happened to their procrastination behavior? and, (2) How did the new approach affect them and what did they learn from it? The results show that core reflection helped students to reduce their study-procrastination. Important tools appear to be learning to be aware of one's emotions, willpower, and valuing one's own character strengths and desires – especially when focusing on a problematic situation.

Introduction

In this chapter, we will describe the results and insights we obtained from a study on the effect of core reflection as an approach to help academic procrastinators overcome their study problems. We were interested in whether the use of core reflection applied in a course would help students reduce their level of procrastination and be able to study to their full potential. And if so, we were interested in learning *how*, through what mechanisms, this would happen. What did they learn that helped them get things done?

Reducing Study Procrastination **149**

Here's an example:

> Law student Lisa talks about her study problems. "I really want to become a good lawyer, and I truly like my studies. Again and again, I tell myself to begin the preparation of an exam early, in order to keep up with the course program. Yet every time I let myself down: I just do nothing. I've lost faith, lost all confidence in myself. Instead of studying I lie in my bed, and pull the blankets over my head. [crying:] I cry myself to sleep most nights, telling myself I'm such a loser. I just don't know what to do anymore."

The example of Lisa illustrates how desperate students suffering from academic procrastination can be. Lisa obviously has no sense of being connected to any of her inner strengths anymore. She seems to completely identify with her idea of being a loser. This leaves her helpless and unable to find a way out. Lisa is not the only student having this problem. Students who chronically procrastinate studying report that they feel as if they no longer control their studying, but that something controls them instead. They feel trapped in the situation. The repeated process of planning to get started, followed by the deception of not being able to follow through, leaves them with a shattered sense of self-esteem. As a consequence, they are more likely than others to suffer from negative emotions, such as fear of failure, anxiety, depression, guilt, and shame (Ferrari, 2004; Lay & Schouwenburg, 1993). Moreover, they are more likely than others to have low self-confidence, self-efficacy and self-esteem, low work-discipline, and they are more pessimistic than non-procrastinators (Ferrari, 2004).

Academic procrastination can be defined as repeatedly postponing intended study tasks, which are perceived by the procrastinator as being important, to the point of failing to accomplish what was intended within a desired timeframe (Milgram, 1991). Figures in the literature on prevalence among university students vary from 20% to 70%, and they vary per study task (Schouwenburg, 2004).

It is important to note that most of these students are intelligent, motivated, and talented young people. The fact that they do not do what they intended to do does not come from a lack of motivation, nor is it a result of inadequacy. However, despite their qualities, study performances are sub-optimal, which is reflected in low course grades and final exam scores (Steel et al., 2001; Wesley, 1994). Moreover, procrastinators report higher stress and more illness late in the term and overall are sicker than non-procrastinators (Tice & Baumeister, 1997). Despite efforts taken to improve their behavior, they seem to be stuck, as if something inside of them prevents them from learning to their full potential.

Procrastination of study tasks is a big problem, not only for academic students. It can develop at early ages; in fact, it occurs even among young elementary school children (Al-Attiyah, 2010). As a result, these children develop a habit of delaying work on their school assignments until the last minute with negative consequences for both their educational performance as well as their psychological state. For those who work with such children, procrastination may also be a problem. Teachers who are confronted with this behavior often tend to feel the same sense of powerlessness as the procrastinator. They try all kinds of interventions to help students get to work, but despite their efforts this does not lead to much improvement. Usually, teachers then become impatient or pessimistic and tend to frame what they observe as laziness or a lack of motivation.

In this chapter, we will first briefly describe the traditional approach to the counseling of academic procrastinators. Next, we describe the outcome of a study on the effect of such a traditional approach in combination with some elements of core reflection. That study was important for us, as it showed that by adding core reflection to the traditional approach, the effectiveness of it improved. Next, we will describe the development of a course solely based on core reflection and explain how we studied the abovementioned questions. Finally, we will present the outcomes of the core reflection course and a discussion of the significance of our study.

Counseling Academic Procrastination: The Traditional Way

Nine out of ten of the approaches to counseling academic procrastinators are based on the principles of cognitive behavioral therapy (Schouwenburg, 2004). The idea is that procrastination is a result of two things. First, students acquire dysfunctional study habits. Somewhere in their personal history, students learned that they gained something from study procrastination, such as additional time for pleasure. Second, this behavior is fed by numerous automatic thoughts that lead to negative emotions as well as to the dysfunctional behavior. For instance, a student who is confronted with a large and difficult text thinks, "Oh no, I will never be able to get that done in time." This may lead to fear or panic and to quitting reading (or not starting at all). Methods used in this approach generally involve a cognitive intervention and/or a behavioral component. Cognitive restructuring and reframing, or Rational Emotive Therapy or Training (Ellis & Knaus, 2002), are frequently used, as well as time monitoring, goal setting, and time-management techniques. Sometimes, just one of these components (either cognitive or behavioral) is used.

Even though these cognitive-behavioral oriented course programs are successful, they have one drawback; the emphasis is put on the problem or problematic behavior (Lay, 2004; Van Horebeek et al., 2004), dysfunctional thoughts (Flett et al., 2004), and/or a combination of the two (Van Essen, Van den Heuvel, & Ossebaard, 2004; Mandel, 2004). As a result students can sometimes get caught up in the problem, as if *they* have *become* the problem. They tend to ruminate a lot about unsuccessful experiences they had over the week. In an attempt to solve their problems, they keep on thinking and talking about it, which may lead to feeling even more incompetent and powerless.

The Traditional Approach With a Touch of Core Reflection

With this drawback in mind, Ossebaard, Oost, Van den Heuvel, & Ossebaard (2008) developed a course based on a multifaceted intervention approach. The course (eight weekly session of 2.5 hours) was an extension of one based on the traditional cognitive behavioral methods, which had been in use for several years and had proven to be effective in itself (Van Essen et al., 2004). The overall format of this course was left intact, but core reflection principles were added in order to improve a person's sense of inner strength and his or her desires or ideals. Interventions included using a weekly structured questionnaire, focusing on personal qualities, and asking questions and giving feedback on the students' personal qualities and true ideals or desires. These interventions were in place throughout the course meetings. The idea was that this would create awareness of the person's core qualities and ideals and that this would lead to an improved sense of self-efficacy and well-being. As a result, this was expected to lead to a stronger reduction of procrastination than when using the traditional cognitive behavioral approach. This was indeed what was found in the research study. The reduction in academic procrastination behavior found was higher in the newly adapted course than in the original cognitive behavioral approach (Ossebaard et al., 2008). Moreover, study motivation improved more than in the traditional course without core reflection. This is a remarkable result, considering the fact that the interventions added made up a relatively small part of the total course.

Hence, we became interested in what the effect would be of a completely new course model, based only on the principles of core reflection. What would happen if we would let go of the cognitive behavioral interventions completely? Would it be possible to design an effective course aiming solely at nurturing what is best, instead of fixing what is broken? And, *if* a course based on core reflection leads to reduced study-procrastination, through what learning processes does this occur?

We decided to perform an in-depth study to see what would happen and developed a course based solely on the principles of core reflection. Our main research questions were:

1. What is the difference in academic procrastination behavior of the participants before and after the core reflection based course?
2. What, according to the participants, were the most important learning outcomes to them?

Course Development, Aim, and Format

We asked one of the founders of the core reflection approach, Angelo Vasalos (from now on referred to as the 'trainer'), to develop and lead a course for students who suffer from academic procrastination. The course had to be based solely on the core reflection approach, and the aim of the course had to be the reduction of academic procrastination. The trainer had never worked with procrastinators before, nor was he familiar with the literature in the domain of procrastination. He was basically asked to apply the core reflection methodology in a way that he used it in other settings, such as when working with school teachers on guiding students. To give him the opportunity to develop a course that in his view would be effective, we proceeded in two stages. First, in order to optimize the course program and the method of data collection, a trial meeting of 2.5 hours was organized with three students. Second, based on his experience with this trial, the trainer developed a larger trial course (three weekly meetings of 2.5 hours each) in which eight students participated. After this, the trainer decided that he had a good idea of the optimal course design meeting both criteria. Based on his experience with the trial course, the trainer designed the final course, consisting of three weekly meetings of 2.5 hours. In this course, no written course material was used, except one article with background information on the core reflection approach and a couple of handouts with some key words describing the basic principles of core reflection.

The trainer defined the aim of the course as "learning to apply the core reflection approach in such a way that a person gets in touch with his or her inspiration in order to stop procrastinating study tasks, to develop awareness of other ideals and needs that need to be taken care of, and to stop suppressing these needs." This implies that the traditional aim of getting students to study is abandoned. Students are encouraged to follow their inspiration instead and to let their behavior result from that, no matter what that behavior is. For example, a student with a strong need of social activities may not allow himself to get involved in such activities because he feels this will take up too much of his time, and he feels he should be studying instead. He considers this need problematic and may even tell himself that he is a weak person because he wants to have a good time with friends, instead of wanting to study. The suppression of his desire takes up a lot of his energy. In this case, the aim of the course is to help him create awareness of this fact and to help him realize that he will be better off stopping this process of suppression. He will then be encouraged to value his ideal, to value himself as a person *with* these needs, and to give it the attention it deserves. The idea, then, is that this will create a sense of space and energy for him to study at another moment. By doing this, an important obstacle in the student's learning process will be eliminated. This – postponing study tasks to a latter moment and choosing to do something more pleasurable – seems like a paradox when viewed from the traditional theory on procrastination. However, the deliberate postponing of tasks to a later point in time in order to better perform on that task later is considered wise planning rather than procrastination in the literature (Schouwenburg, 2004).

The trainer works by using experiences of the students, which are either situations from the week before the meeting or situations that occur in the here-

and-now, during the meeting. Such a situation is used to reflect upon using the core reflection approach, either in a conversation between a group member and the trainer or in the whole group (in which case all group members can participate in the conversation). The next abbreviated transcript is a typical example of a core reflection conversation between the trainer (T) and a student (S). The excerpt starts halfway into the conversation with a discussion on what exactly happens when S gets distracted from studying.

T: Well then, what could be the distraction?

S: . . . when someone gets home I think, "Oh, now we can hang out together and chat with her."

T: OK, suppose that's what happens. The first thing you need to do then is: accept it. That's rule number 1: you neither fight it nor deny it. The next thing to do is to be truly interested in what goes on in your mind. What is it about chatting with this person that I like so much? What comes to mind? Is it the coziness of being together?

S: Yes, I think so. And also, I'm interested in other people . . . Wow, a core quality!

T: Yes, right! Step 1 is acceptance. Step 2 is questioning yourself: what is nice about talking to that person? Coziness. And what is it about coziness that attracts you? That question helps you to become aware of your core qualities.

S: Some kind of affirmation. Maybe then some of my core qualities will be seen and recognized by the other person.

T: In a way that it tells you that you matter, that you are a valuable person?

S: Yes!

T: So now we've discovered a very important need. The need for your core qualities to be recognized and the need to experience coziness with a friend. Can you imagine that? Such an important aspect of yourself, and you are fighting it all the time! I believe that if you really honor this inner need, you will fulfill it. And by fulfilling it you will find the ease you need to study. But if you deny your needs, if you keep on fighting your need for distraction and coziness, you will give in at a certain point, and you will seek distraction anyway.

After such a conversation, the training continued in either of two possible ways: (a) core reflection theory was explained to help the participants gain insight in the core reflection principles; or (b) the coaching skills demonstrated by the trainer were practiced in pairs. It is important that the trainer consequently served as a model by applying the principles of the core reflection approach throughout the entire course meetings. Homework assignments were given every week, which basically meant practicing what was learned during the meetings in small groups, individually, and in conversations with friends, family, and with oneself (self-reflection).

Research Method and Findings

In order to be able to perform an in-depth study, the number of participants was limited to six. Before the start of the course, they were informed about the experimental nature of the course. Participation was free. During the meetings video-recordings were made, and the students were informed about this beforehand. There were two males and four females.

The procrastination of the participants has been measured with a pre-test and post-test using a valid (Schouwenburg, 1994) and reliable (Cronbach's $\alpha = .94$) Dutch questionnaire, the APSI: 'Academic Procrastination as State Inventory' (Schouwenburg, 1994). The total score on the APSI scale indicates the person's current procrastination level, which makes it a useful tool to measure pre-test and post-test levels of procrastination and to compare them (Schouwenburg, 1994). The questionnaire consists of 31 questions, starting with 'Looking back on last week, how often did you . . .?' The student is asked to fill in the answers on a five-point Likert-like scale. The complete list of questions can be found in Schouwenburg (1994). All participants filled in the APSI the week before the first meeting (pre-test) and at the end of the last course meeting (post-test). A t-test was performed on the average difference between the pre-test and post-test scores on the APSI to measure change, if any, in the procrastination levels after the course.

For the qualitative part of the study, we used in-depth interviews based on stimulated recall, as well as learner reports. For the stimulated recall interviews, all course meetings were video-taped. After each meeting, a stimulated recall interview was conducted with one or two course participants. None of the participants were interviewed more than once. The interviewee was asked to mention a maximum of five events that he or she considered the most effective learning moments. Next, the first of these moments was shown to the interviewee on video in order to have him or her recall the moment. The interviewee was asked to indicate when something happened that was really important and from which he or she had learned a lot. The video was then stopped, and the interview started. Two open questions were addressed: (1) What happened that was important to you? (2) What did you learn from this? The other fragments were discussed in the same manner.

The complete stimulated-recall interview was videotaped for the purpose of an in-depth analysis. The interviews were analyzed by marking themes often mentioned by all participants. The marked fragments were transcribed. Next, we counted how often a certain type of learning outcome was mentioned by the participants. Those that were addressed most were further analyzed by identifying shared characteristics.

The learner reports were simple questionnaires, filled in by the students at the end of every meeting. Two questions were asked: (1) What, to you, was the most important moment during this meeting (please describe what happened)? (2) What exactly did you become aware of or did you learn from that?

Results

After three weekly meetings of 2.5 hours, students indicated less procrastination than before, with every individual student showing lower procrastination levels afterwards (see Figure 10.1). A paired-sample t-test on the difference between pre-test and post-test scores on the APSI showed a significant reduction in procrastination ($p < 0.05$). The average post-test score is comparable to what is normal in a student population (Schouwenburg, 1994). This indicates that after the course these students do not procrastinate more than the 'average' student, a level that is in general considered to be non-problematic.

We then looked into the question of how this change had been realized. In the learner reports, students most often indicated that they gained new insights, rather than new skills or attitudes. The insights obtained most often involved a new perspective on the core reflection approach. We combined their reports with the results from the stimulated recall interviews and found four main categories of new insights:

1. The importance of awareness of positive emotions and core qualities.
2. The importance of awareness of negative emotions when reflecting on inner barriers.
3. The importance of feeling willpower.
4. The importance of simultaneous reflection on desire, emotions, cognitions, and behavior when reflecting on an experience.

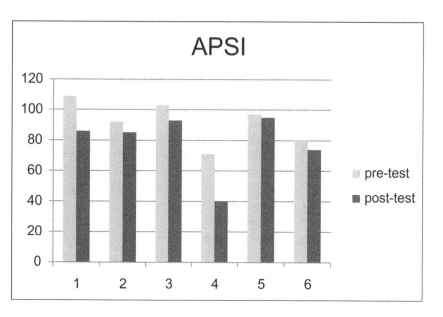

FIGURE 10.1 Procrastination levels of six students before and after the course

The Importance of Awareness of Positive Emotions and Core Qualities

The importance of fully being aware of any emotion in the process of self-reflection is considered valuable to five of the six students. They understand that a power comes from focusing on positive emotions. They realize that they are used to paying attention to the negative a lot, and that this brings them down. They also realized that they can actually choose the focus of their attention and shift toward feeling positive emotions. This prevents them from getting stuck in a gloomy state of mind and in the problem. Moreover, they learn that focusing on core qualities can create awareness of the positive feelings that go with it, something that is typical for the core reflection approach. They were surprised to learn that it is possible to reflect on inner strengths and potential and on feeling positive emotions *even* when focusing on problems. Staying in touch with their inner potential during reflection on a problematic situation is considered a useful tool. We selected three remarks to illustrate this:

> "I have become aware that I get a positive sense of willpower by focusing on my core qualities rather than on my weaknesses whenever I reflect on my inner barriers."

> "Linking my core qualities to such a difficult situation prevents me from drowning in the negative aspects of it."

> "What really touched me were the moments when my fellow students noticed and mentioned my core qualities, as I talked about how I felt and what I really wanted. At those moments I felt a strong sense of self-esteem and self confidence."

The Importance of Awareness of Negative Emotions When Reflecting on Inner Barriers

An important insight to the students is that feeling less pleasant emotions, such as emotional pain, can be crucial for actually making a change. They tell us that they are used to ignoring these emotions. They now realize that this avoidance behavior causes them to get stuck in procrastination, and that actually *is* an important inner obstacle that prevents them from getting things done. One student now frames the inner barrier that prevents her from getting things done in time as her inability to stay connected to unpleasant feelings:

> We discussed the importance of feeling painful emotions to get connected to your inner self. At that moment I realized that I had never allowed myself to feel the pain. And that by avoiding awareness of these painful feelings, I kept the circle of procrastination alive.

Another student described:

> I do not pay enough attention to the barriers and my negative feelings. I do not use them in any way, other than obtaining negative energy from them.

The Importance of Feeling Willpower

The feeling of willpower is mentioned as valuable by four students. They value the moments when they were asked to focus attention on an ideal situation. By visualizing it, they got a sense of how they would feel about themselves after they reached that situation. One example of a student statement is: *"I learned the importance of becoming aware of what it is I really want (ideals), of imagining what it feels like if I reach that situation, and of expressing that in words."* Another student specifically mentions the relationship he now sees between the awareness of willpower, on the one hand, and procrastination on the other hand:

> The most important thing that I learned was the importance of being aware of what I really want. To not lose confidence in my strengths, but rather to stay in touch with what I want. I realize now that a strong willpower, and really feeling that power, will almost certainly lead to action.

The Importance of the Combined Reflection on Wanting, Feeling, Thinking and Doing When Reflecting on An Experience

Three students describe that they are used to reflecting on a situation only in a cognitive way, by thinking about it. They notice that this does not lead to any changes. It is new to them to feel how their experience changes when they extend the reflection beyond thinking and actively include feeling, as well as feeling willpower to it:

> The most important thing I learned was to make a connection between thinking, wanting, feeling and doing. And that this will improve my ability to switch to a modus of self-regulation.

Another student explained:

> Usually I think a lot about myself. I think about how I feel, about what I do and don't do, and about how that affects me. It was valuable to me to experience what happens if I make a connection with my feeling: to actually feel my feelings, and to actively use them to understand a certain situation.

All students found the combination of the one-to-one coaching and the explanation of theory to be very useful. Moreover, they mentioned that the trainer was an inspiring role model to them. Some of them were a bit skeptical at first as they did not understand how core reflection could help them overcome their procrastination problem. One student described that this changed because after a while he felt that the trainer embodied the method. He mentioned [with respect to a one-to-one coaching] that it felt so authentic and that he really felt a desire to learn to be able to apply core reflection himself:

> The way [the trainer] applied the method showed his integrity. It gave me a "wow-experience": "Wow, I want that too!" It gave me respect for the teacher as well as for the method. I saw that he was truly involved, he was there to help her with her problem, to support her, that there was no hidden agenda. It came from the right kind of motivation. This really inspired me to learn this method. It gave me hope: this is something I had rarely seen, yet I really longed for it.

Conclusion and Discussion

First, our research study challenges the widespread assumption that teaching skills, such as goal setting and time-management, are necessary elements in courses for academic procrastinators. Our core reflection course contains none of these elements, yet, after three weekly meetings of 2.5 hours each, all participants show a decreased level of study procrastination. The trainer was not familiar with the literature on study procrastination, nor had he ever worked with procrastinators before. He used a completely new pedagogical approach. The most important goal of the course was to help students reconnect with their inspiration in such a way that either they stopped procrastinating and started studying or they discovered which important ideals needed attention and fulfillment.

We found no explanation in the literature on study procrastination for the effects reported here. Based on our study, we propose a hypothetical explanation: procrastination may be caused by inadequate self-reflection, characterized by insufficient attention to one's feelings, willpower, inner needs, and core qualities. The participants in this study told us that the elements they valued most were learning to be aware of their emotions and willpower and valuing their core qualities and desires, especially when focusing on a problematic situation. They also valued the combined reflection on emotions, thoughts, desires, and behavior. Hence, we conclude that the core reflection approach helps by creating awareness that extends beyond thinking about core qualities, ideals (willpower), and emotions, and this awareness may contribute to the reduction of the existing procrastination.

In summary, we suspect the balanced attention paid to the cognitive, emotional, motivational, and behavioral aspects of the students is an important explanation for our findings. This is in line with what Kachgal, Hansen, and Nutter (2001) state: using a multifaceted intervention approach is beneficial, since procrastination involves a complex interaction of behavioral, cognitive, and affective components. This hypothesis is further supported by the theory on *presence* developed by Senge et al. (2004), and Scharmer (2007). They emphasize the importance of connecting to one's 'self' as a premise to functioning optimally as a person; this requires an 'open mind,' 'open heart,' and 'open will.' In other words, these authors also emphasize the importance of awareness of thoughts, feelings, and desires. A research study by Van der Padt (2007) confirmed that the interventions of the core reflection trainer indeed aimed at restoring the balance between thoughts, feelings, and desires: 5% of all interventions were about the context (situation, problem); 17% about thinking; 51% about feeling; 15% about wanting; and 13% about doing. This is consistent with the core reflection theory, which assumes that in coaching settings such as the ones we studied, 'feeling' requires special attention, since it is an aspect that is usually underappreciated in our society. Thus, a strong focus on feelings is necessary to restoring inner balance.

Since study-procrastination is a problem at all educational levels, our findings may be relevant beyond academic settings. We believe that core reflection can be an important tool for teachers, whether at universities or when working with younger children. Until now, counseling of procrastinators has often occurred either in specific courses or in therapeutic settings. If core reflection would become part of the regular expertise of teachers, it could be applied in the classroom at any contact moment between the teacher and students – before a problem develops to the point where young people experience high levels of distress. Instead, teachers can then guide them to use their core qualities in an optimal way and help prevent learning problems from developing.

The view presented in this chapter may even be broadened to many other aspects of education. Currently, we see a strong emphasis in education on competencies and behavioral training in almost all content areas. This emphasis may be counterproductive to the most fundamental goals of education. In a core reflection view of learning, competencies and behavior are only two of the relevant levels, and they are a result of what is going on at deeper levels in the person. In order to promote deep learning, with sustainable outcomes at the behavioral level, it may be crucial to pay attention to these deeper levels and to people's inner potential, as well as to frictions between the layers and obstacles to enacting core qualities. In this respect, we believe that our study reveals a truth about the essence of deep and sustainable learning and challenges many current attempts to improve student learning at the level of behavior or competence.

The most important lesson, in our opinion, is that by systematically applying the principles of core reflection when communicating with students, teachers can help these students stay in touch with their feelings, ideals, and inner potentials. On that basis, students will get involved in learning activities in a more natural and effortless manner. We believe that the teacher's modeling behavior is an important factor because it gives hope and inspiration to the students. It is thus important that teachers embody the approach. This requires their ability to stay connected to their own inner strengths, feelings, and willpower whenever working with students as well as their awareness of how they can deal with their own inner obstacles. We believe this needs to be practiced thoroughly – for instance, in specific courses on core reflection combined with supervision for teachers – in order to become fully integrated into the teacher's daily practice.

References

Al-Attiyah, A. (2010). Academic procrastination and its relation to motivation and self-efficacy: The case of Qatari primary school students. *International Journal of Learning, 17* (8), 173–186.

Ellis, A., & Knaus, W. (2002). *Overcoming procrastination* (Rev. edn). New York: New American Library.

Ferrari, J. R. (2004). Trait procrastination in academic settings: An overview of students who engage in task delay. In H. C. Schouwenburg, C. H. Lay, T. A. Pychyl, & J. R. Ferrari (Eds.), *Counseling the procrastinator in academic setting* (pp. 19–27). Washington, DC: APA.

Flett, G. L., Hewitt, P. L., Davis, R. A., & Sherry, S. B. (2004). Description and counseling of the perfectionist procrastinator. In H. C. Schouwenburg, C. H. Lay, T. A. Pychyl, & J. R. Ferrari (Eds.), *Counseling the procrastinator in academic setting* (pp. 181–194). Washington, DC: APA.

Kachgal, M. M., Hansen, L. S. & Nutter, K. J. (2001). Academic procrastination prevention: Strategies and recommendations. *Journal of Developmental Education, 25* (1), 14–24.

Lay, C. H., & Schouwenburg, H. C. (1993). Trait procrastination, time management, and academic behavior. *Journal of Social Behavior and Personality, 8* (4), 647–662.

Lay, C. H. (2004). Some basic elements in counseling procrastinators. In H. C. Schouwenburg, C. H. Lay, T. A. Pychyl, & J. R. Ferrari (Eds.), *Counseling the procrastinator in academic setting* (pp. 43–58). Washington, DC: APA.

Mandel, H. P. (2004). Constructive confrontation: cognitive-behavioral therapy with one type of procrastinating underachiever. In H. C. Schouwenburg, C. H. Lay, T. A. Pychyl, & J. R. Ferrari (Eds.), *Counseling the procrastinator in academic setting* (pp. 119–132). Washington, DC: APA.

Milgram, N. (1991) *Procrastination* (Vol. 6). New York: Academic Press.

Ossebaard M. E., Oost, H., Heuvel, S. van den, & Ossebaard C. A. (2008). *The effect of a positive psychological intervention on academic procrastination*, www.i2l.nl/pdf/4ArticleMHS.pdf.

Scharmer, C. O. (2007). *Theory U: Leading from the future as it emerges.* Cambridge, MA: Society for Organizational learning.

Schouwenburg, H. C. (1994). *Uitstelgedrag bij studenten* [Procrastination behavior in students.]. Dissertatie. Rijksuniversiteit Groningen, Groningen.

Schouwenburg, H. C. (2004). Procrastination in academic setting: general introduction. In H. C. Schouwenburg, C. H. Lay, T. A. Pychyl, & J. R. Ferrari (Eds.), *Counseling the procrastinator in academic setting* (pp. 3–17). Washington, DC: APA.

Senge, P., Scharmer, C. O., Jaworski, J., & Flowers, B. S. (2004). *Presence: Exploring profound change in people, organizations and society.* London: Nicolas Brealey.

Steel, P., Brothen, T., & Wambach, C. (2001). Procrastination and personality, performance, and mood. *Personality and individual differences, 30*(1), 95–106.

Tice, D. M., & Baumeister, R. F. (1997). Longitudinal study of procrastination, performance, stress, and health: the costs and benefits of dawdling. *Psychological Science, 8,* 454–458.

Van der Padt, J. (2007). *Tot de kern komen bij uitstelgedrag* [Getting to the core of procrastination behavior]. Master thesis. Utrecht: Universiteit Utrecht.

Van Eerde, W. (2004). Procrastination in academic settings and the big five model of personality. In H. C. Schouwenburg, C. H. Lay, T. A. Pychyl, & J. R. Ferrari (Eds.), *Counseling the procrastinator in academic setting* (pp. 29–40). Washington, DC: APA.

Van Essen, T., Van den Heuvel, S., & Ossebaard, M.E. (2004). A student course on self-management for procrastinators. In H. C. Schouwenburg, C. H. Lay, T. A. Pychyl, & J. R. Ferrari (Eds.), *Counseling the procrastinator in academic setting* (59–73). Washington, DC: APA.

Van Horebeek, W., Michielsen, S., Neyskens, A., & Depreeuw, E. (2004). A cognitive-behavioral approach in group treatment of procrastinators in academic setting. In H. C. Schouwenburg, C. H. Lay, T. A. Pychyl, & J. R. Ferrari (Eds.), *Counseling the procrastinator in academic setting* (pp. 105–118). Washington, DC: APA.

Wesley, J. C. (1994). Effects of ability, high school achievement, and procrastinatory behavior on college performance. *Educational and Psychological Measurement, 54*(2), 404–408.

PART IV

Core Reflection with Teacher Educators

In Part IV of the book, the focus is on *teacher educators*. What can core reflection mean for faculty of schools of education? In the first of the following two chapters, the two teacher educators describe their three-year self-study on their development as teacher educators using core reflection. The next chapter provides another description of how teacher educators as a whole in a university discovered and implemented the core reflection model in their work.

11

ALIGNING PROFESSIONAL AND PERSONAL IDENTITIES

Applying Core Reflection in Teacher Education Practice[5]

Younghee M. Kim and William L. Greene

In this chapter, Younghee Kim and William Greene describe a three-year collaborative self-study examining the impact of core reflection on their identities and practices as teacher educators. They identify four themes defining the core identity issues in their study: (a) understanding the contradictory nature of core qualities; (b) confronting hypocrisies; (c) holding ambiguity; and (d) sustaining authenticity in everyday practice. Various categories of change in the authors' teaching identities and practice are outlined. Moreover, the chapter presents some anecdotal evidence of the beneficial influences of these teacher educators' own development on their student teachers. The authors conclude that core reflection serves as a useful approach for aligning professional and personal identities with a sense of purpose, passion, and teaching ideals.

Introduction

Being a teacher educator means not only preparing our students to teach but also preparing ourselves to teach. Cultivating our inner qualities and the "capacity to teach with greater consciousness, self-awareness, and integrity" looms large in the literature on reforming the profession of teaching and is posited as a necessary

---

5   This chapter is an adapted version of Kim, Y. M. & Greene, W. L. (2011). Aligning professional and personal identities: Applying core reflection in teacher education practice, *Studying Teacher Education, 7(2), 109–119.*

condition for successful professional development (Intrator & Kunzman, 2006, p. 39). Such teaching inspires the best in both teachers and students; it elevates the learning experience for all by tapping the human potential in ways that cannot be quantified, mandated, tested, or standardized. Heart, passion, and a sense of connectedness are qualities often associated with this kind of teaching (Intrator & Kunzman, 2006). These qualities "emerge from the inner or core landscape of a teacher's life and represent the integral feature of inspired and memorable teaching" (p. 17). In this chapter, we focus the lens of our inquiry inward on how we strive to bring the fullest fruits of our potential to the moments that define us as teachers and as human beings.

Context of the Study

The core reflection approach has had a profound impact on our view of teaching and of teacher education. Synthesizing insights from psychology, psychotherapy, various wisdom traditions, and research into human consciousness, core reflection seeks to put individuals back in touch with their essence (Almaas, 1987), with the ultimate goal of unlocking human potential. The idea behind core reflection is that a teacher's awareness of her core qualities, including her identity and mission, determines to a great degree how she will answer the questions, "Who am I, and how do I reflect who I am?" (Korthagen & Verkuyl, 2002, p. 44). This is a critical point of intersection in the process of exploring one's inner landscape as a teacher: the point where one's identity as a human being intersects with one's professional development (Korthagen, 2004; Korthagen & Verkuyl, 2002; Palmer, 1998), where one's identity as a teacher educator emerges from one's identity as a person. Alignment in this relationship creates the conditions for experiencing what Csikszentmihalyi (1997) calls *flow* – a state of optimal functioning in which individuals feel a sense of effortless action and completeness in the moment. In this state, there exists an integrated sense of identity and potential.

The self-study design described in this paper was conceived after we attended our first four-day workshop on core reflection in April 2007. Core reflection provided us with coaching and questioning strategies to use in our regular meetings with each other in order to reveal how the inner tensions and conflicts we experienced in our work related to our core values and ideals. Believing in the promise of this approach to transform the nature of our work, we embarked on this collaborative self-study to investigate its sustainability and potential in our day-to-day lives as teacher education professors. Doing this together offered greater possibilities for development through shared inquiry as we recognized the inherent limitations of viewing "a situation from one solitary perspective" (Loughran, 2004, p. 21).

The purpose of this study was to examine the impact of core reflection on our professional lives and practices as teacher educators. The two questions that guided this research focused our attention on core qualities and how these were actualized in our professional lives: (1) What insights and challenges emerge through attempts to implement core reflection principles in our work? (2) What changes occur in our teaching practices and relationships with colleagues, students, and others?

Method

Our three-year self-study began in May 2007 when we agreed to meet regularly in order to deepen our understanding and application of core reflection in our lives and work. We realized that, because this would be a highly personal and subjective journey, our method and process for exploring these questions should involve frequent contact in order to articulate thoughts and feelings about the effect of core reflection and to document fresh examples of its use from our teaching practice. We established weekly meetings that provided anchor points for extended conversations, for revisiting questions and raising news ones, and for capturing snapshots of our evolving identities as teacher educators. In addition, we facilitated monthly meetings with new teachers and bi-monthly brown-bag discussions with faculty colleagues, applying our use and awareness of the core reflection approach in teaching and advising contexts. Students' capstone essays and other assignments served as mirrors for us to judge how our efforts to consciously unite core and professional identities in our teaching practice did and did not affect our students.

Our data sources included transcriptions of meetings, journal and book notes, email communications, and students' summary reflections. The written data from year one of the study were compiled into 37 single-spaced pages and ordered chronologically to provide a clearer sense of impact and change over time. The constant comparative method of data analysis (Glaser & Strauss, 1967) was used to analyze these qualitative data following an iterative cycle of simultaneous data collection and analysis (Merriam, 1998). Through multiple readings of the year one data set, and after introducing insights and references from the data into subsequent meetings, we developed broad categories to capture key ideas from repeated examples and to reflect our emerging understanding of the two research questions.

As data continued to accumulate in years 2 and 3 of the study, we used a similar process to read and compare data to previous categories and insights, to generate additional questions, to adjust data collection, and to enact new understandings and strategies in our teaching practices. In this way, multiple readings of the collected data at different points in time over the three years proved helpful in identifying the appearance and recurrence of themes and highlighted the cyclical nature of consciousness and awareness.

Applying core reflection with one another involved using questions to talk through issues that had become a source of tension or inner struggle. As we began to recognize the recurrence of problems and behaviors in our data, we could more quickly visualize how we might address each situation based on the core reflection approach. Frequently, these discoveries were part of our conversations with each other as we sought to validate or to critically examine our previous analysis in light of the growing body of data. In our final analyses, we found that our themes and reported changes continued to seem trustworthy and to represent the reality of our experience. We present our findings in the following two sections, first analyzing our core identities and then turning to the conscious restructuring of our teacher educator identities.

Our data revealed the intersection of our core and professional identities in new and deeper ways. Analysis exposed four themes that defined the core identity issues in our data: (a) understanding the contradictory nature of core qualities; (b) confronting our own hypocrisies; (c) holding ambiguity; and (d) sustaining authenticity in everyday practice. Although some of the issues contained in these themes are interwoven, they serve to distinguish and explain how we consciously reconstructed our teaching identities to align with our awareness of self as person.

Understanding the Contradictory Nature of Core Qualities

We came to accept the notion that core qualities carry with them an ostensibly contradictory appearance. We asked, for instance, whether sensitivity in an individual can be construed as a strength. When is it a weakness? We discussed how the power of a core quality to transform and energize us from within is related to its paradoxical nature. Like other core qualities, sensitivity may be a strength or a weakness depending on how it is actualized. Thus, we had to move beyond the apparent contradiction of an experience in order to find the lesson within it to grow. In our meeting notes and transcripts, we talked about the tensions resulting from contradictions in the way core qualities may be manifested. This realization helped us to be more accepting of these feelings within us and to allow time for learning from them.

An example that surfaced on multiple occasions involved the paradoxical nature of *demands*. When is this a desirable quality and when is it a liability to oneself or another? The paradox is exemplified in this statement:

> I'm having trouble letting go of expecting others to do things the same way I would do them. How do I balance my expectations as a professor with my desire to let go? When I fail at this, I feel disconnected from my core beliefs. (Younghee, meeting notes, March 12, 2009)

This comment led to a discussion of the paradoxical nature of demands. On one hand, it can be helpful to model high expectations and standards for others to achieve and follow. On the other hand, it can create conflicts, tensions, and confusion. We have just begun to explore the dialectic relationship inherent in core qualities, but we think that it is in the tension, the void, and the contradiction that we find an important catalyst for growth.

Confronting our Own Hypocrisies

During the first year of our study, we sometimes referred to ourselves as hypocrites when we did not feel successful in living up to our new levels of awareness or to the practice of core reflection. A gap between what we said we wanted to do or how we wanted to be and what we actually did in practice appeared often enough that it almost felt like we had made no forward progress at all. "I feel I'm not reaching enough of my internal goal, so I'm experiencing some tension or even conflict within myself, and that bothers me because I'm more aware of it" (Younghee, email, July 26, 2007). Younghee's confrontation with hypocrisy in this 2007 email exchange illuminates the contradiction she experienced between ideal and practice. A similar conflict much later in the study seems to have served as a catalyst for deeper learning and growth.

> I feel I failed to live up to my ideals . . . Maybe I'm more aware that I'm not meeting my own ideals to live core reflection in my daily life. So this is a deeper level of awareness, a realization that I'm not living up to . . . It's painful to say that.
> (Younghee, meeting notes, March 12, 2009)

While the impact of acknowledging the persistence of this conflict is not clear in the above comment, Younghee's reflection two weeks later reveals a much stronger and more positive sense of her growing ability to apply core reflection and to move beyond the mental trap of idealization or perfection.

> I feel less split in my thoughts and actions and more aligned in the bigger part. When I can stay connected with my inner essence and my own being, I have stronger flow to notice who I am and what I want to become. I am more aware of my own values, feelings, and wants.
> (Younghee, email, March 23, 2009)

Both of us found that we "still have trouble changing thought patterns with certain issues" and that embracing the paradoxes in our lives for the purpose of inner growth is an inconsistent pattern at best. However, the appearance of the hypocrisy theme in our self-study served to remind us that, as our awareness expands, so will our ability to notice how we may or may not live up to some imagined set of new expectations.

Holding Ambiguity

The capacity to hold our own and other people's tensions or struggles in a way that allowed us to acknowledge but not be consumed by them was a major consequence of practicing core reflection. This theme was defined as a growing sense of recognizing our own strength at balancing conflict, both in ourselves and in others, with objectivity and compassion. The following quotation contains a metaphor that surfaced on several occasions to describe this emergent quality: "I can embrace more. I have a greater capacity for holding the concerns and struggles of others" (Younghee, meeting transcript, May 2007).

In the times when we experienced core connections within ourselves and with our students, we were less vulnerable to those weakening messages of doubt, incompetence, and shallowness that derail or block our flow as teachers, and we were better able to hold the ambiguity of struggle outside of ourselves. At other times, those tensions or struggles became what we called "zingers" that took *the wind out of our sails.* Core connections became blocked, and suddenly we were "out of flow." This sudden inability to hold ambiguity happened many times throughout our study, even shortly after an empowering meeting in which we coached each other with questions. The shift from a state of flow to blocked flow remains a fascinating enigma to us. Why does it happen at some times and not at others? In general, our metaphor of *taking it out from inside and holding the tension in a bowl in front of us* became part of our repertoire for relieving some of the immediate anxiety or worry about difficult situations. We understood that holding ambiguity bought us time to bring personal and professional identities into better alignment and to help avoid a regrettable response to a challenging moment.

Sustaining Authenticity in Everyday Practice

When we talked about how we could sustain core alignment during critical moments throughout the day, several techniques or strategies appeared to be developing as we faced the challenge of putting theory into practice. We both tried to be more mindful of taking the time to build in a regular pattern of preparing ourselves to be fully present. This went hand-in-hand with the strategy of imagining ideal scenarios when we thought about situations we might find ourselves in, as these examples show.

> I was weak last week, and I came away from a few interactions feeling powerless and vulnerable. It's like that some days when things happen that your heart, mind, and body are just not prepared for. I continue to wonder about how I attend to these moments and about how to restore my balance, presence, and flow in those unexpected and challenging situations?
>
> (William, meeting notes, August 3, 2007)

I'm reading more of the core reflection articles now and in a reflection mode of how tomorrow might be. I have to envision each student by name and imagine seeing them in person tomorrow. I want to be mentally ready even though I might still be vulnerable to not being all I can be.

(Younghee, email, April 7, 2008)

These comments encompass our use of visualization, taking time to reconnect with our core qualities as teachers prior to meeting our students, and activating self-knowledge and memories of past experience to restore confidence and courage in situations where we start to feel weak or vulnerable. We believe that such strategies helped us stave off the disempowering effects of feeling disconnected from our core strengths. We recognized over time that these critical moments of managing the onset of disempowering thoughts and feelings represented key areas of growth in how to be more consistent within ourselves amid the vicissitudes of daily interactions.

The sub-theme of social support for sustaining awareness and core alignment was very significant for us and threaded through most of our meetings. It was clear to us by the end of the second year that our ability to nurture our use of core reflection in daily teaching and practice was closely linked to regular contact and core levels of communication with each other. Realizing the challenge of sustaining deep awareness without the social support provided in our collegial, *core-to-core* communication, we began to feel that autonomy, paradoxically, could only expand within the context of nurturing relationships.

Every time I reach this point, I realize I'm a stronger person and can face the world better. It's the time I need to explore, to create. I find it much more powerful than anything else . . . It's quite reassuring to be able to reflect back in a safe way.

(Younghee, meeting notes, September 25, 2008)

Younghee's comment from one of our regular core reflection meetings exemplifies the value we found in learning together and sharing in the joy of self-discovery. Similarly:

When others hold a safe space for us to explore, reconstruct, articulate, redefine, and internalize conceptions of ourselves, we engrave them on the heart and in the mind and in the spirit.

(William, meeting notes, March 12, 2009)

We came to realize in our collaboration that self-study is not just about what *is*, but also about what *can* be possible in connecting deeper aspects of self and personhood in our professional lives. This was as true for our collegial relationships as it was for our student relationships, and it was really more than just reframing questions and hearing different perspectives, though they were important elements.

> It's about the opportunity to be who you really are or really want to be. Some people might call it *self-actualization*. Some people might call it *authenticity*, some might call it *flow*, but I'm not sure it's any of those things exactly. I think it's about being human, being very natural in responses, and being very present.
>
> (William, meeting notes, March 12, 2009)

This served as a reminder to us that using core reflection with one another and, as teacher educators, with our students, "requires a purposeful desire to seek the growth of each other's soul." Our comments in the data revealed a growing sense of belief and confidence that, like the examples here, teaching and learning would be optimized when anchored in the act of honoring and encouraging each other's most essential nature.

Conscious Restructuring of Our Teacher Educator Identities

In understanding our shifting identities as teacher educators, it became clear that we were establishing new priorities in our philosophies and practices of teaching. A framework developed by Korthagen and Lagerwerf (2008), also presented in Chapter 13 of this book (see Figure 13.1), illustrates two polar views or perspectives of teaching and learning: one featuring more traditional characteristics and the other featuring principles of core reflection. We used the original framework as a starting point for analyzing our findings and then revised it to better describe the changes we were noticing. Some of the changes included here are examples in our data of the subtle shifts in our teaching practices; other changes are more dramatic. Our own shifts or changes do not represent dichotomous relationships; that is, everything we suggest here should be taken as movement along a trajectory of development rather than a jump from one category to another. We use the labels here as markers to show the contrast in our development and not as markers that identify one perspective to the exclusion of the other. Yet, these do represent evidence of an evolving emphasis in our identities and practices as teacher educators.

From Subject-Centered toward Person-Centered Relationships

In their framework, Korthagen and Lagerwerf (2008) characterize one view of traditional teaching as a tendency to maintain a level of distance between the teacher and her students in order to get the business of education done. In this perspective, teaching is seen as less about learning who students really are or what they really want and more about who the teacher is and what she wants for her students. Our study has revealed to us a clear contrast to this in our own practices in that, by applying principles of core reflection, we feature the student or person more prominently in our awareness and decision-making as teachers.

> It matters much more to me now how I treat my students, make connections, and model for them how they could reach out to their own students. What's most important may not be stated in our competencies and standards. I realize that it's more about the core values that my students hold than a quantitative measure of their teaching proficiency.
>
> (Younghee, meeting notes, May 18, 2007)

As a result of this shift in perspective, we found ourselves focusing more intentionally on making deeper contact with students through interactions that foster core levels of communication. Additionally, we realized that unintentional community building occurred when we focused on the individual strengths of our students. As students' feedback helped us discover later, we had also been building a collective sense of strength through the affinities and trust created in our core reflection exercises and practices. The values of community and of trusting relationships had always been important to us in our teaching, but understanding these concepts in the context of this study has deepened our commitment to using core reflection with this intention.

From Focus on Product toward Focus on Process

Degree and licensure outcomes in teacher preparation programs generally lead to products that demonstrate a specified level of mastery or competence. While our teaching maintains a level of connection to these institutional goals, this study has shown us how our application of core reflection in our teaching moved us with greater confidence toward valuing, accepting, and recognizing each student's developmental process as evidence of growth and competence. Younghee's comment highlights this shift in emphasis "from an outcome oriented mindset to valuing students for who they are and what the process means to them" (Meeting notes, May, 2009). As the following quotation from the work of an undergraduate student suggests, her development as a teacher seems to have been influenced by the process of self-discovery and awareness facilitated by our regular use of core reflection in her classes.

> Whenever I got discouraged, I would remember my core strengths and would be revived and encouraged to keep going. This year I have grown to love the real me, imperfections and all, and admitting so brings tears to my eyes. Now that I have identified my core qualities and have accepted

> myself, I will not only be a better teacher, but I will inspire my students
> to find their strengths and teach them how to love themselves.
>
> (J. C., student teacher, portfolio synthesis paper, May 2009)

Products, as final outcomes, are still an important part of student assessment, but they are not the only significant measure. The significance of the *process* has become even clearer to us through comments such as the student teacher's above. Our use of core reflection with our students has provided us a vehicle to discern what is truly significant in our students' lives and to be more attuned to their needs and passions.

From Thinking and Doing Toward Integrating Thinking, Feeling, Doing, and Wanting

Many perspectives on teaching represent learning as a sequential, linear process of moving from thinking to doing, part to whole, or theory to practice. Our practice has incorporated elements of a *gestalt* nature with more sensitivity to promoting deep learning through experiences that integrate simultaneous dimensions of our awareness and being. Thus we have become less prone to hanging on to our own agendas and more flexible about adapting to the holistic needs of our students. Our data indicate that students noticed and, in some cases, internalized our effort to model holistic practices in our teaching. Two examples come from final papers written for end-of-program portfolios.

> Teaching had become so much more to me than a career. This program became more than coursework. To be a teacher is to completely alter your lifestyle. It is about looking at and evaluating the individuals in your classroom as well as yourself, and it is about constantly modifying your methods and procedures. While being a good teacher takes knowledge and skill, it also takes heart. I suppose this heart for teaching is something that I have had all along; it just took actually doing it for me to realize that it was there.
>
> (E.H., student teacher, portfolio synthesis paper, May 2009)

> Throughout the program my professors frequently asked me to look at my core qualities. At first I was hesitant, but as the year progressed, I realized why they demanded this of us. My core qualities hugely define who I am as a teacher. I realized that compassion and caring are qualities that helped me through times when I felt that teaching was too emotionally demanding . . . I began to realize that who I am inside is incredibly indicative of who I am as a teacher. When I stand in front of a classroom I am not performing the "role" of a teacher, I am being who I am.
>
> (K.H., student teacher, portfolio synthesis paper, May 2009)

One strategy we employed to help students integrate their thoughts, feelings, and ideals involved *guided coaching activities*. With peer partners, students identified areas in which they experienced conflict or tension between their growing awareness of themselves and their emerging identities as teachers. By asking each other a series of thinking, feeling, and wanting questions (see Figure 3.4, *the Elevator,* in Chapter 3), students were able to shift from a tendency to over-analyze a problem to bringing more of who they are as people into the moment. The same strategy we employed in our self-study to align our identities as people with our identities as teacher educators became a feature of our classroom teaching. Interestingly, some of our students indicated that they, too, were beginning to use thinking, feeling, and wanting questions to re-adjust awareness when certain tensions or problems surfaced in their own classrooms.

From Seeking Answers Toward Holding Ambiguity

Changing awareness about our capacity for managing our and others' struggles altered some of our ways of knowing and meeting our students, as in Younghee's observation:

> I see some of my students who are struggling in a different light. I feel more empowered to reach out to understand who they are and where they come from. Their perceived problems or past experiences are smaller than who they are, and I feel I'm more ready to accept them for who they are.
> (Meeting transcript, May 18, 2007)

A quotation from an email exchange acknowledges Younghee's self-realization that establishing core connections with students is part of our teaching mission, regardless of what tensions compete for our awareness in the classroom.

> I can do only so much, and I want to do it with grace and by honoring the students. I'll try to focus on the core qualities students bring. That should be the focus, not the assignments or due dates but our students' transformation process and the joy of being with them. When I see myself as a serving and understanding teacher, my desire to control diminishes.
> (Younghee, email, July 20, 2008)

The idea of meeting our students in this way led us to the notion of being fully present to meet them when they are ready to arrive, and not necessarily when we would have them arrive. Transformational learning requires relinquishing control to the learner. We questioned our well-intended impulses to provide the right answers or solutions for students by embracing the state of ambiguity as another priority to foster in ourselves. This was a liberating idea, one that we hope will help us to remember that sometimes just being fully present is enough.

From Role/Identity Orientation Toward Core Orientation

The process of this study deepened our awareness of the influence our core qualities had on our evolving and emergent identities as teacher educators. This resulted in strengthening our understanding of what it means to teach who we are, as Palmer (1998) discusses, and the implications of this to our views and philosophy of teaching. Because of this, we have learned or re-learned that essential features of our values and work as teacher educators are the following: (a) reminding our students who they are as people; (b) facilitating their discovery of characteristics inherent in who they are as teachers, and not by just "playing the role" of a teacher; and (c) guiding them to help their own students find their core qualities through their teaching. The following quotations represent two examples of students' responses to our application of this process in our teaching.

> It has been an amazing journey to be able to really sit back and reflect not only on lessons planned and taught, but on me and who I am as a person, deep down. It is the true me that I pass along to my students. It is my compassion, empathy, enthusiasm, silliness, authenticity, drive, commitment, open heart, and many more core qualities that allow me to teach from my heart and be the teacher I have become. I find myself reflecting on everything that I do. I dig deep and consider, "Is the way I am teaching truly from my heart?"
>
> (K.H., student teacher, final portfolio reflection, May 2009)

> At this time in the program core reflections became an impetus to stimulate a rebirthing of hope that I doubtlessly necessitated. As core qualities were introduced I started peeling back the layers of my individualistic ideals and uncovered something buried deep within me. I discovered that I am capable of caring more about others than I initially imagined. With this realization I started to actualize that I am a compassionate person who wants to bring the joy of learning to my students.
>
> (J.G., student teacher, final portfolio reflection, May 2009)

Our students' reflections from two cohorts have, for the most part, indicated a high level of interest and resonance with the core reflection approach and contained numerous examples of how their awareness of their teaching changed as a result.

Conclusion

Through regular practice with core reflection, we have grown in our ability to look at our practice through a lens that unifies, rather than separates, self as teacher educator and self as person. We have learned that when we can respond to challenges by engaging the core qualities we recognize within ourselves, we are less likely to feel the disempowering effects of a professional identity somehow estranged from a personal identity. While we previously looked at behavior as a validation of our authenticity as teacher educators, we realized through the course of this self-study how misleading that perception can be. We believe that this change has strengthened our ability to remain authentic in critically challenging moments.

The shifts in our understanding of who we are as teacher educators have resulted in several significant implications for the decisions we make in our work with students. In our curriculum, class assignments are less task-oriented and more holistically focused on student growth. We allow students more time to explore their inner lives as future teachers through selected readings, more class time is spent discussing personal development, and assignments are much more integrated. We accomplish this by sacrificing some of the more traditional course content but with new awareness of the value of that sacrifice. We still seek some of the same course and program outcomes, but our focus is much more strongly aimed at connecting with students' core strengths and aligning those to the outcomes of their coursework. Applying our own process from this study, we have sought to build time into our teaching for students to realize and understand their emerging identities as teacher and self.

Core reflection has served as a powerful approach for aligning our conscious-ness with our sense of purpose, passion, and potential as teachers and as human beings. This directly influenced the priorities we enacted in relationships with others and in our teaching practices. With more conviction than when we began this study three years ago, we share the belief that the need to address the spiritual or inner condition of both teachers and students is an essential role of teaching in current times. It is important, if for no grander reason than because the truthful connection we have with our students has considerable influence on how and at what level they will learn, on their motivation, on their trust, and on the way they interact with others – in short, on virtually everything we strive to model in teaching that is responsive and meaningful.

References

Almaas, A. H. (1987). *Diamond heart: book one.* Boston, MA: Shambhala Publications.

Csikszentmihalyi, M. (1997). *Finding flow: The psychology of engagement with everyday life.* New York: Basic Books.

Glaser, B. G., & Strauss, A. L. (1967). *The discovery of grounded theory.* Dallas, TX: Houghton Mifflin.

Intrator, S., & Kunzman, R. (2006). Starting with the soul. *Educational Leadership, 63*(6), 38–42.

Korthagen, F. A. J. (2004). In search of the essence of a good teacher: Towards a more holistic approach in teacher education. *Teaching and Teacher Education, 20,* 77–97.

Korthagen, F. A. J., & Lagerwerf, B. (2008). *Leren van binnenuit: Onderwijsontwikkeling in een nieuwe tijd.* [Learning from within: Educational development in a new era]. Soest: Nelissen.

Korthagen, F. A. J., & Vasalos, A. (2005). Levels in reflection: Core reflection as a means to enhance professional growth. *Teachers and Teaching: Theory and Practice, 11*, 47–71.

Korthagen, F. A. J., & Verkuyl, H. (2002). Do you meet your students or yourself? Reflection on professional identity as an essential component of teacher education. In C. Kosnik, A. Freese, & A. P. Samaras (Eds.), *Making a difference in teacher education through self-study*. Proceedings of the Fourth International Conference on Self-Study of Teacher Education Practices (Vol. 2, pp. 43–47). Toronto, ON: OISE/University of Toronto.

Loughran, J. J. (2004). A history and context of self-study of teaching and teacher education practices. In J. J. Loughran, M. L. Hamilton, V. K. LaBoskey, & T. Russell, (Eds.), *International handbook of self-study of teaching and teacher education practices* (pp. 7–39). Dordrecht, The Netherlands: Kluwer.

Merriam, S. B. (1998). *Qualitative research and case study applications in education*. San Francisco, CA: Jossey-Bass.

Ofman, D. (2000). *Core qualities: A gateway to human resources*. Schiedam, The Netherlands: Scriptum.

Palmer, P. J. (1998). *The courage to teach: Exploring the inner landscape of a teacher's life*. San Francisco, CA: Jossey-Bass.

12

CORE REFLECTION AS A CATALYST FOR CHANGE IN TEACHER EDUCATION

*Erin M. Wilder, William L. Greene,
and Younghee M. Kim*

This chapter shows how teacher educators in the School of Education at Southern Oregon University used core reflection with one another and with students in different degree programs at the university. As such, this chapter offers an insight into how core reflection can work at two interrelated levels: the level of faculty and the level of students. The authors explore many changes that occurred by following stories of teacher educators who continue to study core reflection and apply it in their teaching, advising, and guidance of students. Changes personally, professionally, and programmatically have shown the impact of core reflection on teacher educators and students and the benefits of sustaining this practice.

It can be scary to expose who we truly are to one another. Yet, because the culture in the School of Education supports being open and honest about our strengths and what we bring to the field of teaching, we can better help students become authentic practitioners in the craft of teaching.

> (Katherine, Assistant Professor, third year faculty member)

Teacher educators impart their values to students in both conscious and unconscious ways. Living up to that responsibility of modeling behavior, words, and states of mind to future teachers requires a strong commitment to the cultivation of self-awareness in order to encourage each other's highest potential. It is with that commitment that a group of faculty, along with their Chair and Dean, attended one or more workshops on core reflection, and as a result they have been exploring deeper aspects of how they teach, advise, guide, supervise, and mentor their students and each other. This chapter describes some of the changes that occurred among faculty – individually and collectively – within the School of Education at Southern Oregon University over five years since their introduction to core reflection.

In the spring of 2007, two of the authors of this chapter attended a four-day workshop in Chicago on core reflection, the first of its kind in the United States. Excited by this work and its connection to positive psychology, they discussed with their Dean the "potential power" of introducing core reflection to others in the School. Together, they wondered what it could look like to provide professional development for the whole staff around core reflection. The Dean secured funding for Fred Korthagen and Angelo Vasalos, co-founders of core reflection, to come to the university in Oregon during the fall of 2007 and again in the fall of 2009 to conduct four-day workshops introducing core reflection. Participation in the two workshops was voluntary, though a majority of School faculty attended at least one. In the aftermath of those workshops, many of the participants found ways to apply what they learned and experienced to their practices as teacher educators. Currently, approximately half of the School faculty of 22 continue to apply core reflection five years after the first training was offered.

Data Collection

In an effort to investigate post-workshop changes among the faculty in the School, the authors created a list of interview questions as a starting point for studying about the influence of core reflection on their practice. The faculty was asked the following questions:

1. How did you begin your work with core reflection? Where do you stand in the process of implementing core reflection in your teaching practice?
2. In your view, how has core reflection affected the culture in the School of Education?
3. How has your work with students and core reflection helped students to discover and facilitate the realization of their potential?

Additionally, program coordinators were asked this question: How has your work with core reflection affected your approach to the job of coordination?

Following are excerpts of individual reflections and stories from faculty, ten of whom agreed to be interviewed and three of whom submitted written responses to the questions. Their responses provided a significant portion of the data used to write this chapter. The first author conducted audio-recorded interviews that lasted 30–90 minutes for each faculty member and then transcribed these data for analysis. As both co-authors and subjects for this chapter, we had also previously attended the core reflection workshops and applied it with our students and with one another. The authors interviewed each other using the same set of questions. Excerpts from all participants' responses, including the authors' responses, are represented in this chapter.

In putting these interview findings together, the authors have taken a personal narrative rather than a descriptive research approach because we believe that each of the examples identify a certain unique truth and highlight the diversity of how core reflection is manifested. The interview findings, examples, and quotations are organized according to topics surfacing in the interview process. This chapter also includes anecdotal evidence from students to underscore and illustrate faculty statements related to student learning and teacher development.

Faculty Use of Core reflection with Students

Faculty have applied core reflection with students in various contexts: mentoring and supervising student teachers, teaching and planning education curriculum, and advising. How each approached the process of core reflection depended on the personal connection they felt with the process and on their comfort level in using the principles of core reflection. These faculty shared the core belief that helping students become teachers is a serious responsibility and begins when they first come through our doors as advisees. Faculty guide students to get to know themselves more deeply through identifying their core strengths while they navigate through rigorous academic programs at the university. The following vignettes illustrate how faculty have applied core reflection with students.

Jacob is one of the coordinators of the Masters of Arts in Teaching (MAT) program and teaches graduate students in its courses. Of his advising and teaching he says,

> I embed core reflection terminology, concepts and techniques in all of my classes. In particular, I use the onion model as a framework for helping students begin to articulate their personal sense of mission and core beliefs about the aims and purposes of education, for how these might impact how they understand and enact their role as teachers, and then for identifying the environmental factors that either constrain or help sustain their ability to manifest their authentic selves within the classroom.

Shelley is the Elementary Education Coordinator of the undergraduate licensure and non-licensure programs, teaching both undergraduate and graduate students. She has implemented core reflection in her work with students and gave this example from her course on diversity.

> I find opportunities to discuss, nurture, and identify my students' core qualities as we address the content of the coursework. In my Multicultural Education class, students learn to recognize their values, beliefs, and biases

to discern where and from whom they were learned. I ask them to consider whether the values and beliefs they have learned will serve them in their developing identities as future teachers.

Victoria, an instructor in both the graduate and undergraduate programs, feels that core reflection has given her the tools she needs to build strong relationships with students. Prior to receiving training in core reflection she said, "I simply found myself telling my students what they were doing wrong and how they could fix it. This resulted in barriers in our relationships based on frustration, disappointment, and anger." Having worked with core reflection for the past few years, Victoria now says, "I have focused on discovering the core values of each pre-service teacher from the beginning and building on that. The relationships are built on the fact that I honor their core and want to help them discover how to use those strengths to become an outstanding educator." Using the strengths-based approach of core reflection, Victoria feels, "By midyear, they are more open to demands I place on them. They know me and realize that everything I say and do is my best effort to impact their growth. By the end of our time together, the celebration is truly from the heart."

As an instructor and advisor, Michelle has seen the key impacts of core reflection take hold in her life, and it has changed her personal relationships as well as her relationships with students. She spoke about the need for students to complete many tasks in the classroom and how core reflection helps students feel more grounded in such a complex environment. Core reflection has also enabled her to identify with the qualities that are important to her in her teaching. Student autonomy and engagement are at the heart of what she wants for her students, and over the last year, her courses have changed dramatically. She has shifted to a constructivist model of instruction where student choice is valued. She described the process she has gone through as her teaching philosophy changed: "My whole structure of letting go and taking risks . . . Why did it happen? I'm still thinking about it. How did it happen? It was a total empowerment of the class." When she gave students more choice and voice in the classroom, she found that more learning occurred and that they were engaged in what they were learning.

Katherine has just finished her second year of teaching in the teacher education program at the university. She completed the core reflection workshop in 2009 and has continued to use core reflection in her teaching. She prompted students to identify their own strengths and reinforced those strengths through authentic praise in conversation and written communications. Katherine is now moving toward giving students more freedom and choice in their learning because she believes that when students have control of what they are learning, they are more invested and will find the learning to be more applicable to their teaching. Through her work with core reflection she has realized that, at her core, she values hands-on, authentic learning and strives to be more transparent with students about what they are doing in class. "I find great joy in helping students identify their core qualities that will allow them to inspire, motivate, and form meaningful relationships with one another and their own students. I do this through modeling these same concepts in my courses."

This section has looked at examples of faculty who applied their core values along with stories of how they identified core qualities in their work with students. The next section describes how faculty have used core reflection to support one another and continue to grow and develop in their roles as teacher educators and within the university.

Faculty Use of Core Reflection with Each Other and Within Themselves

Forging Personal and Professional Identities

In August 2008, the Dean of the School of Education presented a conference paper titled, "Saving Self in a Self-less Environment: Core reflections of a Dean." In the paper he wrote that he had struggled to save self in the face of professional and personal assaults from then university supervisors. He described a challenging situation that he recorded in his journal over a two-year period. Of his own core reflection he wrote "In my quest to learn about being a university administrator and what it takes to retain a sense of self when working, in what I have termed, a 'self-less' university environment" (Mills, 2008, p. 2). Through reflecting on his core qualities, he was able to identify strategies that he used "in order to survive (and perhaps thrive) in a work environment that frequently challenges my core qualities" (Mills, 2008, p. 3). The paper described power differentials in the relationship between the dean, administrators, faculty, and students. When an abuse of power by one of the supervisors was perceived, the dean relied on his "own sense of self and the core values I live by in order to survive . . . It was only through my self-study work through the lens of core reflection that I was able to sustain my sense of self and stay true to my core values" (Mills, 2008, p. 4).

Core reflection helped Morris, the School's Chair, recognize when a core tension was occurring in his work and, in those moments, he found he was more willing to acknowledge and accept it and "not let it disconnect me from the place that I need to be inside." He added, "I feel I am likely to recover more quickly from my most challenging situations than I was before learning about core reflection." As he put it, core reflection has helped him stay connected in his awareness to a bigger perspective and in touch with what is truly important to him in his day-to-day life.

Several years after attending the initial workshop in Chicago, Julia strives to live core reflection through her teaching and work with faculty:

> I feel it's important to move on, not go back to my old habits of doing things in reactive ways. I have to continue to remind myself about who I

am, my core qualities, and examine my identity as a teacher educator. My role is to remind my students of who they are, help them get in touch with their inner truth, reconnect with the greatness within, and honor and cultivate their souls.

The process of core reflection serves as a reminder to her of the need for ongoing reflection of her own strengths and values so that she can continue to nurture the souls of her students to be aligned with what is truly important to them.

The Case of Laura: A Personal Story

Laura teaches in the MAT program and is also a guide to student teachers in the field. She encountered core reflection at a time in her life where she needed some insight and guidance to who she was on a personal and professional level. Laura had moved away from the university with her family and continued to teach part-time online courses. Two years later, when she and her family moved back and she began to work again at the university she noticed some dramatic changes in the faculty. At this point the faculty had already attended the first workshop on core reflection and Laura knew that she wanted to be a part of the change she saw in some of her colleagues. At the same time, Laura was in the process of applying for promotion and tenure at the university and found the process to be a great opportunity to get to know herself better through exploring her growth as an educator in higher education. However, through the process she found that she wasn't being authentic to herself and that her tenure packet was lacking her core qualities that she identified within her work with students. While she was going through this process, the questions she sought to answer at the time and continued to think about were: Who do I want to be when I'm in my classroom? Who do I want my students to know when I'm teaching? She sought out information on core reflection and became a regular attendee to faculty brownbag sessions. She also found articles on core reflection and started implementing the elements of the work into her personal life at home as well as in her work with students and colleagues in the School.

Laura shifted her focus from the content of the course to teaching from the heart. She felt that teaching the content of the course was more automatic for her, and that teaching from the heart was more challenging, but at the same time very rewarding. "There was a real sense of relief that I didn't have to be someone that somebody externally had told me I had to be by saying 'teach this curriculum.' It gave me more joy in teaching. It was hard, but it gave me more joy." This shift in her teaching allowed her to feel more connected to students and that in allowing them to truly know her, she grew to know them on a much deeper level. This created the space for Laura to appreciate the different developmental levels of her students and allowed them to experience and acknowledge their own growth throughout her courses.

Laura believes in the concepts of core reflection and applies this reflective practice to her personal and professional life. Like other faculty in the School she has changed her courses to reflect the nature of core reflection and help students find their own core strengths. Her interactions with students and faculty are based on connection and collaboration. After attending the second workshop that was offered in 2009, Laura has continued to evolve in her use of core reflection. She serves as an inspiring example of how one can encounter core reflection at a specific time in life, and actively seek out the necessary information to apply it in the different facets of life in both the personal and professional realms.

Collegial Mentoring

In addition to implementing core reflection in their teaching, faculty use core reflection in their interactions with one another. All of the faculty who were interviewed have cited trust as being a major change that they shared with other faculty who were engaged in the practice of core reflection. Victoria said: "It has helped shape our identities as teacher educators and helped us grow closer and stronger as a faculty." Core reflection has given the faculty a common language that our students are now beginning to use as well. "Core reflection has helped to provide a common vocabulary among both students and faculty so that all come to recognize purpose-centered teaching, concern for personal authenticity, and a strength-based approach as distinguishing factors of the program," stated Shelley.

There is an appreciation and special bond among the faculty who share the belief in core reflection. Victoria described how this bond forms:

> We can talk through the process together-knowing that we are engaging in a discovery that will help us at a much deeper level. It has built an unusual and deeper trust between us; we are more connected by our joint belief in core strengths and values than we are people who work in the same building.

Marisa teaches both graduate and undergraduate students and supervises student teachers in the field. This past year, she was struggling with what felt to her like an insurmountable issue. She opened up to her colleagues about her conflict with a new cohort of students. She hadn't worked with this cohort in the previous quarters, yet the group had already formed a community among themselves having taken many courses together over the year. During the first class meeting, Marisa focused on the course content instead of focusing more on building a classroom community, as she normally would have done during the first class meeting. This resulted in a disrespectful response from some of her students. The first class didn't go as well as she had hoped, which she feared would set the tone of the course for the rest of the quarter. After the first class meeting, Marisa was disappointed with the negative communication she received from students via email, as she explained here:

> This was the first time I'd been faced with such an issue in my professional life; I didn't know what to do. It just wasn't coming to me. I don't know if it was because I was so emotionally wrapped up that I couldn't see clearly.

Following a committee meeting where Marisa shared with her colleagues the issues she was having in the class, Julia stayed with her to do core reflection coaching in support of her. In going through the process of core reflection with Julia, Marisa was able to open herself up to new ideas. In the end, she felt such strong support from her colleagues that she gained enough confidence to find relief from all of the stress she was feeling. She reports:

> In doing core reflection the answers emerged and I felt really supported. My colleagues were reflecting back to me my strength and my diligence, my past successes and being able to pull from that it just gave me confidence to be relieved of all the emotional stuff I was feeling so I could stay true to myself and do something really authentic to address the issue.

Marisa then goes on to say, "We all have this common approach that we know is really effective and supportive and helps us feel empowered again in order to address the issues, and move on in a way that helps us stay and feel connected to our core, like I know I'm doing the right thing because it's coming from my inner layer." She went into her next class meeting knowing that she wanted to do something authentic to address the issues in her class. She talked with students from her heart and explained how she was feeling as a result of their first class together. She shared her ideal for the class as a community of learners and gave them the chance to really get to know her as a person. Marisa continued to use core reflection with the students through the remainder of the quarter and felt strongly connected to the class at the end of the term.

Some faculty members reported that they were hesitant implementing core reflection with students following the three-day workshop. Instead, some felt more comfortable applying core reflection into their personal lives first, and later brought it into their practice with students. According to Marshall, the coordinator and professor of the Masters in Education (MEd) program, whether one practices core reflection or not, it is still important that teacher educators develop personal relationships with students and that they teach from a student-oriented approach. He implements reflective practices in his classes through the use of case studies and also takes a strengths-based approach in his advising and teaching of students, though he distinguishes his approach from the principles and vocabulary of a "dedicated" core reflection approach that he sees other faculty employing.

One element related to sustaining faculty development among those interested in core reflection is the convening of quarterly brownbag lunches. Faculty are free to come and go during a 90-minute block of time where the agenda is sharing their use of core reflection to address issues, questions, and applications brought to the table for discussion. Julia feels that continual professional support such as the brownbag meetings are key to keeping core reflection in practice among the faculty. Of core reflection she says, "I try to remind myself of it, and live in it in my daily life and practice. The brownbag is a great tool to promoting its organic growth in our everyday work." The next section will explore the programmatic changes that have occurred as a result of the use of core reflection by faculty in each program.

Program Changes and the Impact on Student Outcomes

The faculty who have embraced and implemented core reflection into their daily lives and work with students commented on perceived changes in the culture of the school in the few years since core reflection practice has taken root. The ongoing work has led to changes in the MAT and the undergraduate elementary education licensure and degree programs. In the MAT program, the school has changed the portfolio requirements of student teachers to directly correlate with core reflection. For example, in their portfolios students now pose self-reflective questions, including the following:

* How are my core qualities shaping my identity and behavior as an emerging teacher?
* Who do I want to be as a teacher?
* How do I intend or hope to manifest my core qualities in my future classroom practice?

In addressing and reflecting on these questions, future teachers are invited to explore who they are on a deeper level than what was happening previously.

The undergraduate elementary education licensure and degree programs have also infused core reflection into many aspects of teaching and learning with pre-service teachers before they begin student teaching. Students start the undergraduate elementary education program in their junior year. Many of their instructors use core reflection approaches in the classes during whole group, small group, and one-on-one work with students. During their senior year of the elementary education program, students either go into student teaching to earn their teaching license, or they enter the degree program and earn their degree in education with a goal of earning a teaching license at the master's degree level. The student teachers have faculty, advisors, and supervisors from the program who observe and evaluate their progress over the course of that senior year. In field experience seminar classes, the faculty advisors use core reflection to help students identify their desires, needs, and ideals while working in the classroom setting and developing their identities as teachers. As an example, Heidi, a former undergraduate student, valued the process of core reflection and in one assignment wrote, "When I close my eyes and focus on pushing the outside influences into the environment, I feel a sense of peace wash over me." Core reflection is a powerful way for students like Heidi to learn to identify their strengths and to use the onion model as they address issues related to teaching. She goes on to say, "It takes only a phrase or simple gesture to remind me to stop and breathe. I am reminded to analyze what I have control over and what the ideal situation would be."

Many of the instructors in the undergraduate degree program use core reflection regularly in their work with students. Professor Julia feels that instructors in the program are aware of their own desire to honor students through the use of core reflection. Many of the students in the degree program opt to take online courses that are part of the Early Childhood Development (ECD) online program as well. Julia says that the instructors of both the degree program and some of the same instructors who teach in the ECD program are "more willing to bring core reflection to our online classes. This may bring limitless opportunities for us to help our students to acknowledge themselves for who they are and remind them of their core qualities as early childhood teachers."

In all of the undergraduate programs, students are exposed to the use of core reflection in their courses and interactions with faculty. More students come to value the practice of core reflection as they develop their teaching identities. Former graduate student Madeline wrote about the initial struggle she had incorporating core reflection into her growth as an educator:

> The process of closing my eyes and connecting to my inner core was one I tended to fight, with all my might. Today I fight the process less, and only when I fail to prevent the environment from perforating the layers of my onion and skewing my sense of who I am.

The school year ends with graduating students' portfolio presentations. Students work on their portfolios throughout their senior or final year in the program. They are guided in writing essay reflections for their portfolios that identify and describe their core qualities. The presentations of their portfolios at the end of the year show how much students have learned about themselves through reflecting at a deeper level and how they have come to internalize and apply the main tenants of core reflection in their development as teachers. In her portfolio synthesis paper, a former undergraduate student, Sarah, wrote:

> I have found core qualities in myself that I didn't know I had. I am so passionate about touching the lives of all of my students and bringing out their core qualities. I believe every child deserves to be respected and given the opportunity to reach his/her full potential.

Another former student Alisa wrote, "My experience has led me to develop and deepen my dynamic dispositions. As an educator, these core qualities are the greatest gifts I can bring to my students and my greatest teaching tools because, ultimately, we teach who we are." In teaching students the process of core reflection the faculty are giving them the gift of getting to know themselves on a deep level that translates into the types of teachers they become. This work is reciprocal and, while faculty allow students this kind of opportunity to deeply reflect on who they are, faculty are also doing the work on themselves. The next section is an analysis of the positive impact core reflection has had on the School of Education for both the faculty and students.

Discussion

The institutional and professional culture of the School seems unique to more traditional portrayals of higher education. In this chapter we have seen how core reflection was initially embraced and continues to be implemented by over half of the faculty in the school. Significant changes have occurred in teaching and mentoring work with students, in curriculum and programs, and among the faculty in the years since core reflection was introduced.

A new way of guiding students now encourages exploration into their teaching identities, trust in themselves, and internal growth after they have left our program. Instructors are more transparent about ideals for their students in advising, teaching, and field supervision. Students have responded with work that reveals greater internal awareness of their development, a sense of ownership over their own transformation, and evidence that they place value on their own measurement of these things. In that way, the process of becoming a teacher is more authentic than before when outcomes related to self-accomplishment relied, perhaps too much, on external criteria and measurement.

Using a strengths-based model has created room for students to get to know participating faculty on a more personal level and allowed them to build trust and respect while working together. This encourages students to work at a level that is much richer and truer to the person they *want* to be than in the past. In general, students seem more comfortable taking risks because they know we are seeking the best in them. In standards-based, professional programs such as ours, faculty measurement and evaluation of skills, knowledge, and competence is clearly important and appropriate. However, core reflection has provided a catalyst to define a more inclusive or holistic balance in how development in pre-service teachers is assessed.

Recent graduates of our programs seem to have a clearer vision about why they want to be teachers and how they can realistically reach the goals they have set for themselves and for their students. According to their written statements, it seems core reflection has given pre-service teachers the tools they need to develop a greater vision for their own students and to focus not just on the academic needs of their students, but on development of the whole person. The current educational climate in the US places an over-emphasis on the measurement of academic progress through testing. In this climate, other dimensions of *holistic education* are too often under-valued, or worse, neglected completely. New teachers, graduates from our school, see this and, through their ongoing exposure to core reflection, many have been able to sustain a connection to what they know to be true about child development and what is best for student learning. It is our hope that, as more teachers enter classrooms with experience in core reflection, we will see its intentional application occurring on a broader scale.

Faculty members who use core reflection have also seen significant changes in their interactions with one another. We feel that core reflection has added a common language to our professional dialogues, a language based on shared values of education and how we approach teaching. We are able to share our experiences, issues, and successes in a structured way through listening and through coaching that allows us to problem solve while deepening collegial trust; this happens as faculty gently challenge each other on both professional and personal levels. The collaboration among the faculty that has resulted from core reflection goes beyond the hallway conversations and brownbag meetings to collective projects, programmatic planning, and scholarship. These relationships connect faculty more deeply and more consciously with their students and with one another. Shelley sums up her observation of change in the culture of the School:

> Overall our involvement with core reflection and commitment to support each other in this work has lead directly to increased collaboration among faculty and, I think, a more uniform commitment to greater transparency in our own teaching practice . . . program-level partnerships have provided an alternative to the traditional higher education model in which faculty are fragmented into distinct "disciplinary silos" and largely isolated in their daily teaching practice and research inquiries.

One potential line of inquiry that has resulted from the research and writing of this chapter is to monitor the culture of schools in the area where the university is located. As previously discussed, our university is in a small city where educational change can be readily observed by faculty in the field. Many of the educators around the university and outlying areas are graduates of our programs. The question that arises then is: How will these local schools adopt core reflection as more recent graduates from our programs are hired and have greater influence in these schools?

Conclusion

Core reflection has really sustained itself through the brownbag lunches and the lines of inquiry, and that has impacted about half of the faculty engaged in some form of inquiry related to core reflection. To me, that's a very unique part of it. It's been sustainable in spite of the fact that Fred and Angelo haven't been here since 2009.

(Dean Mills, 2011)

The process of core reflection has encouraged us to continue with our professional development, self-analysis, and self-renewal so that we can be the best colleagues possible to one another while supporting and empowering teachers. The examples in this chapter show how teacher educators are better able to discern essential aspects of their roles. This includes a shift in what we view as significant in our students' development and the courage to reinforce that view in the ways we meet, instruct, and mentor them. In working with our undergraduates, graduates, and new teachers in the field we will continue to grow in how we apply core reflection in our personal and professional lives. We hope that through modeling authentic teaching practices with our students, they will then do the same in their own classrooms with their students, and create classroom environments built on trusting and relationships so that all students can thrive.

References

Mills, G. (2008). *Saving self in a self-less environment: Core reflections of a Dean.* Paper presented at the Self-Study of Teacher Education Practices Conference. Herstmonceux, East Sussex.

PART V
Conclusion

Part V contains one concluding chapter in which we look back on the book as a whole. First, we will discuss how the core reflection approach differs from more traditional views of education. In particular, core reflection is a holistic approach that puts the person at the foreground of learning, focusing on identity and authenticity, on learners' strengths instead of their deficiencies, and on core qualities as the basis for the development of competencies. What could it mean for mankind if education would serve as a springboard for putting identity and integrity, as well as the theme of interconnectedness in the center of our thinking, feeling, and wanting? How might it serve our survival and quality of life on this planet? And, how can education transform itself from the inside out and create hope for the future?

13

TOWARD A NEW VIEW OF TEACHING AND LEARNING

Fred A. J. Korthagen, William L. Greene, and Younghee M. Kim

In this final chapter, we will look back on the book as a whole. The book links theory and practice. In the first chapters, the theory of core reflection is introduced and made transparent, but the approach shows its real merits through reports about its actual use. Chapters 4–12 provide exactly that; they show how the application of core reflection with students, teachers, and teacher educators leads to processes that combine quality with inspiration. Apparently, core reflection leads to deep learning and to learning that connects the human core with effective behavior. This has a long-lasting impact on learners, whether they are young children or veteran teachers, and whether they are beginning teachers or experienced teacher educators. Core reflection is aimed at helping all people grow from who they are and to make optimal use of the qualities and talents they brought into this world when they were born.

The book shows a route toward long-lasting growth that is different from the usual attempts to improve students or educational systems. Most educational approaches or change projects in education are grounded in ideas and ideals of experts outside the everyday classroom, thus creating an immense 'transfer problem.' In contrast, the core reflection approach starts from the qualities already available in people and builds on their psychological capital. It is an approach *from within*. The onion model makes this very visible; by connecting the various layers in the onion, a flow from within is promoted that impacts the environment.

We believe that this book shows it is time to move away from standardized procedures and outcomes and return to the essence of education, the essence of being, and the potential that is waiting within people to be recognized and nurtured. This implies an important and radically new view of the basic goals of education. Core reflection opens a venue toward no longer imposing old and ineffective demands on children, but to supporting them in finding the essence of their own nature, their own "identity and integrity" (Palmer, 1998).

Core reflection is thus grounded in a holistic view of teachers and learners (Miller, 2006, 2010). They are seen as people who are so much more than thinkers; they have feelings, desires, ideals, and empowering personal qualities. By acknowledging all these dimensions of humanness, core reflection puts personal identity and authenticity in the foreground of a new view of education. We are not talking here about an idealized and unrealistic view. We agree that basic competencies are important. Children should learn the fundamental skills of reading and writing, basic knowledge about the world, and the central concepts and principles of math and science. They should explore the limitless depths of their imaginations and creativity through music, art, drama, and other expressive arts. We are not aiming at neglecting these important facets of education, but we are talking about a new view of the *how* that occurs in acquiring all these important learning goals. As the book shows, it is possible to develop competencies from within that align with *who* people *are* and with their unique strengths. This book also presents evidence that competencies that are connected with core qualities are much stronger, more influential, and more enduring as they become realized through a greater sense of inner connectedness. In addition to competencies that are related to dealing with the world around us, we envision that education should also help people learn about *themselves* and to learn how to make use of their potential in an optimal manner.

Organizational Development

Each individual teacher, teacher educator, school principal, or other professional in education can make a difference by applying the principles of core reflection. Many examples in the previous chapters show impressive accounts of the profound impact this approach can have when applied on a one-on-one basis. However, the impact of core reflection will be even stronger if it is embedded in organizational development, such as within a school (see Chapter 8) or among university faculty (see Chapter 12).

At this point, a cautionary word may be needed. We strongly believe that it is not possible to 'implement' the approach in traditional, didactic ways; that would seem contradictory to the basic principles of core reflection. One cannot convey the importance of core reflection to others by simply explaining its merits or 'training' people in the use of the approach and then hoping that the flow will start. The source of flow has to spring from within people. It is our experience that explanations of core reflection principles easily lead to philosophical discussions and to contrasting viewpoints about underlying assumptions. On the other hand, we have seen many organizational changes take place in which core reflection became a pillar in the pedagogical and organizational structures of a school for primary or secondary education or a school of education, but never through attempts to *convince* people of its merits. Too many words *about* core reflection do not create flow; they often create resistance. What is most needed is the genuine human experience of excitement with how the approach works and what it does for people. So, if one wants to interest groups of professionals in core reflection, our advice is: *do* it, create an experience of flow, focus on people's strengths and inspiration, use the broaden-and-build model, and *live* the core reflection approach! In sum, words do not change people, but positive experience does.

Here, the onion model may again be useful but now applied to organizations as a whole. They too have their layers of identity and mission, although sometimes these are implicit. It is very effective to make these deeper layers explicit within an organization and to put emphasis on the core qualities of the organization. Also, barriers at other layers may then become evident, for example, limiting beliefs or insufficient competencies that obstruct the full potential of the organization. But, only if people *themselves* start to feel both the positive impact of core reflection and what is limiting genuine flow within their organization can they become motivated to make next steps in learning about the core reflection approach and in using it. Again, this is not so much our *theory*, but rather it is the lived experience of various contributors to this book.

Small Steps Toward a Great Future

To avoid any misunderstanding, we wish to emphasize that although the approach is revolutionary, it does not necessarily require an overnight transformation. Schools or individual teachers can make their own steps, perhaps small steps, but important ones. In order to support such a process, Table 13.1 summarizes 15 aspects on which a transition is possible from a traditional approach in education toward an approach based on core reflection.

Table 13.1 makes very concrete what the core reflection approach might mean in a practical sense. Again, this is not a vague dream or an illusion devised behind a writing desk in an ivory tower. It has already become reality in many schools, although a change in all 15 aspects at the same time is, for many schools, too big a revolution, asking too much from teachers, students, and parents. We have seen smaller changes happen within schools that gradually grew into big revolutions, and this may be a sound way to apply the ideas from this book. As the Chinese saying goes: "A journey of a thousand miles starts with the first step."

A Broader Perspective

The new view of teaching and learning put forward in this book seems extremely important in today's complex and often confusing world where it is easy to lose touch with who we are. At the same time, remembering who we are may be the most important goal in helping us with our psychological survival. The world

TABLE 13.1 The Transition from a Traditional Approach in Education Toward an Approach Based on Core Reflection

Traditional view of education	The core reflection view
1. Assumption: learning is one-dimensional	1. Assumption: learning is always multi-layered
2. Focus on what is (still) incorrect and should be improved	2. Focus on what is already there, and on successes, in order to build on that
3. Competencies are central	3. Core qualities are central
4. Focus on developing the right 'thinking' in order to influence 'doing' (from knowledge to action)	4. Thinking, feeling, wanting, doing are integrated
5. Focus on abstract knowledge	5. Focus on experiential knowledge
6. Attempts to promote transfer to practical situations	6. Developing awareness in the here-and-now (presence)
7. Depersonalized learning from experts	7. Personal and deep reflection
8. Focus on objects in the world	8. Focus on the person in relation to the environment
9. Distance between teacher and student	9. Relationships are the basis
10. Focus on time-on-task	10. Focus on contact and meeting each other
11. Much emphasis on 'checking' and assessments	11. Much emphasis on promoting growth
12. Based on planning and learning objectives	12. Acceptance of a certain degree of uncertainty
13. Characteristic features are obligations and pressure put on people	13. Characteristic is an emphasis on growth and inspiration, on ideals, desires, and needs
14. Ultimate goal: knowledge	14. Ultimate goal: full awareness
15. Central question: what do I have to learn?	15. Central question: who am I and what is my personal mission?

at large is in a state of big transitions, and some believe it is in a dangerous state of crisis. Increasingly, economists agree that the traditional economic system no longer functions well. Environmental problems have become so big that many believe that the point of no return is close for our planet. These and other troubling realities of the world enter our daily living through television and the internet and increasingly become part of the consciousness of young children. As Barber (1997, p. 17) stated:

> Taken together, these problems present a set of challenges more profound than any in human history . . . This generation and its successors cannot pass the buck. It is their destiny to inherit a unique combination of unparalleled power and terrible responsibility. A well-balanced, thoughtful society would surely give the highest imaginable priority to ensuring that its young people were well-prepared for this awesome destiny. It would examine the upbringing and education provided for its young, and ask whether the arrangements were equal to the task.

Like Barber, we believe education is a crucial factor in overcoming the crises we are facing in this world.

In our view, what is most needed in education is that we prepare students, teachers, and school principals for the important task of solving immense problems for which 'old' solutions no longer exist. People must be able to overcome their old 'downloading' habits (see Chapter 6), their old thought patterns, and their destructive behavioral patterns. This requires that humans are able to connect with their inner being, their core, and to communicate with each other's core. This is what we call *core communication*. Real mutual understanding requires that we are willing to overcome our own limited individual perspectives and that we open ourselves to values different from our own, to other beliefs, to other world views. Hence, what is necessary for core communication is that we are simultaneously connected with our own inner being while transcending our own individual views, needs, and desires. The strength of core reflection is that it connects us with the depths of our intrapersonal being on this planet and with the beauty of authentic interpersonal contact. Core reflection facilitates this connection without contradicting specific religious beliefs, metaphysical experiences, or other spiritual perspectives; on the contrary, it complements many Western and Eastern religions. At the same time, one need not be religious in the traditional sense to understand the transcendental value of core reflection.

Only by making contact with the rich potential that is waiting inside us and others, the potential that is inherent to our humanness, and the wish for genuine connection, can we hope to find new directions in this world. As Senge et al. (2004) state, without a process of reconnecting with our own authenticity and to our connectedness with others and with nature, our role on this planet may soon end. An analysis of possible scenarios for the future of mankind led these authors to the conclusion that the only way out for us is reconnecting the inside and the outside, our own deeper core and the environment. They state that the most pivotal element of a new world view is the notion of *connectedness:*

> . . . connectedness as an organizing principle of the universe, connectedness between 'the outer world' of manifest phenomena and the 'inner world' of lived experience, and ultimately, connectedness among people and between humans and the larger world.
>
> (p. 188)

And as Du Toit (2009) writes, "Our own insignificance, our planet's vulnerability, our total interdependence with life-giving systems are the immanent reality that we must bow to" (p. 250). When we use the core reflection perspective, we highly value natural processes, and we realize the limitations of putting demands and constraints on our environment. We also realize how much we are part of nature, and how much we are connected to everybody on this planet. This concurs with Csikszentmihalyi (1990), who says:

> The task of the next decades and centuries is to realize this underdeveloped component of the mind. Just as we have learned to separate ourselves from each other and from the environment, we now need to learn how to reunite ourselves with other entities around us without losing our hard-won individuality.
>
> (p. 240)

Urgent Questions and a New Perspective

Through a deeper connection with oneself, self-understanding grows and the connection with others deepens, and this may be the vital ingredient for saving this planet. What is the role of education in this respect? How can we support people in reconnecting with their inner world, and help them find their deepest values and personal qualities, their humanness, and to live accordingly given the complexity of life in today's world? How can we teach people how to live in respect of each other and in peace given the many differences in race, ethnic backgrounds, religion, and political opinions? What does this mean for the mission of schools, teachers, and school principals? And what can teacher educators contribute to this on the basis of their mission in education? In our view, these are urgent questions. In terms of the onion model, we have to align the layers in ourselves and connect the inside and the outside with an awareness of our deepest values and qualities. Core reflection offers the method for this beautiful quest.

As the chapters in this book have shown, authentic interpersonal, core-to-core contact is not only possible but creates a flow within and between people that leads to unexpected, highly-valued outcomes. These outcomes may partly resemble the traditional goals of education, but generally they will be new, fresh, and inspiring, presenting new views of ourselves and our world. Such new perspectives enrich our ability to find solutions for problems that are beneficial to everybody involved, as many examples in this book have shown. For education, this means that it is urgent to leave the realm of standardization and control behind us.

Hope for the Future

We hope that this book may serve the development of a broadly applauded new view of education. We believe there is an enormous potential in valuing the human core and prioritizing integrity. And we believe the time is right for this view everywhere in the world. We believe that worldwide there is a hidden longing for the reconnection with our own true nature and a need to understand how we can do this. The core reflection approach is not just a vague dream of some idealistic people, but it is already a reality in many teachers and schools. It is something one can easily learn how to use, and for many it is an approach that will stay with them forever, exactly because the approach is built on the most natural aspects of being human. But, it requires one important thing, namely a conscious decision to go for what is authentic and human. We need people who understand the message of core reflection, the message that people can flourish if they are supported in connecting the inner and outer layers of their being while fully respecting the values of others. We hope that the lived realities and accounts shared by the authors of these chapters will inspire many readers. We are grateful for their work, their commitment to what education is really about, and their willingness to contribute to this book. And we hope that many will follow them, not in exactly the same way of course, but following their *own* authentic route.

Hence, to our readers we say: consider this an invitation to make this first step and try out core reflection or some of its principles. The approach is not very complex, rather it is natural and human, applicable to many everyday situations, small and big. All that is required is the willingness to look at situations from another perspective, not a problem perspective, but a perspective of strength. As discussed above, such a shift in how we look at our experiences and how we perceive other people, may benefit, not only those involved in education, but the whole of humanity.

References

Barber, M. (1997). *The learning game: Arguments for an educational revolution*. London: Indigo/Cassell.

Csikszentmihalyi, M. (1990). *Flow: The psychology of optimal experience*. New York: Harper & Row.

Du Toit, C. W. (2009). Towards a new natural theology based on horizontal transcendence. *HTS Teologiese Studies/Theological Studies, 65*(1), 243–250.

Miller, J. P. (2006). *Educating for wisdom and compassion.* Thousand Oaks, CA: Corwin Press.
Miller, J. P. (2010). *Whole child education.* Toronto, Canada: University of Toronto Press.
Palmer, P. J. (1998). *The courage to teach.* San Francisco, CA: Jossey-Bass.
Senge, P., Scharmer, C. O., Jaworski, J., & Flowers, B. S. (2004). *Presence: Exploring profound change in people, organizations and society.* London: Nicolas Brealey.

CHAPTER CONTRIBUTORS

Roni Adams is an associate professor and coordinator of the Elementary Education program at Southern Oregon University. Her current research explores core reflection, teacher education, social and emotional learning, and issues in diversity and social justice. [adamsr@sou.edu]

Saskia Attema-Noordewier is a teacher educator, trainer and doctoral student working at VU University in the Netherlands. Her main interests are reflection, coaching, and communication in a school environment. The central question guiding her work is: how can people work, learn and live in contact with their full potential? In addition to her work at VU University, she works as a trainer and coach at the Institute of Multi-level Learning (IML). [s.attema-noordewier @vu.nl]

William L. Greene is a professor in the School of Education at Southern Oregon University. His work centers on the spiritual nature of education and human potential in a holistic framework of teaching and learning. [greenew@sou.edu]

Annemarieke Hoekstra received her Ph.D. in Education from Utrecht University, the Netherlands, in 2007. Her dissertation was on informal teacher learning. She has since moved to Alberta, Canada, where she works as a Teaching and Learning Specialist at NAIT. Her current research focuses on faculty development and performance evaluation. [annemarh@nait.ca]

Younghee M. Kim is a professor and coordinator of the Early Childhood Development program at Southern Oregon University. Her current research includes core reflection, holistic learning and teaching, whole child development, the human potential, and reflective/contemplative practices in teacher development. [kimy@sou.edu]

John T. King is an associate professor in the School of Education at Southern Oregon University where he teaches in and administers a pre-service teacher preparation program. His current teaching and research focus on global education, teaching for social justice, and teacher identity development. [kingjo@sou.edu]

Fred A. J. Korthagen is an emeritus professor of teacher education at Utrecht University, the Netherlands. He is currently working at VU University in Amsterdam, specializing in the professional development of teachers and teacher educators. He is co-developer of the core reflection approach and has worked with many schools, both national and international, on the use of this approach. Fred received international awards for his scientific work, for example from the American Association of Teacher Educators (ATE) and the American Educational Research Association (AERA). [fred@korthagen.nl]

Jo-Anne Lau-Smith is an associate professor in the School of Education at Southern Oregon University where she teaches in the pre-service teacher preparation and reading endorsement programs. Her teaching and scholarship evolve around teacher development, literacy education, and the socio-cultural context of teaching and learning. [lausmitj@sou.edu]

Paulien C. Meijer is an associate professor at the Centre for Teaching and Learning, Utrecht University in the Netherlands. Her publications focus on teacher learning and non-learning in different phases of their professional career. As teacher educator and former teacher in social sciences, she is specifically interested in identity issues in teacher learning and development in which transformation and defense mechanisms are central concepts. [p.c.meijer@uu.nl]

Heinze Oost worked as a senior researcher and associate professor in the field of academic skills at Utrecht University. His research focused on 'teaching research skills.' He was co-founder of the Netherlands Centre for Research Schools and Graduate Schools in 2006. Since 2008 he held a position as associate professor at the Research Group for Methodology of Law and Legal Research at Tilburg University. (Deceased)

Marjan E. Ossebaard worked as a teacher and researcher in the field of academic skills at Utrecht University until 2006. Her research focused on the effect of cognitive behavioral interventions and core reflection on study-procrastination. Since 2006 she works as an academic skills trainer and mindfulness trainer at i2L, Institute for Innovation and Learning. Her areas of expertise include study-procrastination and self-regulation. [info@i2l.nl]

Peter Ruit is a senior teacher educator and coach at Driestar University for Teacher Education, Gouda, the Netherlands. He has experience in research and the training of pre-service and in-service teachers. He is also an assessor for the

Dutch Foundation for the Registration of Teacher Educators. [p.ruit@driestar-educatief.nl or ruit.peter@gmail.com]

Jan Stavenga-De Jong worked as a senior researcher and assistant professor in teacher education and HRD at Utrecht University. His research focused on coaching, mentoring, and on-the-job training. In 2006 he started to work as an independent researcher in the field of training and development. Since 2006 he has worked as chief editor of the Dutch HRD journal 'Opleiding & Ontwikkeling. [mail@janstavenga.nl]

Angelo Vasalos is co-developer of the core reflection approach and multi-level learning. With a background as a Gestalt trainer, Angelo works as a senior trainer, educator, and general director at the Institute of Multi-level Learning in Amsterdam, the Netherlands. His experience covers the full range of supervising personal and professional development processes of individual persons, teams, and organizations in the Netherlands, England, the US, and Australia. [a.vasalos@kern reflectie.nl]

Erin M. Wilder is an assistant professor in the School of Education at Southern Oregon University. Her current research includes implementing core reflection with students in the classroom and student teachers in the field, collaborative partnerships in early childhood programs, and reflective practices in teacher education. [wildere@sou.edu]

Rosanne C. Zwart is an assistant professor, teacher educator and trainer at VU University in the Netherlands. Her main interest is the professional development of teachers and teacher educators, especially through coaching and self-study trajectories. In addition to her work at VU University, she works as a scientific staff member at the Centre for Learning of Teachers. [r.c.zwart@vu.nl]

INDEX

Made in the USA
Monee, IL
05 September 2020

41460161R00128